Build Something Great!

Your Reference Manual
of the Best Tips for Startups

David Overhauser
Resve Saleh

Books By Simplex

Copyright © 2015, 2016

All rights reserved. This book or any portion thereof may not be reproduced or used in any manner whatsoever without the express written permission of either Books By Simplex, David Overhauser or Resve Saleh, except for the use of brief quotations in a book review.

Printed in the United States of America

Published by ◆ Books By Simplex

PO Box 93, Cupertino, CA 95015

First Printing, 2015

ISBN   978-0-9970820-0-5

www.BuildSomethingGreat.biz

BUILD SOMETHING GREAT!

Your Reference Manual
of the Best Tips for Startups

Preface

Starting a company is one of the most exciting and exhilarating experiences in a professional career. It is also one of the most difficult challenges because there are so many factors involved in creating a successful company. This book helps budding entrepreneurs by providing specific knowledge that increases their likelihood of success. It is often cited that only 10 out of 1,000 business plans are funded, and only 1 out of 10 funded startups is successful: either going public, being acquired or otherwise delivering a high return on investment to shareholders. One reason for this rather low ratio of 1 in 1,000 is that most entrepreneurs undertaking their first venture are not aware of all the landmines and pitfalls that await them on the road ahead. They often get fixated on the wrong issues and lose focus on what is important. This book provides key tips to help first-time founders and neophytes to the business world to be among those who succeed. While success is never guaranteed, it is possible to increase the probability of success by avoiding mistakes of unsuccessful companies. So let's get started on the road to success!

There are many ways to guide founders and entrepreneurs of startup companies. We believe the most effective way is to provide great tips that have accumulated over the years. Tips are often offered as the keys to success by founders, experienced executives, industry observers, venture capitalists and angel investors. For this reason, we have written this book as a series of tips that are easily remembered, or quickly referenced, to stay on the path to success.

A great tip is a self-contained, bite-size nugget of information with high-value content. It is easily read, understood and digested in a short amount of time, but leads to long-lasting effects and positive outcomes if used properly. We provide the tip as a title in bold followed by a summary of the tip. Key points and takeaways are highlighted when appropriate. For those interested in details, a longer tutorial description is provided. With this format, you can adjust the manner in which you absorb the material based on your circumstances: whether at an airport, on a plane, at work, in a coffee shop or on the beach.

Startup entrepreneurs are usually short of time and want to access information quickly, and then go deeper when they really need to get more information. They do not want to wade through volumes of superfluous content to extract the nuggets of useful information. The knowledge they seek is usually associated with a big decision on some important issue. We know all too well that early decisions have the biggest impact on the long-term success of a startup. So we have collected the best tips that allow you to make good decisions early in the process, thereby increasing the likelihood of success.

The style of this book is one of giving advice in a coffee shop. Anyone involved in a startup, whether a founder, manager or employee, would like to sit in a coffee shop for a few hours with someone who has "been there and done that" to get some good input and advice. This is what this book is all about. We offer big tips and many small tips within the big tips. We hope it provides high value to you no matter your role in your startup or stage of development your company has reached.

Foreword
by Aki Fujimura

I love entrepreneurship and I love teaching. But I find the combination of the two to be quite difficult. I have my thoughts and what I think are my formulas for success. But everyone is different. Every company is different. What are the common factors that would work for everyone?

This is a great book for anyone thinking about starting a company. Although the book is targeted for high technology, I find much of it to be applicable to other types of startups, especially those that are or aim to be venture backed.

Perhaps more importantly, the arrangement of the book in the "tips" format makes this a great reference book. Most of the advice for how to start a company is also about how to continue to grow a company. Scrolling through just the list of tips, I can tell which tips are relevant to me now, and go to that section to read the advice and reminders. In reading through the manuscript, I often caught myself thinking about how a particular tip or anecdote might apply to me right now in growing the eight-year old company I have the privilege to lead.

I have known the authors of this book since 1997 when I joined Simplex as COO. I have been a founder of two software product companies, have helped two other companies grow from tens of employees to public companies while serving as an inside Board member in several operating roles, and have been on the Board of three other companies as an external Board member, all with successful M&A exits.

I can tell you first hand that what the authors founded in Simplex was very special. Simplex's CEO, Penny Herscher, whom the authors had hired, led a very successful public offering in 2001 as one of the first tech companies to go out following a disastrous public market in 2000. Simplex was in the $5B Electronic Design Automation (EDA) market in which there has since been only one other IPO in 15 years. The Simplex story was not of a lucky boat that rode a rising tide. The tips being taught by Resve and David come from their experience in starting a company that went public in a post-bubble environment in a market segment with only 10% annual growth.

There are a thousand ways to fail and only one or two ways to succeed. Trying to learn what not to do from a failure only makes it 1/1000th less likely to fail again. We all make plenty of mistakes of our own. We can learn from failures in real life without reading a book. The only way to learn from a book is to learn about what leads to success. The tips here will guide you to help make your company more likely to succeed.

The best thing about a startup is that we get to create great products and great companies! Enjoy!

Aki Fujimura

About the Authors

We started a company in 1995 that went public in 2001 with a $250M valuation. Our company was a chip-design software startup in a sea of questionable Internet startups. We provided software for integrated circuit designers that solved some serious customer problems arising from an inflection point in the semiconductor industry. We had real products, real customers, real revenue and real profits, almost unheard of in the Internet startup era. In 2000, the tech bubble burst. But we did not! We continued to grow as a company. Our CEO, Penny Herscher, through sheer force of will and persistence, took our company public in 2001 – a time when underwriters and investment bankers were spooked by the carnage on Wall Street the prior year. A year later it was sold to a larger company for $300M.

The genesis of our company began back in 1994. We started by writing conference and journal papers together as professors at Duke University and the University of Illinois. We lived in the land of "publish or perish" where we were changing the world "one student at a time." The university is a great environment for innovation but we yearned to have a bigger impact. We began thinking about starting a company and made the decision in January of 1995 to quit our jobs, move to California and launch our startup.

That company was Simplex Solutions. We started with the lofty goal of solving all of the problems arising from deep-submicron technology by building a set of software tools to inspect chip designs before they were manufactured. We built a great team of cofounders, advisors, investors, managers and of course products. The flagship product gained traction in the marketplace and, along with our follow-on products, eventually led to a public company. Our proudest moment came when the chip manufacturing industry required all chip designers to use our key contribution as an integral part of the design flow before manufacturing silicon chips. Of course, by that time the competition had similar tools so they shared in the glory. But we were first to market with a working killer product. We made the impact we had set off to accomplish.

Looking back, it seems like it was a straight line to success even though it did not feel that way at the time. We made right decisions on major factors that determined success or failure. We did a lot of hard work up front to validate our plans before setting off to build a company. We took all the advice we could get and used it where we felt it was most valuable. We pulled in some heavy hitters as early as possible and combined their experience and know how with ours. We now have a unique perspective on how to build fast-growing startups. One thing we learned is that if you are highly allergic to taking advice, you will fail. We succeeded because we were able to convert advice into action and did not let a "know-it-all" attitude get in the way of building a great company.

Since then, we have been involved individually and together in multiple startups, in both hardware and software. Most of them ended in acquisitions. A few did not make it. Others are still ongoing. But through the initial public offerings, mergers, acquisitions and the ones that did not fly, we identified other criteria that lead to successful startups. We gave talks at MIT entrepreneurship forums and began investing as angels. In that process, we were able to exchange ideas with other entrepreneurs, investors and industry observers about what makes a startup successful. We began to realize why we were able to start a company that went public while others struggled to get theirs off the ground or stay afloat. We compiled a list of the success factors and failure mechanisms, and started giving advice to many new startups.

We have given this advice in countless coffee shops to entrepreneurs eager to know what it's like in a startup and how we succeeded the way we did. We enjoyed doing this, but at some point we realized that we were trying to change the world "one entrepreneur at a time". That's when the concept of writing this book came up. If we took all the knowledge we accumulated about people, products and profits – the three most important ingredients for a successful startup – and put them all in a book, it would allow us to have a wider reach and greater impact.

We decided to team up again to write this book to try to capture what we learned over the past 20 years, and the 15 years before that when we were employed at 3 other startups. All we could think about for months was this book. Pretty much every hour of every day was spent working on it until it was done. We were passionate about our academic lives, passionate about our startups and now passionate about this book describing how to build a successful company. That's the common theme in all our work – passion and teamwork! The book is a combination of our experiences as employees in startups, experiences in starting our own company that went public and recent activities in funding startups. We also draw on our experience serving on advisory boards and as consultants.

Most startups are likely to fail more often than not, and the failure rate of funded startups remains a staggering 90%-95%. We want to change this. While every startup is different, many of the underlying principles, decisions and strategies remain the same. As we started writing this book, we realized that by organizing our advice into a number of tips, the reader can quickly identify which tips are suitable for their particular situation. We hope that everyone will read through all the tips at least once, and then go back to specific tips as situations arise. We believe our advice, along with the willingness of entrepreneurs to remain coachable and open to useful input, will make success possible.

That's the back-story for this book. We wrote it with the intention of reaching the widest possible audience. It targets those starting companies and those thinking about starting a company at some point in the future. It is particularly useful to the management team of a newly-minted startup. We also think it will be especially valuable to employees of a startup. It provides an insider's view of the important issues in a startup. We also believe that some investors new to funding startups will find these tips very helpful.

To summarize our background, we obtained our Ph.D. degrees from University of Illinois and UC Berkeley, and then went on to teach at Duke University, University of Illinois, Stanford University and University of British Columbia. We have written countless academic papers, numerous technical books, received patents, and several national and international awards. As teachers, we are able to synthesize the most important aspects of a subject into an easily understandable form. That is what we did in the classroom every day at the university. That is what we've done in this book. In short, our unique experiences in academia and business allow us to provide the most valuable tips for startups.

That is really all you need to know about us. There is more at the end of the book and on our website if you want further information. Instead of writing further details about us, we are more interested in delivering high-quality information that helps you succeed. No matter what part of the world you live in and what type of company you are starting, you will find something useful in this book. It might be the start of your next great adventure or the one thing that puts you over the top.

David Overhauser
Resve Saleh

www.BuildSomethingGreat.biz

This book is dedicated to
the people of Simplex Solutions
who helped create a great company
and establish life-long friendships

Acknowledgements

We thank the following people for carefully reviewing the manuscript and providing valuable feedback: Lynn Hilchie, Steve Wilton, Penny Herscher, Aki Fujimura, Steffen Rochel, Jody Fast, Isme Alam, Knut Synstad, Art Reidel, Graham Truax, Gareth Keane, Greg Steele, Scott Rodgers, Amit Kedia, Dean Prelazzi, and Paulin Laberge.

Table of Contents

List of Tips ...   xiv

CHAPTER 1: Do You Have the Right Stuff?   1

CHAPTER 2: Build a Solid Foundation   13

CHAPTER 3: Assess Product/Market Fit   51

CHAPTER 4: Start With a Minimum Viable Product   93

CHAPTER 5: Get Properly Funded   135

CHAPTER 6: Operate a Successful Startup   189

CHAPTER 7: Improve Your Success   229

CHAPTER 8: Think Differently   267

Authors' Biographies   270

List of Tips

2.1 ☐ Don't try to BE something Great, Try to BUILD something Great
2.2 ☐ Find the Right Founders
2.3 ☐ Use Make/Buy Decisions to Rapidly Prototype Your Ideas
2.4 ☐ Transform Yourself into a Lean Mean Business Machine
2.5 ☐ Meet Early & Often to Strategize, Plan and Execute
2.6 ☐ Bootstrap as Long as Possible
2.7 ☐ Build an Active Network of Advisors
2.8 ☐ Commit Yourself Completely
3.1 ☐ An Idea is NOT a Product
3.2 ☐ A Working Product is NOT Necessarily a Company
3.3 ☐ Build a "Pain Killer" not a "Vitamin Pill"
3.4 ☐ Identify Your "Unfair" Advantages
3.5 ☐ Market Size Tells You About the Opportunity
3.6 ☐ Competition Tells You About the Degree of Difficulty
3.7 ☐ Know the Ecosystem of Your Product from End-to-end
3.8 ☐ Develop Your Business Plan Iteratively
4.1 ☐ Stay Focused on CASH and the PRODUCT
4.2 ☐ Don't Pack Too Much into One Product
4.3 ☐ Deliver Functionality and Quality on Time
4.4 ☐ Software Quality is a Competitive Advantage
4.5 ☐ Pre-Plan Your Product Pivot Strategy
4.6 ☐ Make Business Decisions from Now On
4.7 ☐ The Product-to-Customer Interface Determines Scalability

5.1 ☐ You Need Angels or VCs to Scale Your Business
5.2 ☐ Make Valuation a Win-Win Negotiation
5.3 ☐ Know What You're Getting for What You're Giving Up
5.4 ☐ Do Your Due Diligence on Angels and VCs
5.5 ☐ Understand the VC Landscape and Timing
5.6 ☐ VCs Expect a 20X ROI
5.7 ☐ Revenue Projections Determine Your Valuation
5.8 ☐ Liquidation Preference is about Who Gets Paid First
5.9 ☐ Convertible Notes Must be Handled with Extra Care
6.1 ☐ Start with a Solid Board of Directors
6.2 ☐ Startups Be Nimble, Startups Be Quick
6.3 ☐ Bad Hires Cost Time and Money
6.4 ☐ Get the Right CEO
6.5 ☐ Cooperate Internally, Compete Externally
6.6 ☐ Systems and Processes Save Time and Money
6.7 ☐ Always Negotiate Win-Win Outcomes
6.8 ☐ Exude Confidence, Not Arrogance
6.9 ☐ Leave Marketing Strategy to the CEO
7.1 ☐ Ten Decisions Determine Your Destiny
7.2 ☐ Keep Your Priorities Straight
7.3 ☐ Work on Things that are Important but not Urgent
7.4 ☐ Always have Action, Backup and Contingency Plans
7.5 ☐ It's a Marathon AND a Sprint so Stay Healthy
7.6 ☐ Avoid Legal Entanglements
7.7 ☐ Selling Your Company is a Business Decision
7.8 ☐ Make Your Own Luck
7.9 ☐ Embrace Change to Support Growth

CHAPTER 1
Do You Have the Right Stuff?

In the beginning, there is an idea followed by a series of events that eventually leads to the formation of a startup. But where does the idea come from in the first place? In the 1960's, the technically inclined would tinker in the family garage with various kits that could be ordered and assembled to build ham radios and other electronics. In doing so, some of these early engineers would generate new ideas and eventually start their own companies. In the 1970's, the next generation of creative thinkers began soldering chips onto boards to build homemade computers and other types of one-of-a-kind products. The first hackers began to develop software for these hobby computers and for commercial "main-frame" computers typically available at large universities around the country. Many ideas developed in this period were commercialized with great success, but high-tech entrepreneurship was restricted to a small group of specialized engineers who had early access to these technologies.

This is not the case anymore. Today, ideas can come from anywhere: hacking code in a dorm room, playing with leading-edge technology in a college lab, working on a cool app in a home office, writing down thoughts on the back of a napkin, exchanging ideas at a technical conference, or just thinking up a new concept in the shower that "just might have some commercial value." Regardless of how it happens or where it happens, when the light bulb goes on, it may be time to spring into action.

2   Build Something Great!

Anyone with the right mindset can be an entrepreneur. If you identify a problem encountered by many businesses or individuals who would pay for a solution you are capable of developing, you should think about becoming an entrepreneur. In fact, anyone in STEM (science, technology, engineering and math) has the potential to start a high-tech company today. Considering the number of people in the world with a STEM background, this is a staggering number. As a result, this century will be defined by technology and talent.

Today, there are technology startups in software, hardware, semiconductors, networking, automotive, biotech, clean energy, business services, and consumer goods and services, to name a few. Software startups tend to dominate the landscape because they are much easier to get off the ground than ever before. They are cheaper due to the availability of open source development tools and open access architectures. The emergence of public cloud computing platforms provides direct access to significant hardware and software resources to test the viability of new ideas with minimal upfront cost.

It is now possible to launch a company with founders and a few engineers. In fact, many small and medium-size businesses (SMBs) have sprouted up in the past five years with the potential to scale up quickly if the appropriate funding can be secured. Often, these companies will start off with developers, engineers, consultants, advisors, and data entry people in different locations, thus forming what is ostensibly a virtual company. Once it reaches critical mass, some consolidation into one or two locations may be needed because of the economies of scale. However, until that point, it is quite possible to operate in a distributed fashion using the cloud-based infrastructure available today on the Internet.

Similarly, building hardware with embedded software is not as expensive or difficult as it was in the past. At the present time, a single-board computer (SBC) can be quickly designed using off-the-shelf parts with proprietary software running on it. There are well-known groups generating very innovative SBC's that can shorten development time for new startups. It is much easier to iterate on prototypes and determine if they have potential value in industry. In addition, relatively inexpensive offshore manufacturing and three-dimensional (3D) printing are readily available to shorten the time for hardware design revisions.

While hardware and software startups are easier to launch, the hard part is making them successful. Actually, this is true regardless of the type of startup. Most entrepreneurs believe their technical expertise will carry them a long way on the road to success. On the contrary, **it is the ability to make the right business decisions, build a team of talented people, negotiate contracts, attract funding and handle the myriad of business issues that will determine success**. Only a small but essential part of a successful startup is due to the technical prowess of the founders. Their **business acumen is much more important**. Fortunately, there are many ways to gain the skill set, knowledge and connections needed to succeed. This book is a first step in filling gaps for anyone currently involved in a startup. But if your goal is to start a company at some point in the future, there are many things you can do in preparation.

First, **generate lots of ideas on how to improve things**. These ideas can be small, medium, large or even grandiose. Thinking, tinkering and trying different approaches will produce many more ideas. Act on these ideas by developing solutions to specific problems. Many people spend hours on Facebook, playing video games or binge-watching TV programs. Instead, use that time to write software programs or assemble hardware systems. If you are not completely consumed (or possessed) by the excitement of building systems and trying to solve different problems in new ways, a startup may not be for you. But if you love to immerse yourself in problem-solving tasks and lose yourself in the technology, you are definitely well suited to starting a company.

Second, **become an expert in an emerging field and become highly skilled in that field**. You can do this at the graduate level in a college or in your spare time. This will take many hours over many weeks, months and years. When you consider the high skill levels of Michael Jordan and Wayne Gretzky, you should realize that they practiced their craft continuously over many years to reach the level of "best in their sport." **Likewise, you must work hard and be very passionate about what you are doing to reach a high level of proficiency in your field.** Skills are developed over time, trying different things, testing different ideas, and pushing yourself constantly to do better. It is no different in high-tech. There are no shortcuts here, no matter how smart you are. You have to put in mega hours to be at the top of your game. This is, without exception, a trait of all successful high-tech entrepreneurs going back to David Packard, Bill Gates and Steve Wozniak, just to name a few.

Third, **work on your communication and writing skills**. While this may not seem critical, you will be pitching your ideas to many people over many years if you start a company: initially to recruit other founders and advisors, then to raise seed funds, later to attract employees and management, and then to demonstrate products and attract customers. A strong ability to communicate, in both oral and written forms, is extremely useful. At least one person on the founding team must be outstanding in this category.

Fourth, **network with as many people as you can** at conferences, universities, business mixers, etc. You must maximize your contacts in the business and technical worlds. Likewise, it is important to build strong relationships with as many technical and business people as possible. You will need them later as information sources, leads for funding, sources of technology and potential employees.

Fifth, **spend time reading business books**, weekly technical news articles and technical publications. You must be a voracious reader to stay on top of what is going on in business and industry. Keep track of the trends, inflection points and areas of growth so you can direct your ideas to the problems of large emerging markets. Take classes and attend workshops on startups, if available, or watch videos on these topics on the Internet. Basically, keep your eyes and ears open to any opportunities that may arise.

And sixth, if you are still unsure about your preparedness, **consider working for a startup for 2 or more years**. In fact, working at a number of different startups in your career is not only exciting but may be lucrative as well. Here you will gain experience and be witness to the inner workings of a real startup. This will serve you well in the future. In the meantime, this book will provide you with key insights from inside a startup environment.

With the right preparation, you will be ready to go when the light bulb turns on. But even if you are doing all of these things, you still need a product idea, a large market opportunity and the right timing. More broadly, you need to consider the following reasons why you should start a company, reasons why you should not start one and some timing considerations. Your motivation for starting a company and your personal drive will be major factors in your success.

Reasons you should start a company:

- You recognize an opportunity to convert a new idea or technology into a product.
- You see a very large market opportunity for the product.
- Your "pain killer" product solves real customer problems.
- There is an inflection point in the industry that requires new solutions.
- A small team of people can be recruited to start the venture.
- **You think of starting the company night and day, and day and night.**
- You love the idea of building something from scratch.

We believe all of these reasons must be present in some form to launch a company. If one is missing, it may limit your ability to be successful. They are all great reasons to start a company.

6   Build Something Great!

Reasons you should not start a company:

- You want to get rich quick.
- You want to be famous and receive many awards.
- You want to prove the naysayers wrong.
- You want to show the world how clever you are.
- You have a lot of free time and you want to be busy.

In this case, even one of these reasons is either a red flag or a showstopper. There are many ways to get rich quick. A startup is not one of them. It may take many years from the date you decide to take the leap to the time you are cashing out, if you are one of the fortunate few. Remember only 1 out of 10 funded startups actually makes it, so you have a high probability of failure. Do not start a company to feed a large ego. It will never be satisfied anyway. And if you want to keep busy and engaged, join a startup to get experience.

When you should not start a company:

- You are in the midst of life-changing events (divorce, health issues, lawsuits, etc.).
- **Minimal funds to bootstrap a company are not available.**
- Venture capital (VC) or angel funding is unavailable due to a weak economy.
- You have no intention of leaving your current employer.
- You do not have enough funds to survive 6 months without income.

The right time to start a company is when you cannot think of anything else but getting a company off the ground. It consumes your every thought. You have the ideas spinning in your head, the timing seems right, the market opportunity exists, the right team can be assembled and funding can be secured. It's go time! That's when you really know you should start a company.

In addition to a strong desire to start a company, you need to have certain personal traits to succeed:

- The tenacity to persevere in the face of great obstacles
- The discipline to stay focused on one goal for many years
- **The strength to overcome the endless setbacks that will occur**
- A strong work ethic over a long period of time
- A level of confidence and mindset to do whatever it takes to get across the finish line
- The wisdom and humility to chart a new course of action due to changing market conditions and unexpected circumstances

If you possess all these qualities and the light bulb goes on, the tips in this book come into play.

Today, tips seem to rule the day. Everything is either a Top 10 list or a set of tips. It is the nature of our fast-paced society. Our attention span is short; we multi-task and we want things encapsulated into useful nuggets of information. Terms can be easily searched on the Internet, so the use of jargon, abbreviations and the like are more acceptable. If you want to know about something specific, it can be found with a simple search, which returns over a million items in a fraction of a second. What cannot be web searched is the knowledge gained through the experience of living in a startup for many years.

Most of this valuable knowledge is buried in people's heads. The movers and shakers are busy moving and shaking so they do not have time to put pen to paper, or fingers to keyboards, to provide the best tips for the next generation of entrepreneurs. Some knowledge may appear in blogs written by industry experts but information flow is somewhat sporadic. And while some key tips exist on the Internet, it is difficult for first-time entrepreneurs to sort out the good from the bad. What is not available is a comprehensive list of the best tips for startups all in one location.

8   Build Something Great!

We decided to build such a list in this book. There are many startup books available and they all have their merits. Some provide step-by-step guidance to build a startup. The main problem with this approach is that a startup does not lend itself to a step-by-step approach. It is not like baking a cake where you just follow the recipe and voila! **You cannot use a cookie-cutter approach to building a startup**. Every startup is different. Things do not happen sequentially. It is about doing things in parallel, sometimes using out-of-order execution, sometimes iteratively, and occasionally chaotically, all the while going 100 miles per hour.

Other books may provide insight through anecdotal information. While useful for the particular type of situation described, it may not translate to your situation. The lessons to be learned must be extracted from stories of trials and tribulations. A third category of book is one that goes into details about financing but gets you lost in the details rather than allowing you to see the big picture in order to make solid decisions about how to make your company successful. Still others introduce new concepts and coin new terms and catchy phrases to be adopted as part of the startup lexicon. However, they do not provide practical details to implement ideas and move the ball forward. As such, their theories seem elegant but fluffy and without the substance needed to resolve real issues in a startup. They do not attempt fill in the missing gaps of knowledge critical to success for most people at a startup. That is what is really missing in other books available today.

Everyone who starts a company for the first time begins with a different starting point than others. Their knowledge is uneven in the sense that they are experts on some things, knowledgeable on others and weak in remaining areas. There is no "one-size-fits-all" approach to fixing this problem. Instead, this book provides a series of tips that help you regardless of your starting point. It is intended to fill in gaps. Some of these tips may be critical to your company's success, while others may be informative. The rest will serve as useful reminders of what you may already know. But they are all helpful at some point along the way. The book addresses issues that arise primarily over the first few years of a high-growth startup.

Do You Have the Right Stuff? 9

Most tips are also valuable if you are trying to bootstrap a company, grow it organically and retain majority ownership.

The main objective of this book is to present the tips that have the highest impact on your business because we have witnessed what happens if you don't follow them. We have been in the trenches in countless startups at all stages of their development, and have seen what works and what does not work. A few tips provide software product examples for illustrative purposes only, as it is a familiar subject matter for most people in high-tech. However, the main message in all tips applies regardless of the type of startup you are building.

The most successful first-time founders are open to taking advice and input, seeking information and knowledge they may lack, and are always striving to learn more. Unfortunately, many founders think they already know it all. They love ideas, but only their own. They believe they are uniquely qualified to convert their idea into a moneymaker. This is often the source of their undoing. The best way to succeed is to be a sponge for knowledge, not a rock that will not absorb new ideas, inputs or suggestions. This prototypical founder may be the reason why a high percentage of startups fail. If founders set their sights on building a great company and realize that it will take a lot of people, money and time and just the right amount of luck to pull it off, they will be much more successful. It is wise to read all the tips with this in mind and apply the ones of most value to move your company forward.

The target audience for this book includes entrepreneurs, founders and early management at a startup. But we believe it will also be valuable to those joining a startup or currently employed in a startup, as well as those thinking about starting a company in the future who want to be well prepared in advance. If you are an employee at a startup, this book is extremely useful to gain some understanding of the inner workings of your startup. It is important for you to know the success factors and failure mechanisms described in this book through the tips. **The more tips in use at** your startup, the higher the likelihood of success. You could make a quick assessment of your own startup by checking off all the tips you are using that are listed after the table of contents.

Success comes in many forms for startups. It is not just getting to an initial public offering (IPO). It can be the creation of a profitable business through bootstrapping, the development of a valuable technology that is acquired before revenue or product completion, or a company that has product and revenue and is acquired before building a sales channel. It depends on the outcome you define for your startup. These tips cover all such exit strategies because they all build value for customers, employees and investors.

Some may wonder why write another book on startups when there are so many out there already. The answer is simple: we believe that tips are the best way to convey information to those interested in startups. You use them when you need them most. The rest of it has to do with details that are situation specific and cannot be covered by books. Instead, this book emphasizes the fact that all successful startups are built on people, products and profits. The right people working on the right products for a large market with a clear path to profitability will lead to success. We have devoted much of the book to these three topics.

This book provides a vast amount of information and advice that are critical to success. But in the early days of a startup there are only a few issues to deal with and the entrepreneur must be hyper-focused on them. Specifically, the focus should be on validating, through extensive customer and stakeholder interaction, that the problem is big enough to support a sustainable business. In that context, the entrepreneur should stay focused on the immediate priorities of effectively executing a rigorous approach to testing and iterating their problem–solution hypotheses and then later more broadly their business model hypotheses. Therefore, **the tips in this book should be read using a just-in-time approach** rather than an all-you-can-eat approach. A laser-like focus on the right priorities (everything leading to an initial comfort level with product-market fit) is needed in the very early stages.

Do You Have the Right Stuff?   11

The best way to use this book is to skim through all tip titles listed at the front of the book and identify the one or two tips that are most valuable to you in your current situation. Stick with those tips until your situation allows the introduction of more tips. Another approach is to read one tip a day over a two-month period. You should seek other resources to study each tip in more depth, if needed. It is not recommended to read all the tips in this book from cover to cover in one sitting. **They are packed full of valuable information so it is best to study only a few at a time, not all at once! You cannot afford to be distracted so keep it simple.** These tips are intended to serve as guideposts on your journey to building a successful company. You need to spend some time thinking about each one and how it applies to your startup. We selected the tips based on ones that were critical, very important or important to the success of startups.

First things first: Let's start by digging into Your Reference Manual of the Best Tips for Startups ... Starting now!

12 Build Something Great!

CHAPTER 2
Build a Solid Foundation

2.1. **Don't try to BE something Great, Try to BUILD something Great**

2.2. **Find the Right Founders**

2.3. **Use Make/Buy Decisions to Rapidly Prototype Your Ideas**

2.4. **Transform Yourself into a Lean Mean Business Machine**

2.5. **Meet Early & Often to Strategize, Plan and Execute**

2.6. **Bootstrap as Long as Possible**

2.7. **Build an Active Network of Advisors**

2.8. **Commit Yourself Completely**

Tip 2.1

Don't try to BE something Great, Try to BUILD something Great

In order to build a great company, you need to change the way you think about startups. The first change is to realize you cannot do it yourself. You need a team of people pulling in the same direction to succeed. Unfortunately, large egos often collide in a startup causing it to fail before it gets very far. **Do not let your ego, or anyone else's ego, get in the way of success. This is a leading cause of failure of most startups according to founders, investors and advisors.** The strength of a startup is in the team not the individual. Therefore, talented individuals must learn to work cooperatively as a team in order to succeed.

First-time entrepreneurs also need to be a sponge, not a rock, when taking advice or input from more experienced people. Many founders tend to be very stubborn and reluctant to change their approach even when good advice is given. The very idea they may be wrong runs counter to their own beliefs. If you are trying to build a company to prove everyone else wrong, or to show how great you are at business and technology, you will to fail at some point along the startup road.

When you start a company, the learning curve is very steep for approximately 3 to 4 years. Imagine drinking from a fire hose for that period of time. The information given here is intended to help you quickly move up the learning curve to avoid mistakes that led others to failure. Those who generally do not take advice may find themselves unexpectedly closing the business. Startup founders tend to greatly underestimate what it takes to build a company and overestimate their own abilities. This eventually leads to failure. Typically, 10 business plans are funded for every 1,000 business plans sent to investors and only 1 of those funded startups is successful. Clearly, the probability of being successful is very small. We believe there is a way to greatly increase this number by changing the way founders think about their role in the startup.

Our message to founders and entrepreneurs is simple. Don't try to be something great, try to build something great. This shift in your thinking puts you on the path to success. Your motivation for starting the company must be very clear in order to be successful. **Think of what you are building, not what you are becoming.** Viewing your goals in this way allows you to be much more open to working as part of a team and taking advice whenever it is offered.

Reframe your goals as if **you are the Chief Architect** about to embark on building a great masterpiece. Regardless of all your great ideas and initiative, you need a team of people, lots of money and enough time to successfully execute this goal. How many people will be interested in your enterprise if you give out orders and do not accept any input? They will be discouraged by your ego-driven approach. If the leader is not a team player, no one else will be one either. On the other hand, if you get them excited about the vision and mission of creating the next great architecture, they will line up to join in the effort.

Always keep the ultimate goal in mind. If you want to build a great company, make sure you have a clear vision of the desired outcome and keep this big picture in your mind at all times. Your fundamental role as a leader in a startup is to get people to share in the passion and excitement of building something great together. If you can sell them on the vision and convince them they will have an important and vital role in its success, you can attract a lot of great people who will work very hard to achieve it.

Tip 2.2

Find the Right Founders

Summary: If you have a great idea for a viable product with a large market opportunity and a good product/market fit, the first step is to build a great founding team to help you to start a company. When you begin to consider potential founders, there are many things to keep in mind. Founders must be technically competent, extremely passionate about starting a company, trustworthy, reliable and have a strong work ethic. You will be living with them for years. You will be trying to solve new and unexpected problems with them. You will have disagreements on all matters. You will be sharing successes and failures, both big and small. Therefore, **the selection of the founding team is the first and perhaps most important decision you will make in starting the company. It may be the difference between success and failure.** Likewise, if you are approached to join a founding team, you will be making a similar important decision for yourself.

Key point: The founders must all have strong technical abilities and specialized knowledge critical to the startup. If one of the founders lacks this expertise, they can (and will) be replaced at some point. **Business experience with strong technical skills is ideal for a startup.** Additionally, prior startup experience is a major asset. Once you decide to start a company, you must view yourself as a business person with technical skills, not the other way around. Technical competence is an important criterion when picking co-founders for the team. However, this is only a necessary requirement, but not sufficient. The success of the startup will depend on how quickly you make the transition to thinking about issues from a business perspective. A pure business person is not as valuable at this stage unless the person is a very seasoned executive in your industry. It must be a combination of technical skills and business acumen.

Tutorial: Startups often fail before anyone ever knew they existed. This is due to fundamental disagreements between the founders that lead to irreconcilable differences and an eventual dissolution of the founding team. Rather than beginning by describing what can go wrong, let's examine the proper way to assemble the founding team.

If you are the lead founder, your job is to sell the vision of the new company to other potential founders. It will be your first selling job so you need to learn how to be successful at it. Later, you will sell the concept to early hires, early sources of funding, then perhaps the venture capitalists (VCs) or angels, and then more hires and your initial customers. This sales job to attract other founders is the first step in building a successful company. If you are being recruited to be a founder, the same principles will apply. You must be sold on the idea, the person pitching the idea and the concept of starting a company. Then you must believe in it strongly enough to sell it to others going forward. **You have to become good at selling your vision for the company!**

The first requirement is that each member of the founding team must be exceptional in their technical talents. This is a must. If any members are also business types, or have some business acumen, then the team has a very good chance of succeeding. If not, then the odds of succeeding drop precipitously. A pure business person with no technical expertise may be useful, but only in the early days of the startup. Unless they are CEO material, their value reduces over time whereas a technical expert with business savvy provides the same value or more value over time. So the founders must be irreplaceable in terms of the product expertise and business savvy.

The right number of founders appears to be three. This is not a hard and fast rule. Many startups have succeeded with two founders, especially if they have a history of working well together. On the other hand, it will be much harder with only one founder. It will certainly be difficult to explain to investors how one person can build a company as a first-time founder, so at least one other founder is needed. While four founders is also a possibility, especially for complex products, there may be too many cooks in the kitchen for things to progress smoothly. Three is preferable at the start, as one may leave sooner or later "to go in a different direction," or will be jettisoned from the team for being difficult to work with, and you will be left with two. It is just the norm in a startup, not the exception. Furthermore, with three founders there are opportunities for each to take short breaks when needed while the others cover their daily duties. Otherwise, you risk burn out.

Team chemistry is very important. You must have at least one founder you know very well and with whom you get along easily. If any pair cannot get along, the whole thing could come to a screeching halt. This has stopped many companies from getting off the ground. Investors will evaluate the team based on their camaraderie, interaction style with one another and shared vision. Start with two or three, figure out what number is in your comfort zone and form founding a team.

Collectively, the founding team should have the following skill sets and knowledge:

- a clear vision of the opportunity
- some experience within startups as an employee
- strong business acumen or business savvy
- connections to large networks of people
- current industry and product knowledge
- market and competition knowledge
- ability to deliver high-quality commercial products
- product demonstration skills with customers
- strong communication, presentation and Q&A skills

The founders should also fit the following criteria:

- you have a long history working with at least one of them
- they are very energetic and have a strong work ethic
- they are ready for the next discussion about a company
- they have the ability to leave their current employer with "clean hands"

- they are willing to move to another location closer to the action if required
- they are full of new ideas to improve things
- they are constantly engaging with you to figure out how to get the company moving forward
- they are not going through some major personal crisis

From the above description, you should realize that one founder does not usually possess all these characteristics. It is difficult to cover all of these points with even two founders. That is why a founding team of three is recommended. You may need the coverage of three founders to reduce the number of holes in your own background or knowledge. Everyone brings a different skill set, personality and knowledge to the table. The technical skills may be the most critical, but the business skills that accompany those technical skills are more important. In addition, the workload is so high at the start that it is better to distribute it across three founders, rather than two or one.

In search of two additional founders for your venture, keep in mind each one must bring valuable and complementary qualities to the group. Think of three circles in a Venn diagram. There should be a mutually overlapping goal of building a great company with a shared vision and shared values. Next, there are areas of technical or business overlap between each pair of founders. And finally, there are areas of no overlap where each person brings a unique but essential set of skills to the company.

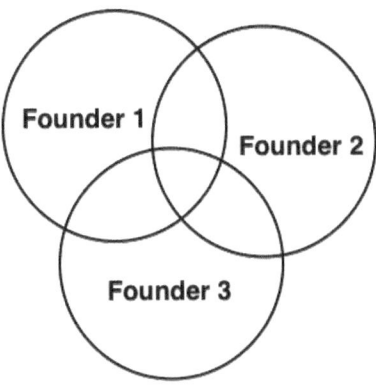

With three founders, there should be some clarity as to who is leading the effort. The leader must be agreed upon by the team, either due to the fact they have the vision and leadership skills, or lots of experience in business and/or startups. It should be someone who can be the face of the company and get the initial goals accomplished through the first round of financing and perhaps the hiring of a CEO. If a founder disagrees about who should lead, you may need to proceed with only two founders. In that case, two equal founders need to work cooperatively to run the company, or one founder needs to lead in the case of a senior/junior partnership. However, if the two remaining founders cannot work together harmoniously, the entire company is at risk. For all these reasons, a three-person founding team is a reasonable place to start.

When investors are evaluating the company, they put a premium on the quality of the founding and management team, so a strong track record of accomplishment in business drives up the valuation of the company. As you build the team, think of how it will be evaluated by investors.

The initial roles and responsibilities of a three-person founding team can be represented with a more detailed Venn diagram as shown below.

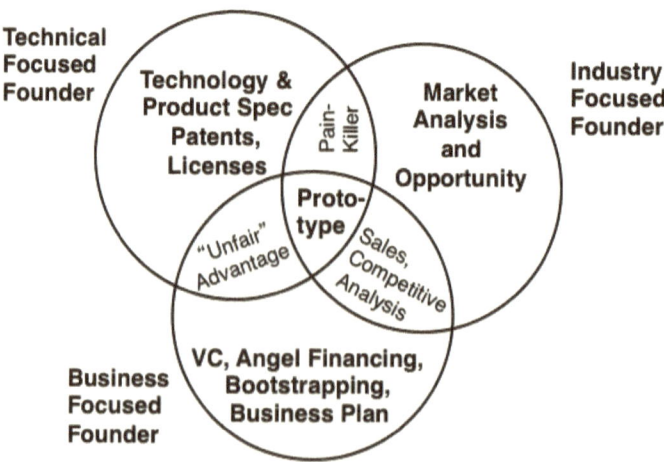

The areas of focus for each founder have been divided into technical, industry and business. While all founders will likely be involved in all activities in the diagram, each area should be the primary responsibility of one founder based on best fit. All three founders must also work together to develop initial prototypes to demonstrate capabilities of the proposed products.

Not listed above, but still along for the ride, are a few other characteristics that are worth noting. Each may bring a large ego with them. If not kept in check, it will be difficult to succeed. While it is true that ego can drive the desire to build a company, it can also destroy the company and personal relationships. There are notable examples of successful companies founded by individuals with larger than life egos, but in the early stages of starting a company, it is detrimental to the effort. It is not always clear how to address this problem as it depends on the people involved. Everyone is different. Their egos are satisfied in different ways, so no specific advice can be given on how to handle this situation. However, it is important to keep everyone focused on the big picture and what you are trying to accomplish as opposed to constantly satisfying everyone's ego in every decision.

Another issue is the potential for numerous disagreements between founders. One founder may not be on board with the intended goal of the company ("exit strategy"), or the first product to be developed, or their role in the company, or percentage ownership relative to the other two founders. A second founder may believe a certain founder is not adding value or is being particularly difficult. A third founder may think the other two are not carrying their load and are not focused on the startup, which requires all their energies to have a chance to succeed. These issues are real and have caused potential startups to end up in the ditch. **It is important to openly discuss these issues before launching a company.**

Assigning initial titles and percentage ownership can be fraught with peril. These issues should be discussed near the end of the initial meetings about starting the company. Most founders seek titles such as CEO, President or VP. Be aware that these titles will change as the company grows and as people who actually fit the title are hired. However, before deciding on titles, it would be prudent to get a sense of what the roles, responsibilities and expectations are of each founder prior to incorporation. Ask why they are interested in starting a company and get a sense of what they expect to get out of it. If it's on the list of "Why you should not start a company," then you may need to reframe their answer for them. If the reasons are not show stoppers in your mind, then you can continue with them. However, if their reasons are unacceptable, you may need to replace the founder candidate with a more suitable person.

Of course, percentage ownership will be an interesting exercise in negotiations. It may be shifting dynamically in the early days. Over the first few months, you should assess what the ownership levels should be and discuss it with each founder individually. Once an agreement is reached you can communicate it to the whole team in one of the meetings and continue with building the company. An initial base amount can be agreed upon and adjusted as more information about the contribution of each founder becomes clear, perhaps on a vesting schedule to allow for changes when needed. In fact, it is subject to change until the company is incorporated. **Keep track of the percentage ownership using a capitalization table.**

While there are no guidelines on founder ownership at incorporation, some actual cases can be helpful. The sample percentages shown below reflect the specific skill, knowledge or level of participation of each founder. For example, in case (c), the professor has chosen to stay at the university but is involved with the company 2 days/week.

Founders	A	B	C
a) Equal partners	50%	50%	
b) Senior/junior partners	60%	40%	
c) Prof/Phd Grad	30%	70%	
d) Prof/Prof/Phd Grad	40%	40%	20%
e) Prof/Prof/Industry	34%	33%	33%

There are many startups that spin out of a university lab where research and development has produced a prototype that may yield a short window to commercialization. The professor and Ph.D. student usually form a founding team and begin working on converting the prototype into a product. Often, the university encourages this type of entrepreneurship and may provide incubator offices to help bootstrap a company. A person with business experience may be added later to round out the founding team. In this situation, it is important to re-establish the pecking order. All the ground rules have changed. The academic hierarchy no longer applies in the company setting. The professor and student are now colleagues along with the third founder (who could also be another professor, a business person, or another student). The founding team must have discussions about the new working relationships. In addition, each professor desiring significant ownership must take a leave of absence to work solely on company business and must be willing to quit their job at the end of the leave.

Advanced notes:
1. Be aware that founder issues that have not been addressed satisfactorily up front may become an issue once the company is up and running. **It is critical to ensure each founder is satisfied with their ownership, title, role and responsibility. Any dissatisfaction must be solicited as early as possible.**
2. Do not underestimate the cost of leaving a founder issue unresolved. **As the company moves to each new stage in its growth, the cost of fixing a founder issue grows in magnitude.** An eruption at the wrong time puts the company at risk. Customers may be reluctant to buy your product and employees will leave if they believe a founder issue creates too much risk to company success.

Take Away: Selection of the founding team is the most important decision in starting a company. Some have argued this is the one critical "make or break" decision for success. It may take a several tries to get it right, but if you get it right, the rest of the ride will be relatively smoother.

Tip 2.3

Use Make/Buy Decisions to Rapidly Prototype Your Ideas

Summary: The key to success is to convert innovative ideas into commercial products in an organized and efficient manner. There are four major phases involved in this process. Every phase delivers a tangible result and there is time for planning and scheduling between phases, and within phases. It is important for everyone in the startup to know which phase you are operating in and its purpose. The first phase is the **[1] prototype phase**, where the ideas are validated quickly with a combination of hardware and/or software implementation. It is used to convince yourself and perhaps some pre-seed investors that you may be on to something. The next phase is the **[2] alpha phase** where the key features of the product can be demonstrated to potential customers to gauge their interest and obtain feedback. In the **[3] beta phase**, the product has enough functionality and stability to be used by a larger set of customers to validate the product and market. And finally, the **[4] production release phase** is defined as a full-featured working product that can be sold to the broader market.

Key Point: **It is very important that a startup continue to innovate as part of the company culture.** Innovation is the heart and soul of a startup. New ideas are always popping up around the company and creating excitement and enthusiasm. Without ideas and innovation, the next set of products cannot be developed; the company will not be able to sustain its competitive advantage; it may not have options to pivot if market forces dictate. So before the company is started, and after it gets off the ground, continue to place a strong emphasis on generating big innovative ideas that may eventually end up in a product.

Build a Solid Foundation   25

Tutorial: There are four phases of product development: prototype, alpha, beta and release. These four phases are shown in the diagram below.

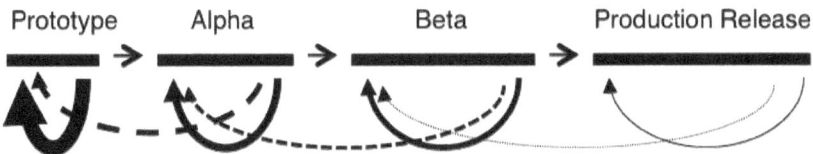

Each phase is longer than the previous one due to the amount of testing, validation and quality assurance carried out concurrently with the development. However, each successive phase allows for fewer and fewer loop-back iterations, as indicated by the weights on the feedback arrows. There are too many unknowns at the beginning. Development can only proceed to a certain point before new requirements are obtained. New information may arrive and require returning to an earlier portion of a phase, or an earlier phase, to make the necessary changes. These loop-back iterations will require additional testing and verification whenever they occur. But as you move from prototype to release, the number of unknowns decreases and the necessary requirements of the product are established. However, if a bug or design flaw is encountered, the cost of fixing the problem often increases by an order of magnitude in each phase as you move from prototype to release.

In the early days, prior to starting a company, ideas must be validated through the prototyping process. This **prototype phase** is often ad hoc in nature where bad ideas are eliminated quickly and good ideas are developed further. This is the time to experiment with bold new ideas, build on them and then start over if they do not work. It is important to set up a methodology for rapid prototyping of ideas in software and hardware, depending on the type of idea. There are many universities that offer free software for various industries. Open source development tools are available on the Internet along with source code, libraries and frameworks. Hardware components can be purchased easily, and often cheaply, to build systems. Hardware prototyping systems called FPGAs (field-programmable gate arrays) are popular for this purpose.

There are no real consequences of implementing bad ideas or getting it wrong at this point. In fact, the more things you try, the better, because you will need to have many options for products. Usually one product idea is not enough to build a successful high-growth company. Consider what you would do if the product failed in the marketplace. With multiple founders and a few engineers, it is time to brainstorm and come up with a variety of product options. Later, you will have to decide which product to launch first but at this point you need to create all your options.

Today, open-source software libraries and cloud-based computing platforms provide significant opportunities for software prototyping to test out ideas and determine if they can gain traction in the marketplace and whether they are scalable. If you are building a software company, there are a plethora of programming languages to choose from including Python, Ruby on Rails, Java, JavaScript, PHP, SQL, C, C++ and other variants of C. The right combination of languages depends on many factors so the selection must be done with careful consideration of the application.

The development platform of web-based or mobile (iOS/Android) introduces additional factors in language selection. Once established, a suitable integrated development environment (IDE) must be chosen. In addition, distributed revision control systems, such as git (available at GitHub and BitBucket), file storage and exchange (available at Dropbox) and online software Q&A services (available at StackOverflow) provide software support facilities. Using these available online systems allows the engineers to quickly build prototypes at little or no cost.

Next, in the **alpha phase**, the main idea is to demonstrate the actual capabilities of the first product to potential customers to determine if you have the makings of a startup. Here, the key objective is to build a minimum viable product (MVP). It does not need all the bells and whistles, but the significant selling points of the eventual product must be present and working. There must be some discipline introduced into the development process in the alpha phase because the beta phase will be built on the foundations of the alpha phase. Testing methodologies must be introduced at this point. There may be multiple loop-back iterations involved in the development of the alpha product because of the number of unknowns is still high, although not as high as during the prototype phase.

During the alpha phase, it is important to shorten the development time as much as possible by not re-inventing the wheel or creating a technology that may already exist. The idea is to get something out there as fast as possible so that experimentation and learning can begin. There are many options to pursue as an entrepreneur to expedite the development process. The first option is to find free software and frameworks suitable for your application on the Internet or through universities. For hardware, there are low-cost rapid prototyping boards available to implement hardware solutions.

Second, it is possible to license software for key components of your product from a third-party vendor. Here, an exclusive license must be negotiated and source code should be obtained, if possible. Third, there are companies that may be closing down shop that may be willing to sell the rights to some of their products. And finally, there may be large companies that are willing to license or sell their internal solutions not critical to their business model. The main point here is to be creative about how you develop your initial product. You may need to negotiate deals during the alpha phase for eventual incorporation into the final product.

You can also outsource development to speed up the schedule wherever possible. It may be a lot cheaper to have development done in other parts of the world where salaries are lower but the quality of work is equal, or in some cases higher, than what may be available locally. As a startup, the burn rate can be kept quite low using this approach. **Note that you must own the rights to any outsourced projects.** For example, you need to obtain source code for any externally developed software to protect the company in case the third party goes out of business or you sell your business. If you license object code, then eventually you must negotiate for source code. The same holds true for hardware development and manufacture to third parties. You may need a second source for any manufacturing that is done offshore as your business reaches profitability.

All of these "make vs. buy" decisions are very important to the success of the company. These decisions must be made in the prototype or alpha phases so they can be used in the beta phase. Any decision to buy something costs time to negotiate, and money or perhaps stock options to complete. It also takes time to integrate the solutions into your product. For software, you may inherit bugs so some quality assurance must be carried out during the acceptance process. Any bug fixes will have to be done by the third party on their schedule. This is the main reason to consider the "make vs. buy" decision carefully. It is a double-edged sword with many pros and cons. But outsourcing can be used to build a competitive solution quickly. **In the end, all of your out-sourced technology must be in-sourced in order to sell the company to a future acquirer. Keep that in mind.**

In the **beta phase**, the customer actually gets to push buttons and turn knobs on the product. The goal should be to build the MVP that would actually be purchased by the customer. This is important. A prioritized set of features and functions must be defined and their implementation scheduled so that the sales team can begin to contact customers to solicit beta-site interest. The beta product itself must include all the necessary features to allow it to be taken to the customer's site for evaluation and win the business.

The goal in the beta phase is to obtain a purchase order or some initial revenue from the customer. When something does not work, it will require iterations to quickly fix the problem, test the fix and release a new version to the customer. For consumer products, there are usually multiple loop-back iterations at this stage because it will involve direct feedback from them. In the case of business-to-business (B2B) products, potential customers may suggest certain "must-have" features in order to get a purchase order, and you will have to implement the changes as quickly as possible. Eventually a better product will emerge after the customers give their final acceptance to buy the product.

It is important to ensure beta customers are happy so they can be used as reference customers for future clients and investors. The beta customers may provide useful feedback to add to the release version of the product. Only a few high-value changes should be allowed in the product at this point. Each new feature costs significantly more time to validate than most entrepreneurs expect, usually by a factor of 10X, so it must be done with caution. This is because it can destabilize the product and will require more extensive testing and verification.

The final phase is the production **release phase**. All the features and functionality are known at this point and all high-priority requests based on customer feedback should be implemented. The goal is to deliver the complete product that solves the customer problem. Very few feature additions are permitted at this phase beyond what is scheduled. Instead, there is a heavy emphasis on testing and verification. A final product freeze occurs and acceptance testing of the entire product is initiated, both automated and manual, by application engineers. Show-stopper, critical and important problems are fixed and tested to maintain integrity of the release. Installation and licensing tests for software are also carried out. At the end of the production release stage, a full-featured product is ready for market.

The complete product requires additional effort from several groups outside of Engineering. This includes the development of documentation and training materials for customers, if needed. It may include additional hardware and software for integration at the customer's site. There may be post-sales support and services to tailor the product to the needs of the customer. The sales team will likely require supporting materials and demos to pursue customers. Without them, the product may not be saleable or usable by customers. These materials and other supporting activities need to be defined and carried out in the final phases of product development. Their completion should coincide roughly with the completion of the product itself. Many companies have neglected to consider the total product requirements, but eventually they figured it out the hard way after making the first few sales.

Advanced Notes:
1. This book itself was written using the MVP approach. The first prototype was released to a select group of 5 people for review. The alpha publication release was reviewed by 10 people and the beta publication release by 100 people. This release is the final version, and suitable for a global audience.

Tip 2.4

Transform Yourself into a Lean Mean Business Machine

Tutorial: One common shortcoming of a founding team is the lack of business experience, and specifically startup experience. Usually, the entrepreneurs are figuring out what to do as they go along and this has led to countless failures due to rookie mistakes. Technical founders expect to learn quickly through osmosis, but they are basically walking into the teeth of a buzz saw. And they will be shredded. It is difficult to make a rapid transition from inventor to entrepreneur. One approach to address this problem is to add a business-oriented founder to the team but if they have no technical experience or deep understanding of the industry, they are expendable in the long run.

There is another approach if the team is lacking in business skills. Each member must transform themselves into a lean, mean, business machine. It takes 5 to 10 years to gain the needed experience, depending on the starting point, but there is a way to get a thin layer of experience in 5 to 10 months: **read 1 business book per week for 6 months and seek assistance from a team of advisors.**

You must train your brain to think like a business person and the fastest way to get there on your own is to read and study about 25 books ranging from business success stories, high-tech startups, negotiating, accounting, management, marketing, competition, leadership, venture capital financing, etc. It is not sufficient to skim these books. They must be studied and understood in great detail. Superficial knowledge won't cut it. This deep knowledge will pay off after you get started. Stay away from fluffy or trendy books about future businesses. You need the nuts and bolts of how businesses are run today.

Next, you must quickly develop business savvy in today's business world. This is different from business experience. It is the art of thinking two moves ahead, watching out for competitors, preparing for negotiations and meetings, being quick on the uptake, connecting the dots, anticipating potential problems, having contingency plans and not assuming that something will happen until after it happens. The fastest way to do this is to use all your business contacts and meet with different people to discuss startup issues at least once a week, and more frequently if possible. Pick their brains on what to expect and where the trouble spots may be. Continue to do this on every issue that comes up.

Over a 5 to 10 month period, you will begin to understand the key issues associated with starting and running a company by talking to experienced people. Ask them if they will serve as consultants or advisors for the company in the interim so that when new issues arise, you can call them for assistance. This is how you prevent yourself from making rookie mistakes. The waters are shark infested and you have to learn how to skillfully maneuver in this environment.

Next, obtain copies of as many pitch decks and business plans as possible from past companies and study them thoroughly. Develop your own pitch deck and business plan and understand the pitfalls of your venture. Have your consultants review the plan to find weaknesses or missing elements. Finally, watch videos, take short courses and adopt business jargon as part of your speaking style. You should be able to understand terms such as liquidation preferences, convertible notes, dilution, pay-to-play, exit strategy, due diligence and so on. It is useful to know acronyms such as P&L, M&A, JV, SWOT, FY3, Q2 and many other short forms.

At the end of the process, you must strive to be as good at business issues as you are with technical issues. **Even the technical decisions you make must be based on their business impact.** And continue to sharpen your skills as you gain experience. You will become an invaluable asset of the company, and people will rely on your ability to balance technology and business in decision-making. It will take 5 to 10 years to truly have the requisite business experience but this immersion program will help you in the short run.

After you get the company going, you may need to hire a CEO at the appropriate time to grow the company based on their actual business experience. If that occurs, you will need to identify a key role that maximizes your value to the company. The position that combines technical and business expertise is the VP of Engineering where your job is to deliver the products for the company. The VP of R&D typically works on the next set of products or product enhancements. The CTO is the technical guru of the company. There are other positions such as Director or Manager that are suitable for those who want to lead small teams.

You will have to decide where you add the most value and work out the most suitable title with the other founders and management. Then continue to hone your craft on both the business and technical sides of the company. As the company grows, you will need to be the best at a specific job and make significant contributions to the success of the company. **Do not become jack-of-all-trades.** Become the master of one or two.

Advanced notes:
1. A business perspective is critical for anyone making decisions about product features. All proposed features must be scrutinized for business impact. Customers ask for many improvements having no impact on current or future sales. But each new feature has an impact on product schedules, testing and quality.
2. **At least one founder must be, or must become, very business savvy. This is an absolute requirement to succeed.** If this does not happen very quickly, then the founding team may have to be revisited or perhaps reconstituted.

Tip 2.5

Meet Early & Often to Strategize, Plan and Execute

Tutorial: A novice entrepreneur usually starts with a good idea and develops a simple plan to commercialize it: get funding, build the product, and go sell it to customers like hotcakes, and then declare success. Unfortunately it does not happen that way. The above sequence of steps is usually the path to failure. If the entrepreneur used the opposite approach and started by selling the idea to the customers, and then building the right product, and then seeking funds to start a company, it would have a much better chance of success. Today, you have to flip the script to succeed.

Greatness does not happen by accident, it happens by design. When you are getting started, there are many unknowns. In fact, almost everything is an unknown. What you have to do is to convert as many unknowns into known quantities so you can build a strategy to convert your ideas into a commercial product to deliver revenue. In order to do that, you and the founding team must meet early and often. There is a lot of thinking ahead of you. And that requires lots of brainpower. Ideas must be white boarded and battle tested. Prototypes must be built. Markets must be understood through experimentation using a minimum viable product. Underlying assumptions and hypotheses must be validated, and the strategy and plans revised, if necessary. And then you repeat the loop multiple times. In the process, you are literally creating something out of nothing – Something great!

When you build an MVP and begin experimenting in the marketplace, a strategy for the company will begin to emerge. When you sketch out initial plans, you will begin to notice holes in your approach and opportunities that you did not consider before. This is exactly what the frequent meetings are meant to accomplish.

Rather than starting a company without any plans in place, you are actually eliminating hypothetical companies that will likely fail. This is the time to challenge all the assumptions, such as "There's going to be a huge market for this product" or "I think we've struck gold!" These are conclusions based on intuition or hyperbole, not facts.

When you actually figure out the market size and guesstimate how much revenue you could conceivably make, it will give you a first-order idea of what type of company you can build. If the revenue number is too low, then you should check your assumptions again. If the same results are obtained, you can consider it as a failed company because it is unlikely to be profitable. Be smart, think ahead and eliminate companies that are likely to fail through this process. This is the best version of "fail fast" because it is carried out with a spreadsheet. **Actual failure in a startup takes a heavy emotional and physical toll on everyone involved and should be avoided at all cost.** Ruling out bad companies by thinking ahead is much less painful and eventually leads to a company that has a high probability of success.

The process of strategizing and planning is inherently an iterative one because you need to make assumptions that may or may not be true. You decide on a product, study the market, competition and potential revenue to decide whether you have a viable company. At this stage, anything is possible so you should allow yourself a lot of latitude about the product and the market. The only real constraint is the core competence of the team. If the founders have the ability to build a product with a small team of engineers, the product is eligible for consideration at this stage.

To help you at a strategic level, you could develop a vision and mission for the company. **The Vision Statement is your "big hairy audacious goal"** or BHAG. It is the "What" of your company goal. **The Mission Statement is the method by which you will achieve the vision.** It is the "How" of your company goal. Keep them short. It is too early to finalize the Vision and Mission statements because you have a lot of latitude on what you can do, so it will change.

36   Build Something Great!

However, you can cycle through various statements as you change your strategy. It is a good idea to include the word "customer" in every Mission Statement just to remind yourself who provides you with revenue. With every modification at the strategic level, you should reduce the latitude of your possible options. Eventually, you must narrow the scope of the effort until you converge on specifically what you can build now and what market it will serve.

Once you have a set of possible products in mind, you need to decide which one to build first. **You need to define a killer product with one or two barriers to entry.** A prototype should be built to test the viability of the product. You need to develop an alpha version of the minimum viable product and then release it to a small group of users or customers to determine if it has potential. This is the time to experiment and learn as much as possible about the product/market fit and to evaluate customer response to the initial offering. You should use this information to improve the product and perhaps develop prototypes for additional products.

If the first product does not do well in the initial market testing, you need to identify the next product that you would release, whether it is an improved version of the first product with new features and functions, or a wholly new product. Either way, you have not spent a lot of time and money building the wrong product but you have already eliminated a number of hypothetical companies through this process. By testing your hypotheses and validating your assumptions with a very low burn rate, you become much more familiar with the product requirements and the right direction for the business in the target market. This is very important.

After you define your product and market, and estimate your market share and revenue, you need to decide what you plan to do with the company if it successful. This is referred to as the "exit strategy". It is a term used by investors because that is the point at which they take the exit ramp off the company highway. It is either an acquisition of your company by another company or an initial public offering (IPO). Both events give liquidity to shareholders, which include employees and founders (although there may be some restrictions for those in management). You should be able to name potential acquirers of your company.

If one of the founders is interested in building only a moneymaker, or an acquisition target rather than a fast-growing investor-backed company, this is a good time to discuss it to resolve any differences. The decision is really up to you and the team at this point. The best approach is to not think about the liquidation event but consider which companies would be interested in buying your company if it ever made business sense to join forces with a larger company. Then you should decide whether the company will be bootstrapped or pursue angel or VC funding.

As a founder, you have to determine if your team has what it takes to get the job done. As you discuss different strategies and different plans, you should assess the overall quality of the founding team. It also provides an opportunity to work with the team to identify strengths and weaknesses. Determine whether they are in it for the long haul or just participating out of curiosity and interest but without any commitment. Assess whether their personal lives would allow them to start a company and spend countless hours trying to get it off the ground. Find out if they are open to new ways of doing things, or stuck on their own ways. This is the time to decide if you can work with this team, and whether there is team chemistry, a set of complimentary skills, critical needs they each fill, and a collective desire to do something great. Do you have shared goals? If not, then it is time to change one or two of the founders. If you swap out both founders, there is no company at this point, but you have avoided a failed company in the process. Make the "Go/No-Go" decision in this timeframe.

Once you decide to forge ahead, the best way to focus the team is to identify the key business questions that you have to answer in order to succeed. Then, decide what insights you need in order to answer the key business questions. Next, develop prototypes and solicit input from customers to obtain these insights. Collect as much experimental data as possible in the process. Finally, examine the experimental data resulting from the initial prototypes or customer/market investigation to determine if you can create a viable enterprise. Your ability to make high-level decisions based on low-level information will be tested. Most people live at one extreme or the other. Those who can span the gap between these two ends of the spectrum will have the highest probability of success. Perhaps the most important factor to assess is the quality of the product/market fit since this may ultimately decide your fate. **The main point is to drive the activities at each stage with one or two key business decisions that are critical to long-term success of your company.**

Tip 2.6

Bootstrap as Long as Possible

Summary: In order to get started on your company, you need a source of working capital in the early days. Financing your company without the involvement of any sophisticated investors is referred to as bootstrapping. During bootstrapping, the main source of funding is from your bank account, either directly or indirectly. A second source will likely come from friends and family (F&F). Venture capital (VC) financing starts in the range of $1-10M with a very high bar to secure funding. It is not a feasible option for a while and it is not cheap money. Angel investors are a viable option but they are also looking to fund startups much further along than just a small group of founders with a business plan. Their funding levels are in the range of $150K-$1M. Investors expect equity in return for their investment, and the amount of equity is highly dependent on your progress. To maximize your chances of obtaining funding at a later date with a high valuation, you need to bootstrap as long as possible to build up the value of the company.

Key point: While you are bootstrapping, you need to identify sources of future funding and hit milestones necessary for those funding sources. **It is very important to know, in advance, what investors expect in terms of milestones achieved.** In the meantime, the options for paying expenses are generally working for free, personal funds, friends and family. If you are committed to bootstrapping the entire operation for certain consumer products, there are also Internet sites that can be used to obtain funds. The details of these options are available on their respective sites. Some investors look at sales on these crowdsourcing sites as indicators and data points for market demand, especially for early-stage hardware companies. Investigate all the pros and cons before taking such a route.

Tutorial: Once you decide to start a company, you quickly realize you need a certain amount of working capital to get it off the ground. There are obvious expenses associated with any business, no matter how small. You need to identify short-term space to do your work (usually a home office), purchase some computers and other hardware and software, and spend money on miscellaneous items. Unfortunately there is about a 100% probability that your company will fail at this stage, so it is unlikely to be funded by professional investors, such as VCs and angels. Therefore, bootstrapping is the only option. However, the length of time you are bootstrapping depends on the type of company you are trying to build.

Many entrepreneurs are not interested in the VC or angel route and prefer to bootstrap the entire enterprise. They start companies to develop a technology or product on their own terms and in their own time without having investors breathing down their necks. They can play in their own sandbox and do things their own way without someone standing on the other side of the fence telling them how to do things and to do it a lot faster.

Life changes completely when you have sophisticated investors, and many entrepreneurs do not like the nature of these changes. Remember that when you obtain VC financing, you give up an equity stake in your company and the clock starts ticking towards an IPO or acquisition within 5-8 years. So it is wise to build up value in a bootstrapping mode as long as possible. In fact, you should try to get to profitability so that you may not even need angels or VCs. Many successful companies have been built this way.

When bootstrapping, there are a variety of methods that can be used to raise cash from your personal assets in the first few months of operation. If you are planning to start a company at a future date and intend to bootstrap it, save 10% of your current income every month for that purpose. If you are starting one in the near term, the founders must all figure out their own way to extend themselves. This is where each founder puts in "sweat equity" to get the company going and it could take several different forms. It may require the use of someone's home or garage for meetings, cash to purchase items to build a prototype product and the investment of your time without any compensation. However you choose to self-fund your effort, you are officially bootstrapping the company, which is a time-honored tradition for early-stage startups.

As expenses begin to mount, there are several ways to supply the company with higher levels of startup capital. For example, if any of the founders has $20-50K available and would like to invest in the company, then a nominal valuation of $500K could be used to set the percentage ownership for the invested amount. This would come directly out of the founder's shares, so everyone would be diluted by an equal amount to accommodate the investment. If a founder adds $25K, they purchase a 5% stake in the company, along with their diluted percentage ownership as agreed upon previously by all founders. In effect, that founder has acquired a higher percentage of the company. If all founders contribute funds, they are essentially paying for shares they already own. These funds will likely not be recovered if the company reaches the first round of financing because "that's just the cost of doing business".

Another option is to seek funding from friends and family (F&F). This option should be used with great care. If the company fails, your friends and family may be upset that they lost their investment. Therefore, you will need to educate those who offer to invest funds in your startup. If anyone decides to give you a gift to get things rolling with "no strings attached", then you should make a mental note to give them some common stock out of your own pocket some time after the company is funded and while the price per share is very low. In fact, keep a list of those who helped you significantly along the way in the first year and think about giving them some shares at a later date.

If cash gifts are not readily available, the founding team will need to find relatives and friends who can afford to give out funds in the form of a debt that may be converted to company shares when there is a seed or first round of financing. **It is important to incorporate the company before taking any startup funds.** Then, it is the company (not you) that takes on the debt or gives out equity in exchange for funding. The company is solely responsible for paying back the debt with interest, or converting debt to shares, or taking funding in exchange for an equity position in the company. Otherwise, you are personally on the hook for the repayment of funds and that will result in fewer friends and unhappy family members because you were unable to pay them back.

A key step in the process of taking money from F&F groups is to have a business conversation about the funds being transferred to the company. You should not approach those who can neither afford it nor have the funds readily available. If they have to sell shares in their retirement account, or take out a second mortgage or a bank loan, it is not worth the trouble. On the other hand, if they can afford to lose all the money and are still willing to participate, then they are investing in your future because they trust that you will make every effort to build a successful company. Effectively, they are investing in you.

For the unsophisticated investor such as F&F, you should explain how the system works. Let them know that the company is taking a loan from them and will likely pay them back at the next round of financing plus any interest that has accrued. However, if the company fails, they might not be paid back. So their money is at risk. Or they can buy common shares directly and take a long-term position in the company. After a liquidity event, such as an IPO or acquisition, they will receive their investment back plus a return-on-investment. Make sure both you and your F&F are aware that there will be potential future issues related to accredited investors that may impact their actual ownership level and type of shares they receive in the company. There may also be an unwinding of certain deals with F&F if new investors find the terms unacceptable.

The instrument used to carry out this transaction using debt is called a convertible note. Early F&F investors could each receive such a note and convert the note at the first round of financing. Be aware that VCs and angels are only comfortable with 3-5 notes from F&F sources. Having these conversations and working out legal agreements with them will save you many headaches later on downstream. And if you take their money, treat F&F funding as a business transaction and keep them informed from time to time on the progress of the company.

A final option for bootstrapping your company is to investigate government-funding programs for startups (e.g. Small Business Administration (SBA) grants). There may be local, state and national government programs that provide seed funding to get you to a prototype product. These funds are highly competitive and require a business proposal and specific objectives to be met using the funds. In general, they apply many of the same criteria to evaluate startups as used by investors to assess companies. In many cases, they do not take an equity position nor do they require payback of a loan, so they are worth pursuing.

If you have difficulty obtaining funds, it will not get any easier going forward. You will have to convince more sophisticated investors to part with their money at a later date and they will not fall for a set of false promises. They expect results. In fact, during the bootstrapping phase, you will have to produce a working beta product, hire some management and engineering people, and contact a few customers for a potential beta-site testing of the product. Angel investors are suitable as a funding option at this stage. VCs are looking at companies that are further along. They must have some initial revenue, and a path to grow the company quickly. The investors expect you to hit these milestones before approaching them. In some sense, bootstrapping is the easy phase of the startup where you get to create and improvise as you build value, but it is also the hardest part because you have to find working capital when you have almost nothing of value. You have to get through this chicken-and-egg phase until you have enough tangible value to pitch the concept to more sophisticated investors.

Once you obtain enough working capital, you need to operate on a shoestring budget. Use the computers that you already have in your home for your startup-related work. **Ensure that you are not using any equipment or proprietary materials from your previous employer. This is a big mistake, which could lead to lawsuits.** Move your hardware to the space you have identified for the company, whether it is someone's home, a garage, an incubator office or some cheap space that you can sublease temporarily. Purchase items you need to build hardware or write software. Find open source code and frameworks online to help develop prototypes using agile methods. Borrow existing business plans from advisors to help you develop the blueprint for the company. At this point, you have all the necessary ingredients to get down to the real work of creating value for your fledgling startup.

Advanced notes:
1. **Several web sites enable pre-sales of your products or cash contributions toward your product ideas.** Depending on the nature of your business, these sites may provide early funding opportunities. They provide funds without equity obligations or serious milestone obligations.
2. **Several web sites enable investment in startups.** Some of these sites may provide a source of funding in exchange for equity. The terms may be better than angels or VCs, but do not expect much help with the business or future funds. If you plan to pursue angel or VC funds later, educate yourself on issues regarding non-accredited investors prior to accepting these funds.
3. **Incubators** are business or academic entities that provide space, infrastructure, some resources and startup interactions in exchange for equity. Their goal is to seed your effort up to a funding round. They may be quite helpful if they focus on startups with similar needs as yours. They may also have regular competitions to qualify for or to continue use of their facilities. Many different models exist, so study them carefully before signing up.
4. **Accelerators** are business entities that provide high-end mentorship programs for promising startups intending to

pursue angel or VC financing. They help the startup shorten the time to go from a company with a small group of founders and engineers to a company that is ready to scale in exchange for a small amount of equity.
5. Many companies have been funded by way of the founders consulting for the initial customer. Be sure the customer is a partner and you have agreements giving you rights to the IP associated with your product.
6. Many professionals accustomed to working with startups (e.g. lawyers, marketers, sales persons and PR firms) make accommodations during the bootstrap phase. They agree to do work in exchange for payment or stock when you receive funding at a later date. In addition, many successful company founders and potential investors give free advice to entrepreneurs in the bootstrap phase.

Take Away: Bootstrapping is required by necessity and to prove that you are serious and passionate about starting a company. You must demonstrate that you have what it takes to go from idea to revenue using only your wits and ingenuity. You should continue to bootstrap as long as you can, and if you are profitable and growing revenue linearly, you have a sustainable business model.

Tip 2.7

Build an Active Network of Advisors

Tutorial: In the first 18-24 months, you need to make a lot of decisions that may be out of your depth. You don't know what you don't know, but there are people who do know. This is where a network of business and technical advisors is indispensable. **Some have argued that the quality of your network is a critical success factor for first-time entrepreneurs.** You need to assemble this group of individuals and be able to call on them to get advice. Experienced business people actually enjoy giving out advice because it keeps them connected with what is going on and they like to give back to an industry that has served them well. **The key point is to use this network of advisors as often as possible. You never know when that little of gem of critical advice is going to come in handy.** You must have "running dialogues" with these advisors, especially in the early days.

Any number of advisors is useful, but the optimal number appears to be 3 business advisors and 3 technical advisors. This way, you are not leaning too heavily on one or two people, and you can spend some time building good relationships with about 5 or 6 people. Decide based on your comfort zone as to the most suitable number, but have at least 4 at the beginning and add more as you go along.

If you can convince one of your advisors to act as a mentor in the early days, you are greatly increasing your chances of success. A mentor is a close advisor and confidant interested in your success and will spend as much time as needed to get you there. They provide the benefit of many years of experience along with moral support in tough times. The special mentor-protégé relationship is usually established over a period of years, but it can develop quickly over a few months under the right circumstances when an advisor believes they can make a significant impact on the protégé over the first year or two. Mentors receive great satisfaction in seeing their protégés succeed and they do it largely for this reason.

When you are faced with a difficult business issue, contact 2 business advisors and get their thoughts. If they are independently in agreement, then you have the information you need. If they disagree, you may need to call a third advisor. If there is a technical question related to companies and products in your industry, you may already have a handle on the answer, but it is wise to discuss it with 1 or 2 of your technical advisors for confirmation.

Business advisors should have different strengths such as raising funds, knowledge of business models and running a company. When you are writing the business plan, it is useful to run the numbers past the business advisors several times. Ask them to validate your assumptions about the market sizes and competition. If they know of any adjacent markets that may contain large potential competitors who could try to enter your market, this information would be very valuable. At a minimum, they should review your revenue, expenses and profit projections. They should also identify additional risks you may have missed. Their experience will be most useful in the first 2 years.

The technical advisors should also have different strengths such as knowledge of product development, competitive product features and technology in the industry. They may have information on future products being developed in various companies and the timing of their introduction into the market. They may know of a few startups going out of business that may have useful technology for your startup. They may offer methods to solve some of your technical problems outside of product development issues. And they may be able to provide leads for potential hires.

Select advisors based on your areas of weakness because you want to avoid making bad decisions. Imagine yourself walking across a tightrope as a metaphor for making a series of business decisions. Your advisors are like your balance pole to make sure you don't inadvertently slip, and they act as your safety net in case you do.

You dare not try to cross without them!

Advisors can be found through accelerators and incubators available in your region. These are entities that help speed up the initial phases of a startup through intensive programs or provide resources at a relatively inexpensive cost in exchange for a small equity stake in the company. It may be a preferred option for those who have little or no background in startups and wish to make contacts with potential advisors. They can often provide useful connections for hiring, funding and legal counsel.

The early group of advisors forms a virtual advisory board in the initial stages. You should contact them frequently as the need arises. Later, convert this group into a formal Business and Technical Advisory Board (BTAB) that convenes once per quarter, then twice a year and then annually. You should add or remove advisors as the company grows and as your needs change. If possible, recruit professors who are experts in their field and well-known business people in the industry. It gives visibility to the company and increases its credibility. The main take away is to build this group early and use them often.

Tip 2.8

Commit Yourself Completely

Summary: There are five key personal decisions that will affect the success or failure of a startup. If you make all five correctly, you will increase the probability of success. In fact, you cannot predict exactly which decision is the one that will put you over the top. So each one that increases your likelihood of success must be taken or you are, in effect, allowing a known risk factor to be part of your equation.

Decision 1: You must quit your previous employment. This shows investors your commitment, but also demonstrates your own belief in the product and the company. If you are not willing to go "all in", then it will not succeed. This includes professors and students. Working part-time is a signal to everyone you are mitigating your own personal risk at the expense of the company. Be sure to leave with "clean hands". Any intellectual property or "know-how" developed at the company cannot simply walk out the door with you. There may be legal issues depending on the employment contract you signed when you accepted employment. You do not want to deal with lawsuits after you get your startup off the ground.

Decision 2: Move to where the action is. If you are not located near a business hub, you are at a disadvantage. Today, many people believe you can start a company anywhere. But are you willing to stay in a sub-optimal location for your convenience instead of moving to the right place for your company? You need to be near the customers! You also need to be near a talented pool of potential employees, investors, lawyers, advisors, Board members and suppliers. Or you can stay at the second best, or third best location in each category and be at a disadvantage. Today, many high-tech hubs have popped up so it should not be a problem to locate near one if necessary.

Decision 3: You will have to work 70 to 80 hours a week for approximately 5 years or more. This is not avoidable. There are no shortcuts to building a successful company. There are too many ways to fail, and only a few ways to succeed. You have to transform yourself from inventor to entrepreneur, from a technical person to a business person, from a star player to a team player. New issues will take up all your time. If you decide to work less than everyone else in other startups, it is hard to believe you will be successful. But make sure you take short vacations and let one of the other founders cover for you during that time.

Decision 4: You must focus all your energies into the company. You may have to give up on certain parts of your personal life in favor of your company life. You cannot afford to be distracted with hobbies, social media or other time-consuming activities. You need to spend a significant number of cycles thinking only about the company. However, it must not cost you your health because burn-out is a distinct possibility. You will be riding the bucking bronco for years. So you need to take care of yourself. But beyond that, all other activities must be reduced. There is no point in doing a startup unless you have a deep and unwavering passion for it that supersedes all else. You must "get in the zone and stay in the zone." If you lose your passion, you may lose your company.

Decision 5: You may have to ask friends and family (F&F) for money. If you are bootstrapping a company for a while to get to a point where you can go to professional investors, you are likely to run out of money at some point. Even your own savings will run dry as expenses for the company go up. Getting out the tin cup and sitting down with family and friends is difficult. You have to make sure that any money taken is in the form of a legal loan with interest or a convertible note if they want equity in the company. If you don't ask for money and you have no other sources to fund your company, there is no company at that point.

CHAPTER 3
Assess Product/Market Fit

3.1. An Idea is NOT a Product

3.2. A Working Product is NOT Necessarily a Company

3.3. Build a "Pain Killer" not a "Vitamin Pill"

3.4. Identify Your "Unfair" Advantages

3.5. Market Size Tells You About the Opportunity

3.6. Competition Tells You About the Degree of Difficulty

3.7. Know the Ecosystem of Your Product from End-to-end

3.8. Develop Your Business Plan Iteratively

Tip 3.1

An Idea is NOT a Product

Summary: One mistake first-time entrepreneurs make is they believe their new idea will become a great product demanded by the marketplace. The chances of that happening are very small. But they refuse to believe it. It is not until they are far along the path of building a company that they realize their product is of no interest to the market. They learn this when their revenue is $0 while the monthly burn rate is through the roof. This is the wrong time to figure it out. But the inexperienced entrepreneur usually does not realize it until long after the company has closed its doors.

To avoid this fatal mistake, the entrepreneur must learn how to differentiate between ideas that solve a customer problem and ideas that are worthless. **The ratio of good commercial ideas to bad ones is 1 to 10,000, so your task is to determine why the idea won't work before going any further.** And when you do, you need to hit the self-destruct button on the idea and move on to another one that solves a customer problem and serves a large market need.

Key point: Be the harshest critic of your own idea, technology and product. Instead of imagining everyone beating a path to your door to buy the product at a substantial price, imagine no one wanting it even if you gave it away for free. That is a more realistic starting point. It underscores the difficulty of selling products to customers. If you adopt this mindset of how difficult it will be, you stand a much better chance of developing something that customers actually need. And even if they need the product, there will be significant sales and marketing challenges to get them to buy the product.

Assess Product/Market Fit

Tutorial: It is important for founders to understand the fundamental difference between an idea and a product. An idea is a creative concept, which may or may not have commercial value, whereas a product is something a customer wants to buy. Ideas have far less value compared to products. But founders tend to be idea-centric and they place enormous value on them. Oftentimes, they mistakenly believe their idea is the product. Furthermore, they think the hard part is to come up with the original technical idea while it is relatively easy to build a product. In reality, ideas are cheap but it is very difficult to build a complete product that will sell and much more difficult to build a company around the product. Many people have many great ideas, but very few of them lead to a product or a viable company. There are rare exceptions to this rule, like Facebook, and this is unfortunately what leads many entrepreneurs to think their idea is the next big thing.

If you have a new idea for a product, your first job is to figure out the limitations of your idea. The strengths are obvious to you because you do not see any flaws, at least none that cannot be fixed over time. But there is likely to be one major flaw and you must figure out what it is. Bad ideas will sink the company. If you can find the main problem with your idea before others do, it will save everyone a lot of time, money, frustration and failure. More optimistically, it is the first step in making you **think critically about ideas from a business perspective rather than a technical perspective. This shift in thinking is perhaps the most important change to make for first-time entrepreneurs.**

Consider this metaphor. A customer accidently cuts themselves on the foot and is bleeding (red ink). They need a tourniquet to stop the bleeding, then an ointment for rapid healing of the wound. You show up with a pair of socks as your product. You suggest the socks may help stop the bleeding. You are so far away from what they need to solve their problem they show you the door. Another vendor who knows the customer shows up with a tourniquet, and they discuss returning with an ointment for rapid healing. They have an immediate solution and a roadmap for full recovery. They win the business. Although your socks are "nice-to-have" items, you did not know the customer was actually in desperate need of certain "must-have" items.

This metaphor illustrates why an idea is not a product. You have to start by being customer-centric, not product-centric, or technology-centric, or idea-centric. You have to build something that the customer actually wants. Most of your target customers are usually too busy to think of buying a new-fangled product. In fact, they are not interested in it. They have immediate problems they have to solve. If you do not provide your product at the right time, either too early or too late, they will not buy it. **If it is a "must-have" product, they will be interested. If it is a "nice-to-have" product, they will not have the budget for it, especially in tough economic times.** That is the customer's mindset.

The key to a good idea for a product is whether or not a customer is willing to pay for it. If it is not something a customer will buy, that is the major flaw you are missing with your technical idea. In fact, there are countless reasons why a customer won't buy your product. The only reason that they will buy your product is they have a serious problem and your product solves that problem. It saves them money, or time-to-market, or time-to-revenue, or is better in some respect than any other product in the marketplace in solving one of their problems. Otherwise, it is not a viable product.

With that backdrop, you should revisit your technical idea and see if it is still a winner. What customer problem does it solve? Will they pay for your solution? Is that problem pervasive in the industry? **If you can clearly and concisely articulate a customer problem, explain how widespread it is and show how your solution solves the problem, then you may actually have a viable product and, by extension, a viable company. Call this your "elevator pitch."**

On the other hand, if your idea is a new algorithm or technology but you are not sure where it would be useful, then it is the proverbial "solution looking for a problem." You are too detached from the target customer and inventing products in a vacuum. This is an all too common example of an idea that is a long way off from being a product or company. However, it may still be a viable business by licensing the technology to third parties, but is not likely to be a fast-growing company.

One test you can apply to any of your product ideas is to ask yourself if customers were involved in validating your new idea. If your answer is "no involvement", then it is probably appropriate to abandon the idea. A better approach is to visit your customers to see if they have any interest in such an idea if you converted it to a product. If your customers think it would be nice to have your solution, be aware they may just be encouraging you with no intention to buy it, because it's a "nice-to-have" item. Alternatively, you could try to name your first hundred customers. If you cannot name them, that would be a problem for scaling your business. In that case, try to name ten companies and call them up and ask if they would pay for your solution. If not, it is time to push the self-destruct button on your idea and move on. Every idea has one. Make sure you push it first before investors, customers or others do it for you.

When you develop a new idea for a product, you must think about the target customer. In the fast moving high-tech world, you need to be building solutions the customer must buy for its own survival, or to gain a significant advantage over their competition, or to dramatically improve their ability to sell their own products. Until and unless you understand the characteristics of your customers, their business needs, their buying patterns and what they are willing to pay for such a proposed product, your idea has no commercial value. It is nothing more than a hammer looking for a nail. In the metaphor described earlier, you should either be working on tourniquets or ointments. Unfortunately, you are busy designing colorful socks because that's what you want to do; thus, the disconnect.

Take Away: When embarking on the startup adventure, it is important to clearly understand the stage you are at and the things you need to accomplish at that stage. The new entrepreneurs and new companies need to stop trying to do everything at once and focus first on validating the product idea. An initial alpha product must be used to understand and confirm the market need for this product. The purpose of this initial stage is to reach a comfort level with product/market fit. If you can identify the customers for your product and validate the market through an evaluation cycle using a minimum viable product, then you are in a strong position to go forward with building a business. And if you ask the right business questions, and obtain satisfactory answers to these questions during the evaluation period, you will have a high probability of success in your venture.

Tip 3.2

A Working Product is NOT Necessarily a Company

Summary: Behind every successful company is a working product. However, a working product does not necessarily lead to a successful company. This seems counter-intuitive but a working product does not guarantee that a business can be built around it. Many issues exist that make it difficult to convert a working product into a growing revenue stream. First, entrepreneurs will often build products that have no market, as surprising as that may seem. Equally problematic is the development of the wrong product that customers themselves request but later decide they don't need because it is not a "must-have" product. Second, if a working product misses its market window, the company will likely fail. Third, developing a proper business model for a working product is critical to get to profitability. And fourth, if the competition builds a superior product, the fact that your product works may be irrelevant. Therefore, building a successful company is a combination of the right product for a large market, the right timing, a proper business model, weak competition and a heavy-duty sales effort to push the product through the sales channel to customers.

Key Point: Most entrepreneurs think that the product IS the company. They believe the hard part is to build a working product but it will be relatively straight forward to build a company around it because it is a simple step-by-step recipe. This is incorrect. A working product is only the first link in a long chain of requirements that must be satisfied to build a successful company. You must think through all of the major business issues to determine if a successful company can be built with a working product. In fact, funding is not based on just having a working product. It based on whether a business case can be made for a fast-growing company assuming the product works.

Tutorial: In a relative sense, if the Engineering effort required to build a product is 1X, then the effort required to build a successful company is around 5X, or higher. But it may not be worth the effort to build a company because a working product does not necessarily lead to a successful company. It is a necessary condition, but not sufficient. In fact, most of the time, it does not lead to a successful company. The question is, when does it make sense to invest the 5X to build a company, meaning what could possibly prevent the company from being successful when it has a working product?

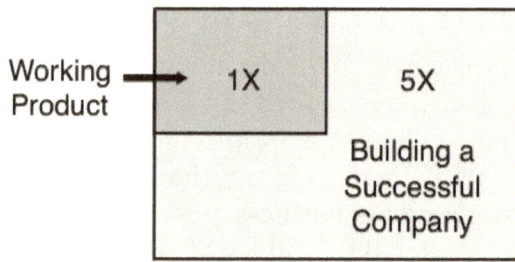

First of all, many startups develop a product that has **no market**. While that seems unthinkable, **it is a leading cause of failure for startups**. There must be a product/market fit with lots of potential customers. Without customers, there is no company but somehow this is lost on first-time founders. Professor, graduate students and industry researchers often pursue product ideas that satisfy themselves rather than a market need. They strive for technical elegance, not marketplace acceptance. Years of publishing papers may have fooled them into thinking they can beat the odds, but they lose that bet almost every time. They believe that customers will all line up to buy their product because it is technically superior to other approaches, not realizing that no one is interested. If they have not worked with customer input from the start, which is typical, they usually develop something no one wants. But they do not care. They continue to build products they think the market should embrace as they merrily drive over the cliff.

Equally problematic is a product that is merely "nice-to-have" for the customers. Most first-time founders will not accept the fact they are building a "nice-to-have" product because they believe they are only capable of building "must-have" products. This is the secondary cause of startup failure. Even so, research-oriented founders believe that they can make a sale of a "nice-to-have" product on the strength of their personality, selling abilities and the quality of their technical solutions. They think the customer is missing the true value of the product. A few customers may kick the tires but even fewer will actually buy it. This type of product rarely makes enough revenue to sustain the company due to the expenses needed to build a company. There may be some initial revenue, which is what gives them hope, but there will not be profits. The market will only accept "must-have" products.

Another common problem is to inadvertently develop the **wrong product**. This is not necessarily the fault of the entrepreneur. Customers may express a strong interest in a certain proposed product when they are initially approached for feedback, but things change from one year to the next. The product may no longer be useful or needed by the customer, even if they were the ones who validated the market for that product. Be aware that **the customer is not responsible for giving you their best advice on what to build. They only provide input but you will have to decide what to build**. You must track the market yourself and ensure that you are working on the right product at all times. When a market shifts to a new set of needs, the company must pivot to the next product quickly based on its internal expertise and core competence. However, if the company moves to another product but is still unable to gain any traction, it will eventually run out of money. That is, if the pivot strategy is reactive, it tends to fail. What is worse is to have no pivot strategy at all, in which case failure is immediate.

A working product may not lead to a successful company if you miss a market window, either being too early or too late. If the product is too early, then the burn rate will be too high relative to revenues and eventually another round of financing will be necessary. Being early to the market is not as serious if you can survive until the market arrives. If the product is too late, then revenue will be gobbled up by the competition. If you are late to the party, you get the leftovers, which may not be sufficient to keep the company afloat. This situation could also arise when a product serves a shrinking market and the market disappears before the product can be delivered.

Market timing is everything. Some have argued that timing is the only thing. If you get it wrong, you are sunk. If you get it right, you win big. Most get it wrong. That's why many companies fail. If you want to succeed, make sure the timing is right for your product. Many high-tech consumer products miss the market window due to delays in product development or sales channel capacity issues. The management team must fully understand the dynamics of the marketplace and avoid these problems. Typically, these issues fall under the banner of time-to-market or time-to-revenue. The goal is to shorten the times associated with these two metrics.

There are other issues that arise even if you have the right product with the right timing in a sizeable market. These issues are associated with the business model. If you get it right, you win big. **Many companies have failed when they get the business model wrong.** The key to a proper business model is to ensure that the business is scalable. Two integral parts of the business model are product pricing and the cost of goods sold. A scalable business has high margins, i.e., the difference between the product price and the cost of goods sold. If the initial sales take place in a growing market, that may still not be sufficient to build a business. It depends on the nature of the sales cycle and the product price. If the sales cycle is very long, the cost of goods sold high and the margins small, it will be difficult to increase revenue year over year. If the price is not sufficient to create a path to profitability, the company will eventually run out of money and fail.

As a simple example of the importance of the business model and pricing, consider a case where a new printer has been developed for home use that runs twice as fast as the competition. It requires color and B&W print cartridges. In this hypothetical example, the cost of making a printer is $150 and the cost of making each cartridge is $5. The company decides to sell the printer for $1000 and the cartridges for $10. What they will find is that very few printers are sold, but for each printer sold there are dozens of cartridges sold. The lack of sales of the printer could sink the company. On the other hand, if the price of the printer is set to $175, which is more competitive, and the cartridges at $25 each, the profits go through the roof because of volume. This is the classic razor-blade revenue model.

But what if the cost of making the printer is $995 due to the use of a new advanced technology? Then there may be a problem with the business model due to the inherent cost of goods sold. At a price of $1000 per printer, margins and volumes would be too small to be sustainable. Even raising the price of the cartridges would not help unless it is increased above $100. At that point, no one would buy the printer or cartridges. There may be optimal printer and cartridge prices that would deliver a profitable business but it would involve a detailed analysis in a spreadsheet, and then trial and error in the marketplace. Even though this is an oversimplified case study, it is clear that the business model is critical to the viability and scalability of the business.

The basic rule is that your business model should be similar to other business models in your industry. If you need to make changes, you will have to develop the strategy and tactics to implement it. If it is a new market opportunity, you may have to cycle through a few business models before deciding on the right one, and that costs time and money. If you do not find one that is scalable and drives revenue and profits up, you will need another round of financing. This is due to the fact that ramping up sales requires building out the sales channel, and that can be very expensive. This process of changing the business model will continue until investors lose faith in the strategy and they will push for a liquidation event when they finally lose patience. An evolving business model has been occurring over the past few years in the Internet of Things (IoT) space, which may explain why companies do not have a high success rate yet.

Social networking companies use another business model variation. These companies depend on recruiting a critical mass of members in order to enable one or more revenue streams. They require large funding to build the infrastructure and recruit members. If they do not succeed in acquiring enough members to enable sufficient revenue or they fail to retain members, the company fails. The strategy here is to shoot for the moon and either succeed or fail spectacularly.

The last issue that could make it difficult to build a business around a working product is **competition**. This is a large topic worthy of a separate discussion because it can take so many forms. A fragmented market with a few small players is ideal, but usually there are two dominant companies in a large market and that is undesirable. It is best to avoid a David and Goliath situation. Large competitors will either squash you or buy you before you get out of their purchase price range. They will attempt to reduce your projected revenues by undercutting you on price, out-competing you in the customer base, or sending a frivolous lawsuit in your direction just to tie up the management team. They are not interested in seeing a small fry eat their lunch. So if you have built a great product that is gaining market share, be prepared for a lot of incoming fire from the competitors, both big and small.

Take Away: A working product is only the first link in the chain to build a successful company. The next two links are a large market for the product and weak competitors in that market. If the competition is not weak, then your product or business model must be far superior to theirs. The last two links are the right timing and a scalable business model. It is a combination of all these requirements that leads to success. If any one of these requirements is missing, then the probability of success may drop precipitously, depending on which one cannot be achieved.

Tip 3.3

Build a "Pain Killer" not a "Vitamin Pill"

Summary: When you are ready to pitch your idea for a business to investors, they will try to quickly assess what type of product you are planning to sell so they can decide whether they want to listen to the rest of your presentation. For professional investors, time is money. And you will be wasting both if they find out at the end that you don't really have a business. As a result, they have developed a shorthand to categorize the product for a given market. In their parlance, a "pain killer" is something that actually solves an existing or near-term customer problem and is guaranteed to sell. It is a *must-have* item. A "vitamin pill" is a *should-have* or *could-have* item. While this type of product may have intrinsic value, the customer may or may not buy it depending on the circumstances. That is, it is not absolutely essential. In economic downturns, the customer is unlikely to purchase it. Therefore, it is important to build products that are pain killers to guarantee funding and to have a high probability of success.

Key point: If you walk into an investor meeting and are able to convince them that you have a product that is a pain killer for a large market, you are likely to get their attention and keep their attention. Perhaps more importantly, you should evaluate your own product beforehand using the "pain killer" vs. "vitamin pill" analogy when deciding whether to build a prototype or launch a company. You do not get to decide if it one or the other. It is up to the customers to tell you if they will pay for your solution. If the majority of customers are in demand of your product, it is a pain killer. Otherwise, it is a vitamin pill.

Tutorial: Technologists inherently love new technology – especially ones they develop themselves. Likewise, the excitement of building a product with a breakthrough technology often overshadows the actual commercial value of the idea. Entrepreneurs usually build the product that satisfies their own interests rather than one that satisfies a market need, and this is a well-beaten path to failure. But you need to view the product differently and think about it from a business perspective. Investors are primarily interested in whether a technology or product can be commercialized and converted into a large revenue stream. All the technical bells and whistles will not impress them. In fact, the less said in the business plan and presentation about the technical details, the better. The first question they actually want to answer in their own minds is whether the product is going to solve a real customer problem in a large market, and whether or not the customer would be willing to pay for it. If you can convince them of that, you get to continue with your presentation.

One way of quickly making that assessment is to label it as either a pain killer or a vitamin pill. While products may not fall neatly into these 2 categories, it turns out to be quite effective at separating the wheat from the chaff. It can also give you a first-order predictor of the sales of the product if you understand the market size and competition. Therefore, it is useful to think of your idea or technology in this context: can it be developed into a product that customers must buy to solve an existing problem or fill an existing market need?

The analogy has merits. A pain killer is something that you will reach for every time you have a headache. It is a *must-have*, not a *nice-to-have*. Similarly, a pain killer product is something that your customer will always buy in order to solve a real problem. A pain killer *with no side-effects* is even better, meaning that the customer does not need to make any extra effort to use the product, and it does not require changes to their environment to integrate the solution. This killer product has the highest value.

Assess Product/Market Fit 65

Likewise, a vitamin pill is something that you may or may not take on a given day. If you skip a day - no harm, no foul. A vitamin pill product is a *should-have* or *could-have* item. These products are very hard to sell. You must convince customers to buy something that is not essential to their business. It does not directly solve an immediate or near-term problem. When times get tough, the customer will not buy such a product, so it depends a lot on the state of the economy or that industry.

Entrepreneurs who understand this way of categorizing product tend to call their product a pain killer even if it is clearly a vitamin pill. They realize that no one will be interested in a vitamin pill so why would they admit that they are building one. In fact, it is difficult to convince them it is a vitamin pill because they have decided it is not. They will only figure it out when they attempt to sell the product to customers. It will be difficult to fool investors or customers that you have a pain killer rather than a vitamin pill. Do not fool yourself into thinking you have a pain killer when you actually have a vitamin pill. Instead, convert your product idea into something that is truly a pain killer.

Recently, a third category has emerged due to social networking sites and video games. These products are akin to highly-addictive drugs. Once you start to use them, you usually cannot stop. "Binge watching" is another form of addiction leveraged by video-streaming companies. These products are very successful because of human nature. Over the next few years, there will be a new wave of social media products, online games, mobile apps and streaming video services. The ones that are highly-addictive and habit-forming will win in the marketplace and dominate this landscape. If your products in these categories do not have this feature, it is best to abandon them before the users do. The sole focus must be on making it habit-forming. This type of company may be funded, but a high degree of skepticism may be encountered from investors as you pitch the next Facebook, Twitter or Netflix.

Finally, there is the "placebo " which is a working product, but does not deliver a tangible value to the customer. An example is a software system to improve office efficiency that does not actually save time or money in the end. The system works well and gives the impression that there is some improvement but there is actually no measurable improvement. This may be due to the fact that the overhead in the total solution offsets the advantages of a new technology embedded inside the product. This problem is often difficult to detect until after the total solution is built and deployed unless the complete system is analyzed front-to-back for bottlenecks and overhead before building the product and launching a company. Eventually, the customers realize that it is more of a placebo than a product and sales begin to drop off.

Take Away: A pain killer product in the enterprise B2B market has well-known characteristics. It must help the customer reduce their cost, reduce their time-to-market, or enhance their own product in some manner to increase sales. For a consumer B2C product, it must be marketable as a *must-have product* or be *highly addictive* with a potentially high volume of sales to be successful.

Tip 3.4

Identify Your "Unfair" Advantages

Tutorial: When you take a product to market you will have a number of competitors to deal with. In order to beat the competition, you need to have a compelling advantage. But not just any advantage. It must be either an outstanding **X-factor in your product** or the abilities of the core team or a unique market strategy that would give your startup a clear and sustainable advantage. This is called your "unfair" advantage. It allows you to walk into a customer's office and replace a competitor's product with yours. It enables you to increase the price of the product commensurate with the value added. It keeps revenue flowing into the company as long as you can maintain that advantage. It would also allow you to defeat other startups with similar product offerings, even if they may have a technically-better solution. For all these reasons, it becomes a key selling point to the VCs and other investors in early-stage financing. Therefore, it is an important factor to consider as you build a team and design a product. What is your "unfair" advantage?

An unfair advantage in a product is its biggest selling point that presents a seemingly insurmountable obstacle for the competition. It may be that it is first to market with the ability to rapidly capture a large market share, or a revolutionary new technique that is a game changer for your market. It is a clear and unambiguous "secret sauce" that you can state very simply. It can also be an unusual capability of the team itself, often referred to as **the core competence of the company**, which would give it a decided advantage in the marketplace. It may be related to the team's unique insights of the market, special connections to the customers, or specialized knowledge of methodologies or the supply chain that is not readily accessible to others. It can also be a strategic marketing approach that other companies are unable to execute.

This is effectively how you block the competition and win in the marketplace. **If you cannot figure out what your unfair advantage would be, you will have difficulty with investors and the competitors.**

When developing your product, you must have many advantages over the competition. In fact, make sure you plan on 3 clear advantages because 2 of them may not work out so you have at least 1 to carry you forward. This mitigates the risk of failure. If all of them can be implemented, you have a better chance of winning the largest market share for products in this category. You need many barriers to entry and one unfair advantage. The probability of success will be increased if you have multiple unfair advantages, and you can sustain one of these advantages over a long period of time. If you can't come up with 3 clear advantages, have at least 2 big ones. If not 2, then have 1 that is truly an unfair advantage. Otherwise, think about a different product.

There are many situations when an unfair advantage may be short lived. If you are first to market, this may constitute an unfair advantage. But not for very long! **Do not underestimate the competition.** If the big competitors are able to replicate your product within a year, they could take your business away. They will reverse engineer your product if it gains any traction in the market. They are not sitting idly by while you soak up all the revenue. They are hard at work duplicating your effort and developing their own unfair advantage. So you will also have to consider if you truly have significant barriers to entry.

As an example, if you have designed a new single-board computer (SBC) with off-the-shelf parts and embedded software, then you have effectively 3 advantages – time, hardware and software. If you are successful in the marketplace, a competitor will replicate the board within weeks, then write the same software within a few months to try to put you out of business. If they have great difficulty developing equivalent software due to your specialized knowledge, that would be your only unfair advantage. Therefore, you need to file patents on the software algorithms to protect the

Assess Product/Market Fit   69

product. The hardware design may also be patentable, and if so, it should also be filed. In fact, the more patents or intellectual property (IP) you can accumulate, the higher your barriers to entry.

An interesting way to gain an unfair advantage is to license a key technology from a third party with exclusive rights in your industry for a number of years. To obtain such a license, you may need to provide cash and stock options to the licensor to carve out exclusivity in your market segment. But you also need to set up two more barriers to entry. Otherwise, the competitors will simply license a similar technology and produce a "MeToo" product and then squeeze you out of the market. Ideally, you need to own the technology by acquiring it from the third party before the competition finds out about it. It is also possible to have exclusive access to a hardware interface from a large company that is selling a high-volume product. However, since you are dependent on the larger company for your success, the merits of this approach are situation dependent.

Yet another case is a proprietary chip design to be used on a board with off-the-shelf parts for the remaining chips, and proprietary software running on it. In this case, the unfair advantages are the proprietary software, the hardware design and the chip. The major downside of this approach is that the chip design is critical to the success of this product and if it fails, the whole company is at risk. Iterations of design and fabrication can be lengthy and expensive. Critical portions of the design must be tested in silicon to reduce the risk of failure. You may not want to bet the whole company on one chip that is critical to the success of the company. You could use off-the-shelf parts in its place but this can be replicated and may affect the form factor of the SBC design. While you still have some notable advantages in software, large competitors could still enter your market with their own chip and try to put you out of business.

The core team of the company may also possess an unfair advantage in several forms. If a team member knows the decision makers in the customer base, these relationships may allow sales to happen more quickly. That may be an unfair advantage if it provides a competitive edge. If there are relationships built up along the supply chain that provides leverage for your startup, this is also an unfair advantage. Many startups have developed strategic marketing plans around relationships in the market or supply chain as their unfair advantage. If the team members have specialized knowledge or have developed ground-breaking methods in their field, this serves as an unfair advantage. Having an unfair advantage in the product and another one in the core competence of the team is a winning combination that would be hard to beat.

Clearly, it is important to have multiple unfair advantages to increase the likelihood of success and mitigate the risk of failure. The advantages have to be tangible, in the form of patents, or exclusive licenses, or proprietary algorithms, or chips. It is specialized knowledge or relationships that the team can uniquely leverage in the marketplace. **An unfair advantage is the main reason you will succeed where others would fail.** It cannot simply be that you think that you are better. Angel investors, VCs and future employees must all be convinced of exactly what you have and what prevents the competition from overtaking you in the market. You need to have a clear answer to that question. However, guard the "secret sauce" like your bank account pin number. The fewer people that know the details, the better, because eventually it will work its way back to the competition.

Tip 3.5

Market Size Tells You About the Opportunity

Summary: Many entrepreneurs believe that "if I build it, they will come." This may be true in movies, but it is not the case in business. You have to build the right product and then you have to chase customers to get them to buy the product. Selling products is very difficult so you need to identify a large market with lots of potential customers to be successful. In fact, it is the market size that tells you about the size of the business opportunity. Even if your product works, you cannot build a viable company unless you know how many customers would be interested in buying your product. You need to take off your technical hat and put on your business hat to determine the size of the market. If the market is too small, it may not matter what product is being developed because it will not lead to a fast-growing company. If the market is large, it is important to determine what part of the market share you can expect to capture. This tells you roughly what type of company you can build and what level of revenue you can expect.

Key point: The market size must be greater than $100M to build a fast-growing company or seek angel funding. Venture capital financing is available to startups pursuing markets that are much greater than $100M. Occasionally, if there is a cap on a market size, such as $250M, it may be of little or no interest to big competitors. A startup can maneuver quickly to establish a beachhead in this type of market before a competitor notices. Markets smaller than $50M are not likely to produce a fast-growing company, although there may still be an opportunity to build viable businesses.

Tutorial: A market is a collection of companies in the same industry, or perhaps adjacent industries, which have potential customers with similar requirements for the products purchased. Market size is the amount of money these customers are spending or will spend on a particular set of products or services. A market is often segmented into smaller collections of companies that purchase a common subset of products. Adjacent markets are segments that share certain common characteristics with a given market segment. Enterprise business-to-business (B2B) transactions comprise industrial markets. Business-to-consumer (B2C) markets are comprised of individuals or groups.

The objective in studying a market is to determine how much money is being spent by customers in that market and whether or not there is an opportunity to provide new or better goods and services to that customer base. The total revenue available in a particular market is called the market size. The revenue of a specific vendor as a percentage of total revenue of all vendors is called the market share. In an established market, there may be one or two dominant vendors (or players). It is difficult to establish a beachhead in such markets unless the product is brand new or greatly superior to existing products (a rule-of-thumb is 10X better). In a fragmented market, there are usually small players or weak products. The market size may be large but it is not being serviced with specific products demanded by the customers. Such a market presents a business opportunity.

The size of a market is usually tracked by industry analysts and published in annual reports. These are perhaps the most accurate sources of market sizes and market segments. They also report the market share of various companies if public information is available. Some startups do not report revenues in order to maintain their stealth-mode status, at least in terms of income. However, public companies are required to report revenue and earnings. Market sizes may also be obtained anecdotally from other vendors in the industry, or from CEOs of other companies. It can also be calculated using a rough bottom-up analysis using product prices and sales volume. All of these approaches should be used to triangulate on and confirm the market size.

Consider for example two hypothetical markets in the figure below. In Market 1, there is a large company and two small companies. The total market size is $200M. If the large company has revenues of $110M each year, then it owns 55% market share. If the other two companies have $40M and $50M in revenue, they own 20% and 25% of the market, respectively. It would be difficult, but not impossible, to penetrate this market. All the slices of the pie seem to be taken. However, if a new product with an order of magnitude of improvement is introduced, it could upset the balance. In that case, all existing vendors would train their sights on the new product and begin to compete against it using a variety of tactics.

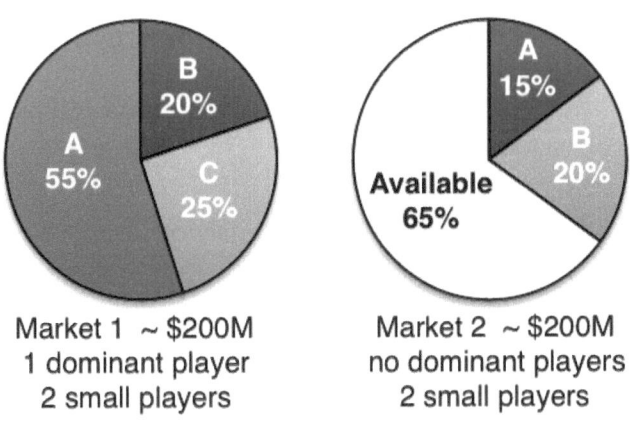

Market 1 ~ $200M
1 dominant player
2 small players

Market 2 ~ $200M
no dominant players
2 small players

In the second example, Market 2 has only two existing vendors with new products and they control only 35% of the market share. A large inviting 65% is untapped and available to any new player, so this fragmented market of about $200M presents a great opportunity for a startup. For angel investors, any market size over $100M is considered to be a large market suitable for funding. Venture capitalists seek markets that are much greater than $100M. Markets in the range of $50-$100M may be funded depending on other aspects of the opportunity. However, markets that are less than $50M are too small to provide the expected return on investment (ROI) for these types of investors. Depending on the type of company you are trying to build, it may still present a good opportunity for a startup, but the doors of the sophisticated investors are effectively closed if the markets are small.

In the high-tech industry, there are points in time when new markets are created and everything changes. These are called inflection points. There have been numerous inflection points in the past few decades. For example, the Internet, deep-submicron technology, digital media, wireless technology, the apps revolution, big data analytics, cognitive computing and Internet of Things (IoT) are all examples of inflection points. Some of these are also referred to as disruptive technologies because they force most companies to change the way they do business. The emergence of social media, which is now ubiquitous and highly addictive, has also changed the way many companies do business. Where there is an inflection point or growing trend, there is an opportunity to start a new business, but only to entrepreneurs with a core competence that fits the characteristics of the inflection point. New emerging markets are more of a Wild West and still require careful consideration for the most suitable products to deliver to that type of market.

As an entrepreneur, you need to obtain information about the size of a target market and whether or not it is growing. Once a large market opportunity has been identified, it is important to identify the customers and their needs. The first step is to list the top 10 largest customers for your proposed product. These are the early adopters if your product is viewed as a "must-have" product. They will buy a brand new product that is not full featured but still functional. They may also help you finalize the features and functions in exchange for first access to it. If you cannot name your top 10 customers, it may be time to go back to the drawing board because your product has no market. If you intend to have only one very big customer who buys your product in large volumes, this may lead to failure. That big company may decide it does not need your product after all. It could select someone else's product over yours. It could even decide to build its own product instead of buying yours. You need many customers to increase the probability of success.

After you have listed the top 10, you need to identify the next 100 customers. You must be able to list all 100 because this is the mass market you need to grow revenue. Their requirements may be

Assess Product/Market Fit   75

different from the top 10 customers. They need a product that is easy to install, easy to use and works reliably. They are not interested in helping you build new features and functions. They simply want the product in order to solve an immediate problem that is costing them time-to-revenue. But unless you can identify the next 100 customers and how to sell to them, your product has a very small market.

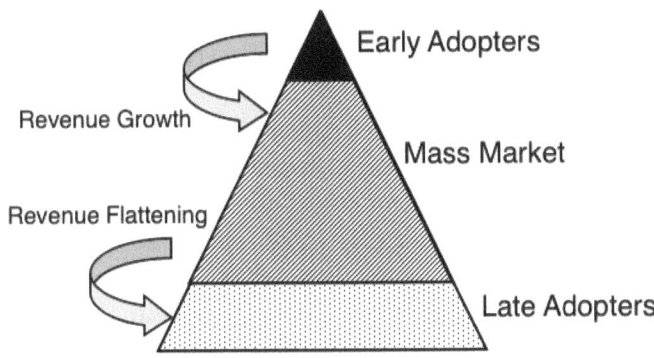

The transition from early adopters to the mass market is shown in the diagram. Making this transition implies rapidly growing your revenue, effectively scaling your business. Three factors related to scaling your business come into play when you address the mass market. The first one is the length of the sales cycle, which is the length of time required to go from a generated lead to a paying customer. The second is the gross margin, which is the price of the product less the cost of goods sold (COGS). And the third is the post-sales support, including customer service, training and maintenance.

You may have to rework your product for this mass market to make your revenues scalable because the sales cycle needs to be much shorter than the time required for the top 10 customers. The margins may be lower than for early adopters, but the volume will be higher. The costs of goods sold and customer support requirements must be as small as possible. If costs rise as you increase the number of customers or users, the business is not scalable.

The revenue/COGS ratio must exceed a certain threshold to be profitable in traditional software businesses. Today, many startups provide software-as-a-service (SaaS) where they gain and lose customers each month. New metrics called the customer acquisition cost (CAC) and lifetime customer value (LTV) are used to assess profitability. The CAC is the total cost of marketing divided by the number of customers acquired in a given period of time. The LTV is the dollar amount generated by a customer over the duration of their use of the product. In this case, it is the LTV/CAC ratio that must be greater than a certain threshold to reach profitability.

After serving the mass market, there will still be other remaining customers that have yet to purchase your product. These are the late adopters. They may be new companies, or companies that were lagging in technology but caught up over time. You don't have to list these companies by name but when you start selling to this group, you should already have your next product ready for the top 10 customers and then repeat the cycle. You will still have revenue from existing customers due to maintenance and upgrades of the first product, but your revenues will begin to flatten out by this point and then drop off if the market is saturated. In order to keep revenues growing, you need to develop the next big thing for your company well before this happens.

Take Away: You should only proceed with launching a startup when you identify a large market and as many customers in that market as possible. The biggest opportunities exist in large markets that are fragmented with many small players. If competitive products are weak in a fairly new market, it presents a great opportunity. If one or two large companies dominate an existing market, it will be difficult to unseat them in the customer base because of inertia. Customers do not want to switch to products from a new company unless there is a very compelling reason to do so. As a result, startups must offer a value proposition that is an order of magnitude better than the competition to gain traction and unseat large dominant incumbents.

Tip 3.6

Competition Tells You About the Degree of Difficulty

Summary: It is hard to get a company off the ground even if you are building the right product for a large market. If the product does not work or you miss the market window, things can unravel very quickly. However, if the product works and you start to gain traction in the marketplace, there is a bigger threat lurking in the shadows and ready to pounce: the competition. This has been a primary cause of failure, as well as untimely M&A exits, for countless startups.

Founders rarely think about competition before they get started. This is like a football team not bothering to find out who they play on Sunday – just go out there and see what happens. This does not work in business. You need to learn what the competition is all about, and how to get the upper hand. It is not a walk in the park to win in the marketplace over the competition. It will be a bare-knuckles, no-holds barred, knockdown, drag-out fight for survival. So if you are starting a business, you would be wise to carefully study the competition in your market, and certain adjacent markets, to size up what you are up against. The best strategy is to avoid competitive markets if possible. However, this is not usually possible.

There is no single way to solve the problem of competition. It is a continuous threat and it comes in many forms. You will have to combat every form thrown at you whereas they only need to find one way to defeat you. When you first start a company, you may be in stealth mode, but eventually the word gets out that you are planning to build a certain type of product. Once alerted, the competition begins to plot against you, and from that point forward you are involved in a battle to survive. The good news is you can win if you know how. There is a clever way to beat the competition. It works almost every time. You start by picking a market that is very large and full of weak players or products. Then you build a product with an "unfair" advantage and erect several technical barriers to entry for your product. And finally, you need to develop business responses and a roadmap to address any potential threats from the competition. In addition, if you avoid directly taking on the 900-lb gorillas of the industry, you can establish a beachhead for your products. Doing this, you are using all your business smarts and business savvy to outsmart the competition.

Key point: A large emerging market with only weak competition is the best-case scenario for startups. If there are fledgling competitors or if their product offerings are not as good as your product plans, there is an opportunity to succeed. A large established market with one or two large companies may pose the most difficult challenge for a startup. You will have to build a killer product to invade their territory, but you will be doing it with a big target on your back.

Tutorial: **When you develop a product based on a new idea, you need to take into account the competitive landscape in the market for your product. Do not fear the competition. They only make you better and more focused.** A lack of competitors may be a red flag for your product, especially if you are having trouble getting customers to engage with you. So competitors actually validate your product plans. Customers help you build the right product; competitors force you to build a better product. Once released, competitors will attempt to duplicate your effort through reverse engineering, or perhaps they have also been working on a similar product during the same period as you. You need to create barriers to entry so you can meet your revenue projections in the presence of competitors. As long as your product is significantly better than the competition, you will be able to gain traction in the marketplace.

Consider the analogy of defending a castle in the middle ages. In order to stop an invading army from overtaking your castle, you need to build a moat and a high wall, and if they get past these two

Assess Product/Market Fit 79

barriers, you fire cannons or drop boiling hot cauldrons of oil on them. In a similar way, you must build business and technical barriers to entry for your products. This metaphor is useful as a constant reminder to build in competitive barriers and safeguards into your product and all your business practices prior to engaging the market. It is a battle for survival and you must win.

The first step is to identify all competitors (both big and small) with products in your market space, and then carry out coarse-grain and fine-grain analyses of product differentiation. This information is used in the business plan to describe the competitive environment for your product and how you expect to mitigate risks associated with the competition.

A coarse grain analysis can be done quickly by categorizing products as being "New" or "MeToo", relative to the competition. A "New" product is first to market. It inherently has a barrier to entry in that any competitor must spend a certain amount of time to replicate the product. So there is a head start in revenue until the competitor catches up and releases their product. However, additional barriers need to be implemented in the product to hit your revenue numbers. A "MeToo" product is one that serves an established market and directly competes with an existing product in its installed base. If you are releasing this type of product, you need to have one or two major points of differentiation to unseat incumbent products, especially if the competitors are large players who rarely lose to an upstart.

Refinements of these two terms are based on the significance of the technical barriers that have been created for each product type.

    New++   = first to market with two barriers to entry
    New+   = first to market with one significant barrier to entry
    New   = first to market with no barrier to entry but trying to grab market share
    New-   = first to market without full functionality but trying to grab customers

MeToo++ = similar to an existing product with two new barriers to entry
MeToo+ = similar to an existing product with one new barrier to entry
MeToo = similar to an existing product but trying to grab a share of a large market
MeToo- = an inferior product with a large market due to lower pricing or trade restrictions

As a startup, you must first attempt to build a New++ or MeToo++ product to have the best chance at success. A New++ product has three barriers to entry because the competition must first duplicate the product, and then surmount two other barriers before they can enter the market. That will delay them long enough for you to soak up more revenue. If you are able to implement only one of the two barriers, at least you will end up with a New+ product. This is why it is better to attempt two barriers to entry in the first product. It may not be possible to implement both for whatever reason. But it is better to aim high and end up at a fallback position due to circumstances than aim low and end up failing because the incrementally better solution was not adopted by the customer. Of course, any barrier will likely be surmounted by the competition over time.

Sometimes, as a tactical move, a startup may release a New- product to beat the competition to an emerging market, win a few accounts, and work with customers to complete the product. Then they release a New+ or New++ product to keep out the competition. In that case, even if the competitors replicate the product, the one or two barriers deny them immediate wins in the customer accounts.

A MeToo++ product is the only way to unseat an incumbent because of the inertia in an installed customer base. Unless it is a full-featured, drop-in replacement, the customers do not want to do extra work to install and learn another product, even if it is slightly better. It must be significantly better and save them time or money or both. A MeToo+ product may also work if the one new barrier is significant. In fact, unless it is an order of magnitude better in some metric, the customer prefers to stick with their current vendor. A

Assess Product/Market Fit   81

strong case must be made in favor of building a MeToo product in the face of the entrenched competition.

A fine-grain comparison needs to be carried out by creating tables or charts indicating details of features, functions, form factor, speed, ease of use and price points. These points of differentiation must be highlighted so the advantages of such a product are clearly conveyed. After this high-level analysis, you must be able to clearly articulate in short form how your product is positioned to succeed, especially for the case of a MeToo+ product in a niche market. A MeToo+ product has a chance to make some headway, but the competition will use various tactics to drive you out of business while they are busy trying to replicate your advantage. A MeToo- may product work in some consumer markets because of either lower pricing, trade restrictions, or other regulatory issues, but in general should be avoided.

When you consider developing a MeToo++ product, you must take into account how the competitors will react to your product when it hits the market. If successful, you will see an immediate response. Three tactics are quite common. The first is to undercut your pricing model. If they are a big company, they can starve you out. They can outsell you because they have more boots on the ground, meaning more capacity in their sales channel. The second approach is to go into your accounts and try to unseat you in some way. They can lengthen the evaluation cycle to slow you down. They can change the evaluation criteria in their favor. Or they could simply state your product does not work, just as you might do regarding their product. A third approach is to bundle a similar product with their other products, effectively tossing it in for free. This is a classic approach used by large 900-lb gorillas in the industry. That is why a fragmented market with smaller players is preferable.

The competitors are not sitting idle while you toil away. They are busy plotting against you. Your job is to think of all the possible ways the competition could react to your product. If your product is superior, they will use business tactics. If your product is weaker, they will use technical tactics. Put yourself in their shoes and figure out how you might respond to your own product if a competitor were to put it out there. If the market is large enough, there may still be room for more than one product. But the competitors do not want you to get any market traction because it eats into their market share. And one day you might grow up and swallow them.

They will also try to hire people from your company. Perhaps they will start with sales people because they are always on the road and easily accessible. They may also try to extract some management people to destabilize the company. Next on the list would be to hire away employees who may know the "secret sauce" and are willing to move to the competitor and share it for a pay increase and more stock.

Another standard tactic is to slap a lawsuit on you just to distract you from the company goals. This lawsuit may come in the form of patent violations or the illegal use of intellectual property. Even if the lawsuit is frivolous, it will tie up the management team, cost money to pay lawyers, and generally cause confusion among the rank and file in the company. They could also make friendly visits to your customers to let them know they are filing a lawsuit for various and sundry violations and you may not make it to the end of the year. They want to create fear, uncertainty and doubt (FUD) in your customer base. And it usually works. Your management and sales people will have to go back into those customer accounts and allay their fears.

A competitor/partner may invite you to integrate your product into their system for a royalty stream in exchange for the use of their sales channel to increase revenue. This is typical in the software industry. However, it distracts you from developing your own product since all your developers are preoccupied coding APIs (application programming interfaces) instead of new features and functions. When the APIs are modified, the developers have to modify their code again. Some APIs disappear or are non-existent, in spite of the deal that you struck. This continues until you run out of money. Beware of being dependent on a large company and their interfaces for your success. It may lead to failure.

Assess Product/Market Fit

The CEO and VP of Engineering have the primary responsibility of dealing with competitive issues. Sales, marketing and the CTO provide input on the business and technical competitive landscape and possible strategies and tactics to respond to the competition. It is a team effort but the CEO owns the business response while the VP Engineering owns the technical response.

Advanced notes:
1. **Patents** are one of the best ways of adding a "+" to your New or MeToo product. Not only does it provide a documented barrier to competition, it is also a basis for higher company valuation. When a patent is published, be aware competitors will study your patents to gain insight into your product as well as devise a way to implement their product around your patent.
2. **Your lawyer may advise you not to study competitor's patents.** If there is proof you knew about a competitor's patent and still infringed it, penalties are multiplied.

Take Away: **Discuss the competition at least once every quarter.** Put yourself in the shoes of the competition and ask yourself how you would compete against your own product. Don't forget to include the potential list of "dirty tricks" in the discussion. The product roadmap for the company should describe technical responses to competitive pressure. It should provide options to maintain your competitive advantage in the face of competition. It should also include follow-on products to grow the company or to pivot to an adjacent market due to competitive pressure. If this is well thought out in advance, the presence of a 900-lb gorilla in the market or another startup will not be as big a threat to your company.

Tip 3.7

Know the Ecosystem of Your Product from End-to-end

Tutorial: There are many ways a product can succeed or fail in the marketplace that are not related to the availability of customers. They are associated with issues along the path from the vendor (you) to the customer and may present either opportunities or risk factors. This path from end-to-end is referred to as the ecosystem of the product. Entrepreneurs need to spend some time thinking about the ecosystem just in case there are potential advantages or disadvantages relative to launching a product in a given market. **It is important to know the ecosystem of the entire industry and a few adjacent industries.** If there are mechanisms that allow the product to be quickly adopted by the customers, it has a higher likelihood of succeeding. Conversely, if the product works but it is difficult to get it into the hands of the customer, it may cause the company to fail.

Examples of potential problems in the ecosystem are: regulatory issues or government approval requirements that may block the sale or use of the product; integration or installation problems at the customer's site; unusual issues that may arise in displacing the competition; significant inertia in the customer base; and, unusually lengthy sales cycles. Any of these problems can sink the company, if severe enough. Before starting your company, ensure that none of these problems exist in the path of sales. Otherwise, they need to be stated as potential risks in the business plan. It is better to recognize these problems and risks in advance instead of wasting a lot of time, money and energy chasing a goal that is not achievable.

The ecosystem may provide certain advantages for your startup to increase sales by making the product more accessible. Examples of opportunities in the ecosystem include APIs (application programming interfaces) that allow you to integrate your product into industry standard formats to allow customers to readily access your product. If there is a standard flow through the supply chain and you can enhance part of that flow, it presents an opportunity to access all customers in that chain. If there are other vendors that have complementary products, there may be an opportunity to form a joint venture (JV) and provide enhanced capabilities. When considering this option, always seek to find JV partners who have similar attributes as your own team and your advisory group. However, the JV option has its own level of complexity and should not be entered into lightly. There may also be an opportunity to jointly build a standard for the industry with the cooperation of multiple companies if your startup can take immediate advantage of it.

The more important of the two are the barriers in the ecosystem because they are failure mechanisms. It is not possible to list all possible scenarios, but it is instructive to examine a few case studies of companies that have failed when neglecting the ecosystem of their industry.

Case 1: A startup develops a new monitor circuit that can be integrated onto a silicon chip to control the speed of a microprocessor. The device works perfectly in the initial test chips that are fabricated. Many companies express interest but they resist buying the product because the integration of a foreign object onto their design increases the likelihood of failure of their own chip. The startup is unable to make any sales because of inertia in the customer base.

Case 2: A software startup designs a product to speed up a portion of a customer design flow significantly. A customer decides to beta-site test the software, but finds that the input and output formats do not match their own. The startup engineers modify the format but the input/output processing becomes the bottleneck. Once that problem is solved, the software runs properly. However, at the second beta site, the same procedure must be repeated because they use a different format for input/output. The startup realizes that every company has their own internal format for this part of the flow and the sales cycle will be long and drawn out, and therefore not scalable.

Case 3: A startup develops a water purification system but cannot get regulatory approval to implement the product at the local, state and federal levels. The company stalls until the government approvals are obtained, which is expected to take over a decade.

Case 4: A startup develops software to speed up the processing of patients at hospitals for x-rays, MRIs and CT scans. The improvement in processing time is significant. However, each sale requires multiple levels of approval from the hospital and the involvement of key management people from the startup. Each installation requires customization at every site using the hospital IT group. The cost of sales is very high and the revenue is not scalable.

Case 5: A company develops a system for big data analytics that ties into APIs of a large company. Unfortunately, the APIs are constantly changing and some are removed entirely. The developers spend most of their time on the APIs and very little time on their own product. Eventually, the company closes its doors.

These are only a few of the countless cases where the product works, but a fatal flaw exists in the ecosystem and leads to failure. If you find out in advance that there is no way to deploy the product in the marketplace, it is best NOT to start the company and waste your time and someone else's money. On the other hand, if you are committed to building the product, then it would be better to remove the barriers or work with the customers to find solutions to problems in the ecosystem BEFORE any major activity on the company is initiated.

Tip 3.8

Develop Your Business Plan Iteratively

Summary: A formal written business plan is not usually required by most investors today. However, they do require key elements of the plan, especially those relating to capital requirements. And for this reason alone, a preliminary business plan is important. In fact, the business plan is an evolving blueprint for your company. It is a collection of documents, pitch decks and spreadsheets developed in stages as the need arises and information becomes available. It should start small and grow over time using continuous improvement and iterative refinement ("kaizen"). It captures your real-time view of how the business will be built and how you expect it to succeed.

Key point: When you begin thinking about your business plan, you are typically in the bootstrapping phase. The most important part of a business plan in the early days is to identify potential risks to the business. This is usually the last consideration, but it should be the first. You want to thoroughly examine what could sink the business, whether it is regulatory barriers, a small market, a low barrier to entry for competition, long timeline to revenue, high investment requirements, or any other factor. If the risks are significant or the barriers are too high to overcome, you should choose a different direction for the company.

Tutorial: A business plan is a useful part of building a great company. It sounds like a boring and tedious task with a lot of guesswork and empty promises to fill in the sections so investors will fund you. That is the prevailing view. But this is not correct. Creating a business plan is a valuable exercise whether you seek funding or not. However, the first draft of the business plan should not be written until there is something to write about. Then the documents should be refined many times over the course of the first year until you have a solid handle on the viability of the company. That is the goal.

Today, a business plan is mostly an internal set of documents that describe your current knowledge about the direction of the company and its viability. You have to boil it down to its key components before you take it on the road. Most investors expect a short 20-30 minute presentation based on your business plan to attract their attention. The presentation slides are referred to as the "Pitch Deck". You need enough content in a pitch deck to serve as a stand-alone document for review, with a large enough font size for use in an actual presentation. Typically, 10-15 slides are used.

A possible list of slides is provided below. The slides per topic and ordering should be adjusted based on the priorities of the target investors. In fact, you may need to modify your pitch to suit the intended audience.

1. Elevator Pitch – Vision/Mission/Product
2. Problem and Current Solutions
3. Market Opportunity and Customer Base
4. Team Members, Advisors, Consultants
5. Your Solution and Unfair Advantages
6. Product or Service Being Developed
7. Customer Traction Milestones & Metrics
8. Competition and Product Positioning
9. Business Model, Financials, ROI, Exit
10. Budget/Cash/Capital Requirements
11-15. Additional Slides as needed above

Since the pitch deck is a summary of the business plan, it is useful to understand how to put one together. Let's start at the beginning. You have an idea for a new product serving an existing market. You pull a team of founders together and a number of developers and start building a prototype. While you are working on the prototype, you should begin thinking about the market size, the competition and potential risks for the product in the marketplace. You want to capture this knowledge and information in a set of materials called the "Business Plan."

Developing a business plan will not only increase your business IQ but it will also allow you to talk intelligently about your company to prospective customers, investors and employees after doing your homework. It is an integral part of transforming yourself into a lean, mean, business machine. Details matter and you will be intimately familiar with all the details in the process of assembling the business plan. A customer or seasoned investor who understands the industry will quickly realize you are out of your depth if you do not study all aspects of the business through a business plan. This is why it is so important.

The time to engage in this activity is roughly when you intend to incorporate the company. One matter to address in parallel is to pick a name for the company. If the founding team can agree on a name to use for the next few years (pick one out of five possible names that you think would be appropriate), then you should purchase the domain name. Use this company name in the business plan. Design a temporary logo and have business cards printed. Assign titles depending on the proposed roles of founders. Then, if you are very serious about starting the company, go ahead and incorporate after deciding the percentage ownership for each founder. Create a Board of Directors with all the founders as initial Board members.

Now the hard part begins. Find a way to present your product plans to a small group of potential users or customers. You can use your pitch deck and demo your prototype and then solicit feedback. Take notes and gauge their response. Ask if this is the type of product they would need and how quickly they would need it. Find out what they will do if such a product is not available. Ask if there are other products that are interesting to them. This may lead to more viable candidates for an initial product for your company. Continue to ask questions along these lines and take plenty of notes.

In parallel, you need to make contact with angels and VCs, if you have the necessary connections. Other founders of companies, CEOs, entrepreneurs and any other business people should be consulted regarding your plans to launch a company. Investigate the best practices of successful startups with these experts. Lunch and dinner meetings are often used for this purpose. Remember that everything you say will eventually get out to the competition so do not divulge any details or proprietary information. On the other hand, you need to obtain as much information on funding levels, market sizes, typical business models, the competition and potential risks.

The diagram below shows how the information should be gathered and the cycle of steps to follow to produce the business plan, starting from the initial idea.

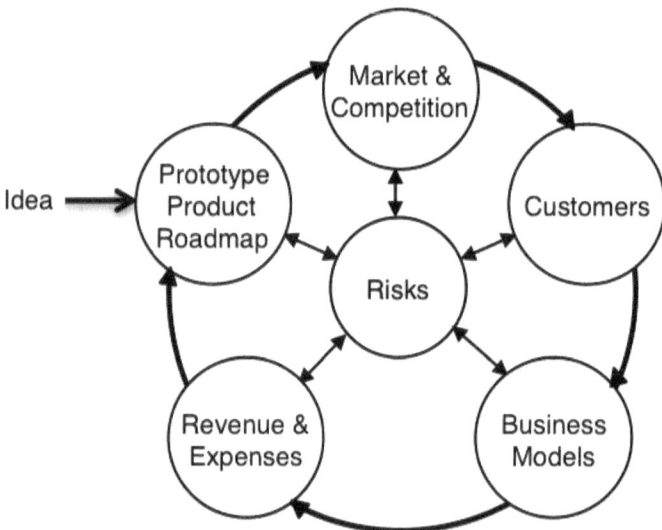

Once you have gathered the necessary information, it is appropriate to revisit the technical plans and make any adjustments needed. In the worst case, you may have to change direction from what you perceived to be the right product. Perhaps a bigger market exists for a different product you did not previously recognize. This is the main reason for meeting with a variety of groups – to validate your

Assess Product/Market Fit 91

plans or modify them. Once validated, you have to figure out the steps necessary to convert your prototype into a minimum viable product and then develop a roadmap for future products. In any case, there will be enough new information to rework the business plan.

There will still be many holes in the business plan but now they will become apparent. You must continue to work on the prototype and technical plans, but you should also plan to engage with other customers, more angels or VCs, additional business people, or perhaps the same ones, to fill the gaps. The Internet provides lots of data that is useful to further improve the business plan and create a pitch deck. Each founder could be assigned the responsibility to provide the input for different sections to streamline the process. Divide and conquer, and share information with the other founders using the business plan as a repository.

The main task to be completed in parallel is the building of a prototype. Later, when an alpha version of the product is ready, the customers who were approached several times already should be contacted again to visit the company for an in-house demonstration of the product and its features. Perhaps ten or more such companies should be consulted. At this point, the features, functions and schedule for the beta product can be defined. Two customers need to be identified to participate in the beta testing process, with an agreement to purchase if certain milestones are met. The product pricing will be based on the business model described in the business plan. When examining the viability of the company, the business model itself comes under scrutiny. If it survives the test, it validates much of the business plan. Note that the business model is always subject to modification.

When you are ready to calculate the revenue, expenses and profits, they must be based on detailed bottom-up analyses. There should be three different versions of these numbers: expected, optimistic and pessimistic. This will put bounds on the range of company that you can build. Inherent in the three versions are the risk factors that would move you from the most optimistic projections to the most pessimistic. It is good practice to always have these three plans and to be able to explain what factors move your company from one plan to another. Investors will likely work with your pessimistic projections and re-label it as the "realistic projections".

Once you've identified all the business questions and have determined credible answers to all of them, it is time to revisit the angels and VCs contacted earlier, along with several other potential investors as backup, just in case. You can write a new executive summary, develop an elevator pitch, and create a pitch deck with 10-15 slides to pursue funding. By this time, you have experienced all aspects of the business plan first hand and are in a strong position to secure funding.

Take Away: Ultimately, the business proposal and pitch deck must contain valuable information about the goals of the company, the market, the competition, revenue projections, hiring plans, expenses, risks, break even points, customer traction metrics, funding requirements and ROI. A subset of the complete business plan should always be tailored for the target reader. Even if you do not intend to pursue angel or VC funding, the process of working through the business plan will give you the confidence you need to succeed.

CHAPTER 4
Start With a Minimum Viable Product

4.1. Stay Focused on CASH and the PRODUCT

4.2. Don't Pack Too Much into One Product

4.3. Deliver Functionality and Quality on Time

4.4. Software Quality is a Competitive Advantage

4.5. Pre-Plan Your Product Pivot Strategy

4.6. Make Business Decisions from Now On

4.7. The Product-to-Customer Interface Determines Scalability

Tip 4.1

Stay Focused on CASH and the PRODUCT

Tutorial: There are two important priorities that must be kept at the top of the list in the early days of a startup: cash and the product. Losing cash due to an excessive burn rate is fatal, and developing a working product is the key to winning market share. Cash is needed to build the first working product which, in turn, is used to raise more cash or bring in revenue. The two are interconnected. This must be clearly understood by all involved. As the company grows, the CEO and VP of Engineering are the two people ultimately responsible for keeping their eye on the ball. As a result, the CEO and VP of Engineering must have a close working relationship in a startup.

Job ONE of the CEO in a startup is to manage cash. The burn rate should be low enough to hit all milestones with some room to spare, typically one or two extra months. This practice should continue until the company is profitable. Keeping an eye on the burn rate in the early days is the only way to delay the next round of financing as long as possible. A burn rate chart can be constructed based on monthly expenses to determine how many months of funding are left and when to begin fund-raising activities. Big budgets and wild spending are for the big companies. As a startup, you need to stretch every dollar and control spending to get the company to profitability, grow the revenue, or get to the next round of funding. **Having just enough money to stay hungry, not too little so that you starve or not so much that you get complacent, is perhaps the best way to operate in the first two years.**

Cash is like an airport runway for a young company. You need enough of a runway to get lift-off. The more you burn, the shorter the runway. There are many things needed to build a company but nothing can be done if you run out of money. In fact, the next round of financing depends so much on the product that the CEO had

Start With a Minimum Viable Product   95

better keep one eye on the status in Engineering and the other eye on the burn rate in the early days. The CEO should monitor the burn rate, the product status and headcount requirements needed to reach the next set of milestones monthly. Everything else is a lower priority. Control the burn rate until you bring in the next round or become profitable. When one of these two events occurs, you should be well-conditioned to managing company expenses.

The length of the runway can be determined by taking the initial cash position and subtracting off the projected burn rate in each subsequent month. Unfortunately, the burn rate is not managed properly in many startups and that eventually leads to failure. To avoid this, the CEO should periodically examine a set of progress metrics used to trigger a change in the operating plan. If the schedule is running late or key functionality in the product is not ready to engage customers, the CEO must be prepared to take some pre-determined actions to adjust expenses and expectations. If these situations are thought out ahead of time, it is less of a shock to the company and investors when they arise. If the CEO prepares both realistic and conservative plans, along with a "red-zone" contingency plan, just in case, the triggers set by the predetermined progress metrics can determine when the company needs to move to the conservative plan. All of management must be prepared for what that entails: project cuts and layoffs are the most common results.

Job ONE of the VP of Engineering is to deliver a working product. This should always be the highest priority. There are some important steps to achieve this goal. Put the best people on the product. Do not waste their time with tasks others can do. Put a process in place and manage the process. The software developers must spend their working hours developing software. The same goes for hardware developers. Make sure tools and systems are in place to develop, build and test software and hardware.

Identify the minimum viable product that would sell in the marketplace and get it working. Use a burn down chart (BDC) to manage the schedule for delivery of the product. If the product does not work, figure out what is wrong and fix it. Have the entire project schedule in your head. Know the critical path. Identify bottlenecks. Prioritize the bug list. There are a number of commercial products that provide tools to monitor the key performance indicators (KPI) of the development process. These tools allow you to construct dashboards for agile methods that display KPIs and metrics for DevOps, continuous delivery and IT management. Once in place, it is much easier to identify bottlenecks and problems in the system. Stay focused and get the product working.

Given that a startup is a high-risk undertaking, one possibility is that you cannot get the product working at all. The VP of Engineering along with the CEO and other team members must identify product pivot strategies using the same technology before this problem arises. Then, the question becomes when to move to the second product, as a medium risk option, or third product, which is the "red-zone" option. If milestones are not met in the given window of time, the team must assemble to determine whether the first product is still viable. If so, a new set of milestones must be established and expectations must be reset. If not, the first product must be abandoned and work must begin on the second product, which should be based on the same technology and targeting the same market. A project cut and an engineering transition to the second product must be undertaken in this case.

The key to avoiding red-zone plans is the proper management of cash and completion of the initial product. A startup is a very stressful environment but the stress is usually the lowest when there is plenty of cash in the bank and the product is working. The atmosphere becomes one of excitement and enthusiasm, especially after the product is sold to the first customer and a purchase order is obtained. This situation allows the team to focus on more sales, strategic marketing and customer support. It allows more people to be hired knowing that there is a high probability of obtaining more revenue from customers. Ultimately, it puts you on the road to becoming a successful company.

Tip 4.2

Don't Pack Too Much into One Product

Summary: Entrepreneurs are overly ambitious by their very nature. This is a good thing. However, they greatly underestimate what it takes to deliver a product and build a company and this is often the cause of their undoing. They believe that taking on many technical challenges is the best way to build a successful startup. Furthermore, they think that VC's will be very impressed by the scope and magnitude of their technical plans, and this will lead to funding for the startup. The truth is that VC's are not interested in getting into the technical details of the products. They are interested in the viability of the business and their own bottom lines. When you present a lot of different technical ideas, they will think that you are taking on too much, or do not really understand business issues, or the development of a product, or building a company. As a result, they may not be willing to take a risk on a group of naïve entrepreneurs and may pass on the deal because of the low probability of success. On the other hand, if your proposal is the design of a minimum viable product (MVP) for a large market and you can make a business case for its viability, it has a high probability of success and will likely be funded.

Key point: Doing too much in one product before validating the market or getting any revenue is a very risky proposition. It is also important to differentiate between a technically elegant product and a product that works. A product that is technically perfect is unattainable whereas a working product generates revenue. **Temper your entrepreneurial enthusiasm with a healthy dose of business savvy. Define the MVP that will produce revenue within 2 years, and then continue growing revenue year over year.** Use the rest of your ideas to define a Roadmap to grow the business after the initial product is successful.

Tutorial: When you start a company with many great ideas for a world-beating product, you are tempted to throw the kitchen sink at the problem. The product is loaded up with features and functions – many of which will never be used or even noticed by the customer. This is typical of a first-time entrepreneur, as they do not know that packing too much into a product tends to reduce the likelihood of success. The problem is usually that the scope of the product is more ambitious than is needed.

When you have a set of big ideas to dramatically improve an existing product in the marketplace, you need to figure out what improvements you want to launch right out of the gate. This is an iterative process whereby you develop an MVP, test it with initial customers, determine what needs to be improved in the next iteration, and repeat. **Every step of the process must be used to answer your toughest business questions that go to the heart of the viability of your startup.** This point is best illustrated through a hypothetical case study.

Assume there is a software product in the marketplace that was developed many years ago but is getting slower over time. It processes large quantities of data, and the amount of data is expected to increase over time slowing it down even further. You decide to start a company to build a MeToo++ product. The definition of a MeToo product is a direct replacement for the existing product. Typically, these products do not sell due to inertia in the installed base of existing customers. To gain any traction, it must be a MeToo+ product with a significant advantage over the existing product, either smaller, faster, or cheaper than the competition. A MeToo++ product is defined as having two significant improvements over the competition.

Through your own R&D effort, you develop a method to process more data by using data caching, and then improve the processing speed by 5X using a new algorithm. You recognize the data can be segmented and processed in parallel across many computers to deliver additional speed improvement. Finally, "to blow the competition out of the water", you consider designing a hardware accelerator that provides a 2X speedup of a bottleneck in the software. The combination of these enhancements would make a very compelling case for the customer to switch to your product.

Overall, you propose a three-tier solution shown below.

Proposed Product

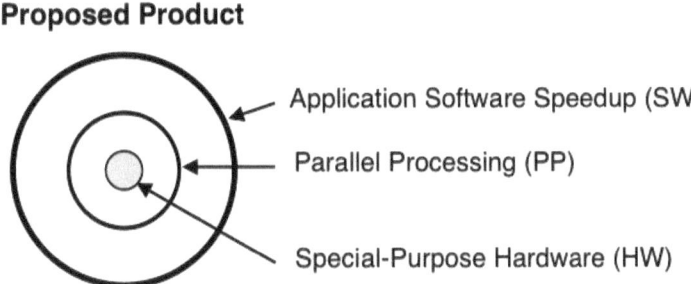

At this point, you need to put your business hat on and strategize over the best approach to build a successful company. When you are developing a solution with multiple enhancements, carefully consider what features to build into the first product. You must decide which of the three enhancements you should implement, and in what order to do them. Consider two scenarios.

Business Strategy A: attack the whole problem at once
Business Strategy B: implement the solution in stages

The two strategies are outlined below along with the likely outcomes.

Business Strategy A: In this case, engineers will be simultaneously speeding up the software (SW), making it run in parallel (PP) and using a board (HW) to speed up the bottleneck. While it may make sense hypothetically, it makes no sense from a business perspective. First consider the probability of success of each part of the solution. It is not 100% guaranteed that they would all be implemented successfully. Even the SW component by itself is not guaranteed; otherwise, all software companies would be successful. Optimistically, the probability can be set to SW=80%. The PP solution has a slightly lower probability since it is still software but there are network and partitioning issues to address. Set PP=70%. Finally, the HW portion requires the purchase of rapid prototyping boards, and then the design, implementation, and test of the product. Therefore, the likelihood of achieving a 2X performance improvement is rather low because of the inherent degree of difficulty of this enhancement. Set HW=50%.

A back of the envelope calculation of the probability of success is simply 0.8 x 0.7 x 0.5 = 0.28. In other words, there is a 28% chance of producing the full capabilities of the product. Whether you believe these probabilities or use your own numbers, the probability of success is low. This alone is a reason to pause and reconsider this business strategy. It is better to go after the software-only solution, which has an 80% chance of success while providing a 5X improvement.

Second, it is important to validate the software product in the marketplace before committing to the parallel and hardware improvements. If the market rejects the software solution, then the rest of it is not worth pursuing. If it accepts the new product then the next two phases can be pursued. Furthermore, the interaction with the customers is a necessary part of delivering the right product. They may have no interest in further speedups but may require other features and functions. That would negate the efforts to develop the parallel and hardware solutions.

Third, consider the time, number of people and the expenses needed to carry out the tasks. The burn rate will be extremely high and it will take longer to complete the product. There is a big difference between a burn rate that is required to get a company off the ground compared to a burn rate that is artificially high because you choose to take on too much. Furthermore, the Engineering Department will be a chaotic environment with hardware and software issues popping up every hour of every day. It will be a very stressful place to work. If the product is not working before you run out of money, you may have to lay off part of the team and raise another round of financing. If that happens, the company itself will be a chaotic environment in which to work. If the product is not on schedule, the burn rate must be reduced, which also implies a painful process of laying people off.

Business Strategy B: The second strategy is to break the product development into phases and address one phase at a time, while constructing an architecture that allows future phases to be implemented easily. Phase 1 implements data caching and a new algorithm to build a fast software product that can handle large quantities of data, with a segmented architecture that allows for a parallel implementation at a future date. Phase 2 is the parallel implementation. Phase 3 is a hardware acceleration of a bottleneck in the software. Initially, the company works exclusively on Phase 1 in which the minimum viable product is built to replace the competitor in a few beta-sites within 18 months. If customers accept the product in Phase 1, there is initial revenue by the end of the second year. The company can then work on the improvements in Phase 2 and then Phase 3, as shown in the Roadmap below.

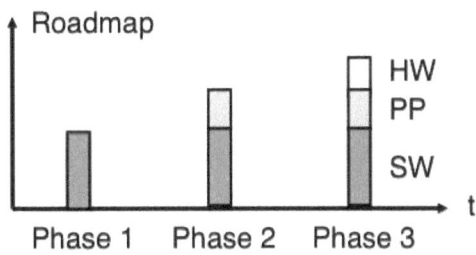

If beta customers are happy with the initial product of Phase 1, the completed product can be sold more widely. But customer support effort may be very high depending on the type of product and the volume of sales. This is usually an unexpected aspect of selling product for first-time entrepreneurs. It costs time and money to acquire and support customers. Furthermore, there are bug fixes and other internal improvements needed on the product even after it is released. Getting these fixes to the customer must be coordinated with the sales team.

At this point, it is important to work with the customers to decide what should be done in Phase 2. They may agree with your approach or request their own improvements that are not in line with what was originally planned in Phase 2. Then, a tough decision is made to either go ahead with Phase 2 or enhance the product based on customer feedback. The answer will depend on which path produces more revenue in the long run. Either way, there will not be painful reduction in force (RIF) since the company did not ramp up Phases 2 or 3. In fact, the same software team from Phase 1 can be shifted to Phase 2 rather seamlessly. The decision to go to Phase 3 can be postponed indefinitely or until the company is profitable and it makes sense to build a hardware group.

These two strategies will produce two different outcomes because of the decision of which product to build first. Think carefully about how to build the right product for a given market. If the proposed solution requires multiple phases, consider the probability of success of each phase to understand the overall probability of success. Determine the burn rate of product development and timelines to complete product enhancements. Consider issues of market validation, and sales and marketing costs as well as customer support issues. **Take the path of lowest risk both in terms of burn rate and time-to-money.** In this way, revenue can be achieved earlier and further improvements can be added over time or abandoned before burning through a lot of cash unnecessarily.

There is one caveat to the approaches described above – the competition. If a competitor improves their product by 10X, you may have no recourse but to include Phase 2 of the Roadmap while working on Phase 1. In that case, the Roadmap should be used as a strategic planning tool in case the competition produces an equivalent or better product and then tries to unseat your product in the customer base. Phase 2 and Phase 3 become your pre-planned responses to a competitive challenge as opposed to a panic reaction to it.

Tip 4.3

Deliver Functionality and Quality on Time

Tutorial: Entrepreneurs in their first startup have great difficulty predicting how long it will take to build a product and how much it will cost to do so. Usually they are off by a factor of two or more on the time and cost they tell investors. They are not purposefully trying to be untruthful. They just do not know how to predict how long it will take, so they make wild guesses and tell investors what they think they want to hear. But investors have heard it all before so they internally adjust all estimates, predictions and projections that entrepreneurs provide to determine more realistic schedules and expenses. There are ways to develop reasonable estimates of time and cost that have proven useful.

It should be stated up front that a software schedule is notoriously difficult to estimate, especially if it s a large software project using many languages across the entire application. They key is to build a credible schedule with a known critical path and then track the project with a burn down chart (BDC). When determining how long a product will take to develop, you can use top-down and bottom-up analyses.

For the top-down analysis, you begin by defining the major components of the product and estimate the time it will take to develop each component. This is highly dependent on the type of product being developed. For illustrative purpose, a software product is assumed since many in high tech are familiar with this type of product. For software, you start by estimating the number of lines of code (locs) in the entire product including testing. Assume that the total is 200k locs. If you have 10 developers, then each is responsible for 20k locs. Assuming that each production quality module requires 50 locs, then each programmer is responsible for 400 modules. If 1 module can be created per day, it will take 400 working days, or about 18 months to develop the product.

A bottom-up analysis for a software product would require sketching out the structure of the code in terms of functional blocks. Each block would be comprised of multiple modules. A total count of the blocks and modules can be made and then assigned to different programmers. Assume that 3200 modules are required with 8 developers working on the product and 2 test engineers writing test scripts and developing test automation tools. Then the longest path through the schedule can be determined. If integration and system testing time is added, then a total time can be estimated. This analysis produces an 18-24 month time frame to complete the project, which includes the four phases of prototype, alpha, beta and release versions. This is only a first-order estimate to get a sense of the time lines for the project.

Carrying out top-down and bottom-up analyses allows you to bound the length of time required to develop the product. The best case would be 18 months to complete the four product phases in this example. It will likely take longer because there are unexpected events that can delay the schedule. A buffer period of 6 months can be added for insurance, which produces an upper bound of 2 years for a large-scale project. The equivalent analysis for hardware is more difficult to carry out because it depends on whether a rapid prototyping board is used, or off-the-shelf parts are utilized or a new chip is designed. Regardless of the type of product, top-down and bottom-up analyses can be carried out in a similar manner.

Next, consider a first-order expense calculation for the cost of the software development. The software group requires 10 engineers in this example. If the fully-loaded headcount cost is $150K/year, then the 2-year cost of development is $3M. In addition, the cost of general and administrative (G&A), sales and customer training personnel is approximately $2M. Therefore, expenses of $5M will be consumed in 24 months. A bottom-up analysis yields a similar result.

While both the schedule and expense calculations above are rudimentary, they can be used as a starting point to carry out a much more detailed analysis to produce more accurate results. For example, consider the quarter in which you would hire a person and start their development clock in the next quarter. Adjust the expense associated with each hire according to their expected salary. Refine the product structure, blocks and modules with each pass of the process and revise the schedule. It is important that several passes of the schedule and expenses be carried out until you converge on a believable schedule and credible expenses.

In some sense, this is the easy part. The hard part is to actually hit the schedule while staying within a reasonable range of the expense budget. The highest priority is to deliver the product on time with the right functionality and quality. The second priority is to keep the burn rate under control during that period. If you have a working product but it costs more than expected, that would be acceptable. But if you blow through the cash without delivering a working product, that is not acceptable. If that happens, you have to go out and raise more cash, which puts the company under significant pressure. This situation can be avoided, or at least mitigated, by using a number of well-known approaches, as described below.

The first approach is to use a product development methodology to deliver the desired functionality in the prescribed timeframe. It is very important to select the right development method, especially for software, that matches the type of product, the phase of development and the experience level in your startup. Today, many software companies **use agile methods** and they come highly recommended because they deliver products that are usually on time and under budget. They are ideally suited to the development of software when the customer requirements are not fully known at the outset because they are iterative methods. If you are using agile methods, documentation should not overly burden the agile process but instead should provide all the information needed by other developers and other parts of the company.

In agile methods, a small team of experienced programmers engage in a series of scrum-sprint iterations. The scrums are used to plan the next 2-3 weeks of coding while the sprints involve the actual coding process. Short stand-up meetings are held daily to identify any problems and to communicate progress to other developers. At the end of each iteration the software has a new working feature that has been tested. The probability of meeting deadlines with the right functionality is very high with agile methods. Testing is done concurrently with development to maintain quality.

Implementing agile methods involves interactions between many different groups and processes as well as many revisions of the software produced on a frequent basis. The overall process must be managed in a coherent manner; otherwise, it may end up being chaotic and less effective. DevOps and continuous delivery are used to facilitate agile methods. DevOps is a collaborative approach between several small teams that allows development, testing, QA and release management to flow smoothly. Continuous delivery is based on automated mechanisms by which new releases are delivered on a consistent basis, either weekly, monthly or annually. The details of these approaches should be understood before using agile methods in a production environment.

A **burn down chart** (BDC) is an effective tool for monitoring the progress of a development schedule, especially in the case of agile methods. If you do not track the schedule, you WILL be surprised by some unexpected issue at some point along the way. So it is good practice to use a BDC. The first step is to list the developers and what percentage of the time they are working on the project. This produces a value for the effective number of developers. Next, the time required to complete the tasks in the project are estimated. Finally, taking into account weekends and holidays, the expected end date for the project is determined based on the amount of work, the number of effective developers, and an efficiency factor (a scaling factor used to cover whatever overhead or non-productive time exists in the period of interest). This information is used to generate the BDC using a spreadsheet.

An example BDC in mid-stream is shown below that compares the ideal trajectory of the project to its actual progress. The solid line represents the actual tasks remaining while the dotted line represents the projected tasks remaining based on the initial estimates of task time lines and dependences. Note that the accuracy of the chart depends on the quality of the original task estimates. Nevertheless, it is a powerful tool for managing projects and delivering results on time.

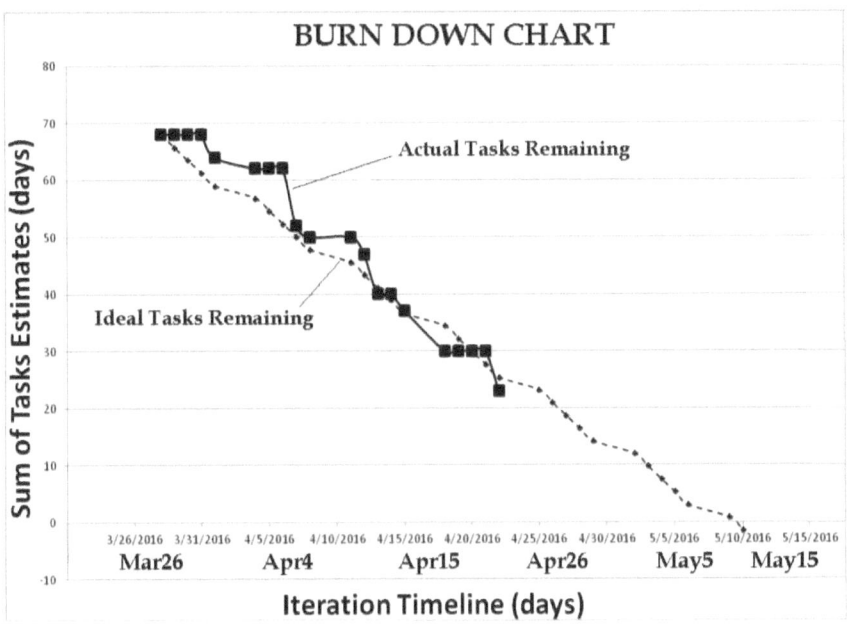

The second approach to improve the likelihood of achieving a deadline on product delivery is to use a high-impact management technique to properly assign developers to tasks. The first step is to develop criteria to **assign the right person to the right task**. For example, use experience level, application knowledge, bug rate of the developer, speed of coding and other such metrics. Then build a matrix of projects and people, and find a best-fit assignment of people to tasks. By placing people in situations where they are likely to be successful, it increases the probability of completing tasks on time. Also, the best programmers should be assigned double duty as a back up for critical projects, or to oversee development of junior programmers. There should also be some knowledge overlap between developers to mitigate risk. If the assignments are carried out with all these factors in mind, the likelihood of hitting the schedule and delivering a quality product will be very high.

A third approach to deliver functionality in a given time frame is to use priority-based scheduling. It uses the "must, should, could" or MSC method of prioritizing the functionality to be implemented in the product. It can be used for agile methods, waterfall methods or any of the other methods. The only difference is the length of the schedule. In this approach, a set of tasks to be implemented are each labeled as M, S and C, respectively. The "M" items are carefully selected as high-priority items that define the minimum viable product and must be completed in the next release. A few of the lower priority "S" items are used to fill empty slots. The "C" items are added after the deadline and are only attempted if M and S items are completed faster than expected. A schedule that illustrates the results of this process is shown below.

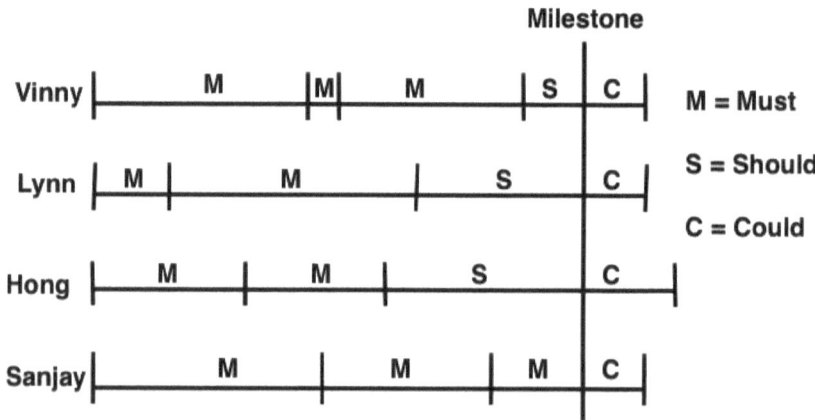

The first items in the schedule are the M items and they are assigned to the developers according to their tasks on the product using best fit. Each engineer or manager must estimate the time required to complete each M task in the schedule taking into account that time must be spent on hot fixes, regular bug fixes, and small adjustments to previous versions. It is difficult to accurately estimate the task sizes for this reason but the uncertainty is accommodated in this approach. The person who is scheduled to complete their M tasks last defines the length of the schedule. Other developers will complete their tasks at earlier times, so the S items can be inserted to fill their available time slots. Similar timing estimates must be carried out for S tasks. Finally, after the milestone, the C items can be included in the schedule after estimating their completion times.

Using this approach developed by Aki Fujimura (in presentation entitled "Quality on Time", 1997), you can increase the likelihood that the product will be completed on time if you promise to deliver only M items and some of the S items by the delivery date. The C items are intended for future implementation. Some would argue that this is just padding the schedule when, in fact, it is an *a priori* sorting of the tasks into the most important to the least important, and then building an achievable schedule. With it, you can confidently commit to delivering the product and you will hit your deadline almost every time.

For best results, the project manager must monitor the schedule and make adjustments as needed using tracking tools called dashboards. If someone is unavailable for any period of time, some of their S items can be removed. If any M items are completed faster than expected, then some S items can be attempted, and perhaps one C item. If an M item is taking longer than expected, those working on S items with overlapping knowledge can be shifted to help on the M item. If a new customer request comes in that must be included, an S item can be taken out and replaced with the new M item.

All of this flexibility is automatically built into the schedule as the priority of each task has been pre-defined and the actions to be taken in a contingency situation have also been pre-determined. The key to this method is to carefully decide what functionality must be included to constitute the next version of the product. Then, an MSC schedule is based on the tasks to implement the functionality. The result of this process is a quality product delivered on time with the required functionality for the target market.

Tip 4.4

Software Quality is a Competitive Advantage

Summary: Quality is a term thrown around quite often but many believe it is just a fictitious goal that is hard to achieve. In a startup, you have to adopt a mentality of building quality into all your products, especially in your software products, and then quantify it via a set of quality metrics. Make it clear to everyone in the company that Engineering is committed to deliver "quality on time". For software, this must be done using a product development process and low-defect coding practices. No short cuts should be taken. The costs later on may sink the company because the success depends upon products being released on time with high quality. There are several widely-accepted methods to achieve this goal for software products.

First, coding standards must be used so developers can easily take over the programming of someone else's function, if needed. This lowers the risk of the product failing to meet the schedule. It also facilitates readability, code reviews and debugging. Second, a software development process must be used to deliver the product on time for the alpha, beta and all subsequent releases. This is needed so the entire project can be properly managed with visibility into all issues that arise in order to quickly address problems and stay on schedule. The company depends on having the initial product ready in a timely manner for its survival. Third, testing must be done concurrently with development so that quality is maintained in the product from beginning to end.

Key point: Programmers want to write code for new features and not fix bugs all day. This requires a set of guidelines that must be followed by all software engineers. The first step is to use the following rule-of-thumb: developers need to write 100 lines of unit test code for every 50 lines of production code in each module. This testing code but is much easier to write since it draws from a well-defined set of test code templates. Both positive (intended use) and negative (improper use) tests should be created. The approach will reduce the number of bugs to a small number that is countable on one hand for every 10,000 lines of code. If all modules are written in this way, the final product will have very few bugs. The overhead of doing this is very small but the payoff is huge, especially during integration and system testing.

Tutorial: Imagine a scenario where you release a bug-riddled product to your customers just to hit a target delivery date. Not long after, you receive reports that the software keeps crashing. Every time it crashes, Engineering goes through a fire drill to fix the bugs over the weekend to stay on schedule for the next release of the product. Soon, the number of bugs coming in forces programmers to spend 80% of their time on bug fixes and only 20% on new features in the next release. It is almost as if you have 1/5 of Engineering doing productive work. Eventually, the rest of the company begins thrashing as much as Engineering because the word is getting out that the software is full of bugs. Employees begin to express concerns about future prospects of the company.

Now imagine the opposite. High-quality software is released on schedule, and customers report they are quite satisfied with the product. Their feedback is related to new features they would like to see in future releases. Engineering is considered as a source of high-quality work and on-time delivery. This message starts to make its way into other parts of the company and they begin to improve their own processes. Sales increase dramatically as word gets out that the product works and provides real customer value. Employees gain confidence about future prospects of the company.

One of these two scenarios plays out in every software startup. The first is much more common. The second is rare except in successful startups. Usually startups begin with buggy code because there is no system in place to enable and encourage high-quality software development. It is driven by functionality and speed of coding, not quality. The reason is the urgency of getting something working quickly to prove the technical idea works in a short amount of time. But once the proof of concept is completed, it is time to introduce approaches that continuously improve the quality of the product.

Today, it is much easier to write code than ever before but it is taking much longer to verify the code actually works. In fact, the ratio of time verifying code to developing code has been increasing, but developers have not been spending the needed time to test their code. Everyone who writes code has their own style and their own idiosyncrasies. They write code at different rates and may have a clever bag of tricks to optimize their code. Each developer has a favorite programming language (relating to familiarity, preference of static or dynamic typing, etc.) and a variety of approaches to debugging their code. In short, you will attract a lot of strong hackers to a startup who like to do things their own way.

In a successful startup you have to adhere to doing things the same way. This seems to run counter to the creative spirit of a startup. Why put developers in a "straight jacket" and then expect them to be creative? The answer is simple: because a startup must be an environment of high productivity, low risk of missing the schedule, and the ability to create high-quality products. As such, it is imperative that certain software best practices be implemented as soon as possible. Engineering must be viewed as a group that keeps delivering the best products time and time again, not a bug-filled chaotic environment that prevents the company from succeeding.

The steps involved in building a well-oiled Engineering team are not complicated, but they are hard to implement. Developers are under heavy pressure while setting up the integrated development environment (IDE) and computer hardware, writing code, fixing bugs, refactoring code, installing tools, fighting with APIs and platform issues, and engaged in a myriad of other priorities. Therefore, **it is best to introduce new steps incrementally as you move to successive product development phases.**

Start With a Minimum Viable Product 113

First, coding standards should be used to write the software. There are well-established coding standards for headers, global/local variables, comments, indentation, function calls, etc. Agree on a set of rules and stick to them. Applying constraints on coding lowers the probability of introducing bugs in the code (e.g., use languages with static types). Keeping the code as simple and readable as possible has the same effect. This is important. It is much easier to catch bugs while coding if the code is self-explanatory. Make sure your code can be easily understood by you when you are debugging at a later date. Furthermore, the use of a coding standard allows others to read your code in code reviews, or take over if someone is sick or unavailable, or leaves the company. Therefore, it reduces the risk in the schedule. By following these steps, the modules are all reusable, reliable and readable. **Rather than discussing the merits of coding standards and which features to include in the standard, the message should be clear – use them!**

Second, **use all the software-debugging tools available in your integrated development environment (IDE)** to verify code coverage, check for memory leaks and identify other potential sources of bugs. Set up systems for revision control, unit/system testing, feature testing, bug tracking and fixing, and automated regression tests. This will further improve the quality of the software. Carry out code reviews of critical modules, especially with junior programmers. In addition, spot-check the adherence by developers to the coding standards and built-in software test (BIST) coding techniques. All of these steps may be met with resistance at first, but the engineers will appreciate it later when they are working on new features 80% of the time and fixing bugs only 20% of the time (or less), instead of the other way around. Furthermore, if you inherit source code from a third party, consider rewriting it using these techniques.

Third, a software development process should be used to produce your alpha code (for product demonstration purposes only), beta code (for beta-site customer testing) and release code (a product available to all customers). Ensure that you have a sign-off checklist to ensure that a quality product is delivered. Before launching any releases to customers, **identify the weakest links in the chain of software** in your product. Trouble spots may be due to timing issues, human intervention or critical data that, if incorrect, may crash downstream software. Once identified, every attempt should be made to safeguard the product from potential disaster in front of the customer or user.

During the development cycle, engineers should interact frequently to discuss problems they are trying to solve. In many cases, a few minutes a day of team interaction can increase productivity substantially and increase quality at the same time. Ensure that documents that are shared between engineers are updated frequently to keep everyone informed on the status of the project. These documents are critical to keeping others in the company synchronized and on schedule. Typically, people in marketing and sales will need to know the features and functions of the product and the delivery schedule with certainty in order to carry out their roles and responsibilities for the company.

Before releasing the initial product to the marketplace, a set of milestones and metrics must be passed called "gates" since many different customers will use the product. These include comprehensive functionality tests, code modification rates, unit/system regression tests, bug rates, remaining bugs review, installation tests, licensing tests, hours of test and quality checks. There may be unexpected problems in each phase that force you to fix a problem in the code written earlier in the schedule requiring that a whole series of tests to be redone. These loop-back iterations are expensive, as are new features that are added to the product due to a new customer request. **Do not allow "feature creep" at the end of the release phase** or you will disrupt the existing code and then have to redo all of the tests to hit the milestone and potentially miss the deadline.

The benefit of doing all of these things is significant. Customers will quickly be aware that there is high quality in the product. Before installing the software at the customer site, in the case of on-premise versions, it is important to test the installation procedure at your own site a few times until it is fool proof. The customers should experience quality from the point of installation onward. Above all, you will have a high-quality product that actually works. That is worth a lot.

Take Away: Introduce processes in stages rather than all at once for low-defect coding, coding standards, software development cycle and product release milestones and metrics. This becomes a competitive advantage and reduces the likelihood of failure. It also reduces stress in the company, and eventually leads to happier customers and employees.

Tip 4.5

Pre-Plan Your Product Pivot Strategy

Tutorial: It has often been said that a company is like an ocean liner – once you set sail towards a particular destination, it takes a long time to change course to another destination. But this is not true for a startup. If something goes wrong, and it will, the startup is agile enough to pivot, both in product development and business strategy. **When launching an MVP, you are trying to answer some big important business questions.** If the answer comes back in the negative and you have to scrap your product plans, you need another option or two to be successful. But **many startups do not consider a pivoting strategy until it is too late.** So pre-plan your product pivot strategy early in the game. It is an insurance policy. You hope you never need it, but it is nice to have it when you do.

When you are planning the products or services for your startup, you should **tackle a growing market and develop a multi-product strategy for that market using the same underlying technology for each product or service**. In fact, you should envision a series of products that you can build using the core competence of the founding team. Each of these potential products should be based on the same underlying technology with variations that target different markets or different customer needs. You want to launch the product that has the best chance of capturing the largest market share first. You also need follow-on products to maintain revenue levels when the first product saturates the market. **You cannot afford to be a one-trick pony in a competitive, fast-paced business environment.**

If the first product fizzles, you may need to pivot to another one – either a variation of the first, or the second product in the roadmap based on the same platform or technology as the first. The second product is both a backup plan for pivoting purposes and a second

Start With a Minimum Viable Product 117

revenue generator if the first product succeeds. A third product should also be planned as a "fail-safe" option. Usually this product is not actually developed because the market conditions will likely change dramatically by the time it is scheduled to be launched. But as a fail-safe measure, it plays an important role in the company roadmap.

When you develop products for a marketplace, you should categorize products as being either "New" or "MeToo". A "New" product is first to market (or a close second). It inherently has a barrier to entry in that any competitor must spend a certain amount of time to reverse engineer the product. You will have a head start in revenue until the competitor catches up and releases their product. As a result, additional barriers need to be implemented in the product to hit your revenue numbers. A "MeToo" product is one that serves an established market with a product that directly competes against an existing product with an installed base. Further refinements of these two terms based on the significance of the technical barriers have been created for each type of product.

```
New++    = first to market with two barriers to entry
New+     = first to market with one significant barrier to entry
New      = first to market with no barrier to entry but trying to grab
           market share
New-     = first to market without full functionality but trying to grab
           customers

MeToo++  = Similar to existing product with two new barriers to entry
MeToo+   = Similar to existing product with one new barrier to entry
MeToo    = Similar to existing product trying to grab a share of a large
           market
MeToo-   = an inferior product with a large market due to lower
           pricing or trade restrictions
```

Several different but related products can be developed during the prototyping phase. If you have only one product, you are basically betting on one number at the roulette wheel. Too many companies fail in the marketplace with their initial product and do not have any backup plans or pivots in place. Think about taking a different approach. Develop a number of product ideas that are either New++, New+, MeToo++ or MeToo+. Then, implement and launch the product that is most likely to succeed in the market. If it fails, go to the backup plan. If that fails, use the contingency plan.

Consider the following realistic scenario. You examine the market and see an opportunity for several products. After prototyping, you decide to build three products related in some manner: New++, MeToo++ and New, according to the definitions above. The first product of interest is a New++ product that you believe will capture a target market within a few months so you decide to launch it first. This is your Plan A, the baseline strategy of the company. Based on this decision, the resources of the company are solely focused on the successful execution of Plan A.

After some amount of experimentation in the marketplace, you realize that there is a need for a modified version of the first product. This improved version would have a better product/market fit based on initial beta-testing results. If many customers require this new capability and you agree to deliver it, you are creating a derivative product and have effectively pivoted to Plan A'. This is a partial pivot, but must be recognized as a pivot nonetheless. Assuming that most of the other customers would require this capability, this sequence of events would validate that Plan A as was correct as a starting point.

But what if there is a problem with getting Plan A or A' working due to unexpected circumstances? In that case, you would need to make a full pivot to Plan B. That means switching to the MeToo++ product that serves as a first line of defense against failure of Plan A. In some sense, this decision is easier to make because the first product is not working. Even though this product must unseat an incumbent product, a MeToo++ product has two new features that make it compelling for the customer. But there will now be a competitive battle to gain market share. Plan B is not as attractive as Plan A, but it still allows the company to be viable.

The fallout of this decision is that many changes must be implemented, projects must be cancelled, people must be transitioned to the new product and the company must be refocused on a new goal. This will be a difficult but necessary transition for survival and will depend on the funding available and the support and approval of the Board of Directors.

If Plan B works, it would allow the company to be sold for a high valuation. But perhaps the prospects of an IPO in the future would be dimmed slightly. On the other hand, if Plan B fails, there is still one last hope to salvage the company in a full pivot to Plan C. The product would be a New product that would need to be developed from scratch. This product could be quickly replicated by the competition but, with a head-start, initial revenue would still be obtained.

Another downside is a second series of difficult internal changes are necessary in the company. There may be many departures of employees from the company, especially sales people, and the Board and investors may become increasingly impatient. However, if successful, it would make the company an attractive acquisition target because of the technical expertise and the existence of a working product. This would be the main selling point to the Board and the employees. The acquisition value would depend on the quality of Plan C, but any acquisition is a successful outcome in the sense that value was delivered to the marketplace and another company recognized that value.

The notion of pre-planning your pivots is another way of saying you should develop a Roadmap for the company products. The plans can be placed in the Roadmap document as shown below. Some partial pivots that are unexpected, such as Plan A', are not usually included because they are in response to customer needs. Pivot decisions of this sort must be made in real time. However, full pivots must be included in the Roadmap. Simple business models can also be developed around Plans B and C in case those plans are brought into play.

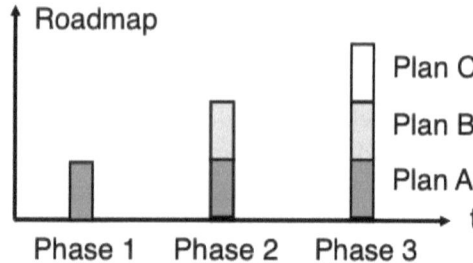

By using this approach of working out a pivot strategy in advance, you will know that you have multiple ways to succeed. The first product idea may not work for a variety of reasons, but unfortunately entrepreneurs have 100% confidence in it and may not bother to develop backup plans. They also believe that it is too much work and a complete waste of time to build a Roadmap. It may seem overkill at the time but not when you actually need to use it. Similarly, never jump out of a plane without a backup parachute, or two.

Tip 4.6

Make Business Decisions from Now On

Tutorial: In a startup, you are going to make decisions you have never made before and at a rate higher than ever before. So get ready to make some very tough decisions. It may be a daunting prospect at the outset so here are some suggestions that may help.

First, you must view all decisions as business decisions. **Even technical decisions must be made in the context of the impact on the business.** Technical founders have great difficulty making this transition. They think of technical improvements to the product without considering whether it would increase sales. In fact, technical elegance is preferred over increased sales by many technical people. Often, technical founders will consider 4 or 5 different approaches to solve an inconsequential problem and then test all of them to decide which one is best. Once implemented, there is a great deal of satisfaction and some consideration to write a conference paper. This works in academia or a research environment but not in a startup. In most cases, it is a waste of time to try all the approaches. Pick one and go with it!

The question is whether all the fanciful technical experimentation will make an impact on the revenue. The answer is usually no. If you are used to making mostly technical decisions, you will have to remind yourself that it is now a business decision. This change in the approach allows you to make better decisions for the startup. **Rewire your brain over time until it is second nature to view every decision as a business decision.** You have to let go of the desire to produce the perfect product that is technically elegant. It should be the minimum viable product that can be developed in the shortest amount of time that can be sold to customers and produce revenue.

Second, you need to realize you do not have to be right every time on every decision. Just on the big decisions. And even those, you just have to be right more often than not. The higher your decision success rate, the more impact you will have on the success of the company. Third, if you do make a mistake, do not dwell on it. Instead, correct it as soon as you can. Fourth, check on the progress of all big decisions to make sure they are going the way you expected. Follow them from beginning to end. Apply any midstream course correction needed. For the smaller decisions, ask the person or persons involved to check back if there are any problems. And fifth, don't make decisions for those to whom you have delegated this responsibility. That is their job. Provide input only if they request it. This is how you build trust and empower your employees to succeed and increase their value to the company over time.

There are many tough decisions to make in the first year or two. If a product does not work, then a decision must be made to terminate the project and begin working on the next one. This will require moving people from one project to another in midstream. You will have to explain why it is being done in one-on-one meetings and answer all their questions. Another option is to continue working on the product and hope the problems can be overcome by some miracle. This option will only prolong the problem and delay the inevitable. It is also possible to look for third-party solutions for pieces that you cannot get working. This will take time and effort. This is what makes it a difficult decision. While there are no simple answers, you will have to pick one and make it work for the company.

Firing someone may be a difficult decision in a small company environment. However, if the person is not working out or creating problems in the company, they must go. There is no room for politics or divisiveness in a small company. The decision must be made without hesitation regardless of what hardship it may cause to the person being fired. Afterwards, an explanation must be made to the rest of the company as to why the person was no longer an asset to the company. Then focus on finding a replacement. In cases

Start With a Minimum Viable Product

where someone unexpectedly quits, you can try to change their mind or just move to hire a new person. It is much better to have a new excited person than a previously disgruntled one.

When the burn rate is too high relative to revenue, another tough decision may be required. Laying people off. Since the headcount is frequently the most significant part of expenses, people must be let go to bring down the burn rate. This is called a reduction in force (RIF). It is a difficult decision because many people are asked to leave the company at the same time. In this situation, you have to let people know that they did nothing wrong. Tell them it was an issue of excessive burn rate and not enough revenue. Offer to serve as references for those who need it. Treating people with respect in the midst of a company RIF is very important because those who remain will be watching how the company handles difficult times.

There will be many other difficult decisions that you will have to make. Realize you will never have 100% of the information you need to make the perfect decision. In fact, the information may not even be of high quality, or may be superfluous to the decision, or may contain biases, or may be based on old data. You can only try to use your best judgment to make good decisions in the midst of incomplete and uneven information, so accept that in the first place.

The decision-making process can be viewed as being comprised of 3 parts:

- 1/3 on information gathered and what you know about the facts
- 1/3 on implications of information based your experience in prior situations
- 1/3 on what your instincts or intuition tells you about the right decision

By this qualitative assessment, only one-third of the decision is based on available information. In fact, too much information may not be desirable since it leads to confusion. Identify the goal of the decision and use only the information pertinent to that decision.

And remember, "you don't know what you don't know". So dig deeper on big decisions to get enough input from your advisors within a reasonable time frame. It is the second component, the implications of the data, where these advisors can add value because you need to find out how to interpret the data that you already have and extract the most important pieces to make the right decision. This is a skill that you have to pick up over time.

Do not underestimate the power of your own intuition or instincts in decision-making. You have to listen more intently to your inner voice. You may already know the right decision in a short amount of time but are hesitant to act upon it for a variety of reasons. This is also very common in startups. The problem is that a big decision usually results in big changes. You do not want to drag out decisions under any circumstances. Your fear of the potential fallout from the decision will likely stall the decision just long enough to prevent you from succeeding. If you hesitate too long, you will lose more often than not.

The earliest big decisions have a long-lasting impact on the success of the company. These are the ones that you have to get right. The rest of the decisions along the way will determine how successful you are in your venture. In the end, the decision is yours - so make it and own it. Some have said there are no bad decisions, only decisions where you didn't work hard enough to make them good. Actually, there are bad decisions: those that you did not recognize quickly enough as bad and therefore do not act fast enough to correct.

There are also decisions that must be made quickly. Situations arise unexpectedly requiring an on-the-spot "Go/No-Go" decision. They occur more frequently than the big decisions. You must be able to think on your feet, quickly carry out a high-level analysis on the information you can access, and then rapidly make a decision. The elements of these types of decisions are the same as the bigger decisions. You have partial information, a certain amount of experience and your intuition. Advisors cannot be consulted due to time constraints. Depending on the decision, pull a small team together to discuss your decision to test if you are missing anything. If not, put the decision into action. If so, adjust the plan accordingly. These decisions will get easier over time as your experience increases.

And finally, do not mix emotions with business decisions. Agonizing over an obvious decision because of emotions will cost the company in the end. However, there is a difference between how you make decisions and how you treat people based on those decisions. People must be treated with dignity and respect at all times. If you cancel a project, take the time to explain it clearly to each member of the group. If there is a layoff, tell people it does not reflect on their abilities but rather a change in the market conditions. If you need to shift or demote someone, spend time with that person explaining the reason for the change. Keep one thing in mind – how you treat people reflects on the company value of teamwork. As long as you deal with people respectfully, you will minimize the potential for emotional upheavals with any business decision.

Tip 4.7

The Product-to-Customer Interface Determines Scalability

Tutorial: A high-growth startup requires annual revenues on the order of $20M or more within 5-8 years. Companies that achieve this level of revenue are likely to have a scalable business model but it depends on the expenses associated with achieving the target revenue. The term "scalable" is tossed around quite a bit during discussions with investors but the exact definition is somewhat elusive to first-time entrepreneurs. It has to do with the nature of the product-to-customer interface, so it is worth studying what goes on at this interface. The enterprise business-to-business (B2B) market has certain well-understood characteristics and is the focus here, as opposed to the business-to-consumer (B2C) market.

An underlying assumption in building a scalable company is that you can find customers for your product. **First-time founders do not realize how hard it is to get customers, especially the large customers. Simply stated, it is extremely difficult.** Before funding your startup, it is typical for investors to interview several of your customers or potential customers to verify that you are solving an important problem and they are willing pay for your solution. So you should contact many customers before you seek funding.

Potential customers must have a need for the product and the budget to pay for it. If you approach a customer with a need but they are at the end of their budget cycle, they will not be able to pay for it. They may become a future customer, but not in the current quarter. There may be another potential customer with a budget but not an immediate need. They may indicate a future need; so another future customer is identified, but not an immediate customer. And there may be cases where the potential customer has neither a need nor the budget. This is the most common situation because the product may not solve their problem. Those with an immediate

Start With a Minimum Viable Product   127

need and enough of a budget may agree to evaluate your product. But even in these cases, they will not engage quickly because they have so many other things on their plate.

Initially, the number of customers that can be pursued will be very small because it is not possible for a fledgling startup to cover a large territory at once. The field sales force, which may be the founders at the beginning, has limited bandwidth and must identify which of the potential customers will be actual customers. They have to go through a maze of decision influencers to reach the decision maker who actually owns the budget. Then, they can begin the process of working out a beta-test evaluation and develop acceptance criteria with the customer to obtain a purchase order. After a lengthy evaluation, if the customer is not satisfied, the whole process may have to be repeated again until some customer finally agrees to purchase the product.

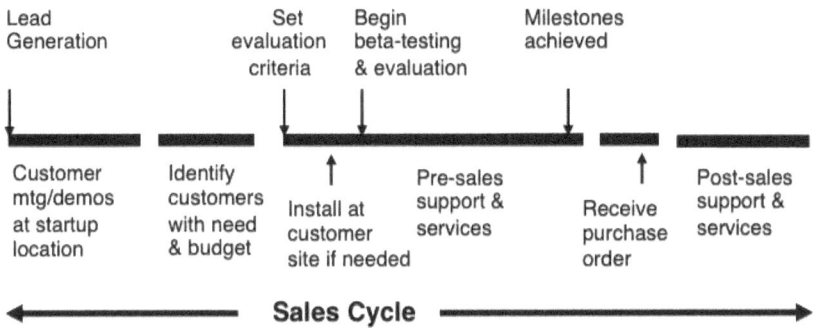

A realistic enterprise business-to-business (B2B) sales cycle is shown in the figure for a field sales team. Clearly the sales process can be labor intensive and expensive. Often, it produces no customers, especially in the first year of operation with an alpha version of the product. In the second year, if a beta version is ready, one or two customers may be convinced to participate in an evaluation without competitors involved. This process may take months to execute and convert into a purchase order, which is typically paid in 60-90 days. Many unexpected things go wrong in the beta-testing period. The whole process from start to finish may take a year rather than the 2 months that is typically allocated for it.

The two most important aspects of the sales cycle are the length and the cost. Ideally, the sales cycle fits into one quarter, since quarterly results are used to measure the success of a business. However, it may span several quarters in practice. At the tail end of each quarter, the sales force is very busy trying to close every possible account while at the same time trying to fill the pipeline with new potential customers to be harvested in the following quarter. So the cost may actually extend past the quarter boundaries even though most work occurs in a flurry at the end of the quarter, right up to midnight on the last day. There are usually large expenses associated with the sales (and marketing) process. The price of the product being sold must offset these sales expenses by a large enough margin to have any chance of being profitable and scalable. For scalability, the length of the sales cycle and expenses must be greatly reduced over time. If the business model involves a product and a service, the scalability will depend on how much service is delivered and at what price and cost.

To better understand how the product-to-customer interface largely controls the scalability of the business, consider two extremes. If you start a consulting company that takes in contracts with partial payment upfront, then you will likely be profitable in the first year. It is a service-oriented company that may require very little cash to start and has immediate bookings. But this type of business is not scalable in the venture capital sense. This is because your team has a finite bandwidth and you will have to increase the number of people and the number of contracts to grow the business. Also, the sales cycle is long because you have to work directly with the customer over the entire period of the contract until it is completed properly. Therefore, the significant interface between the product and the customer over an extended period of time limits the ability to scale.

Start With a Minimum Viable Product 129

The other extreme is a software company that develops a product over a 2-year period with a relatively short and inexpensive sales cycle. There is no income for 2 years as the company burns through cash to build the product and the company. Once completed, the product is downloaded over the Internet and an instruction manual is emailed to the customer along with a live chat option for troubleshooting installation. A user license is updated automatically for the customer each year without customer intervention. This business may not be profitable until the third year but it is highly scalable, assuming a large customer base and a suitable price point for the product. In this case, the interface between the product and customer is minimal and highly desirable.

Note that both types of businesses are profitable and viable but only one is scalable in that the revenue growth rate is exponential after a few years. You must attempt to build the type of company in the second example. If a business offers both products and consulting services to customers, the service component of revenue needs to scale to a small percentage of sales over time because service does not scale easily, as described above. If the consulting component does not produce very high margins, investors may discount this revenue when considering the growth rate of the company and, therefore, the valuation is lower. In fact, **the lower the service cost of each customer, the higher the scalability**.

One of the main issues faced by first-time founders is to determine whether their business is scalable. This is a difficult question to answer with certainty at the outset but there are leading indicators that should be examined before going ahead with the startup. Two factors that determine scalability are the cost of goods sold (COGS) and the revenue from the customer. Embedded in the COGS are production costs, the salaries of the sales people plus commission, sales expenses, cost of pre-sales customer support for product evaluation and cost of post-sales customer support for installation, training and maintenance. Marketing costs may also be included if they are a substantial percentage of the expenses in lead generation.

If the average sales price (ASP) of the product including services, maintenance and upgrades is larger by a given factor than the COGS, it is likely to be scalable. **Typically, this factor is about 3.** More specifically, if company sales and marketing costs are 25% of the total expenses, then the revenue must be 4X this amount to break even. This is to offset expenses that make up the remaining 75% of the company (i.e., G&A, Engineering, capital equipment, manufacturing and miscellaneous expenses).

There are situations where the sheer volume of product sales also leads to a highly-scalable business. This is more typical of a consumer market, which is not addressed here. This may also be true of equipment sales where the volumes are relatively high. The margins can be much smaller as long as the reduction in the sales margin is offset set by a corresponding increase in volume. Therefore, a target ratio of revenue to cost of goods sold cannot be established unless the volume is known. This is why scalability is difficult to assess in many cases.

There are also a number of situations where a company has the appearance of being scalable but fails to scale for one reason or another. For example, if a hardware company does not manage its inventory properly, the cost of excessive warehousing of inventory or the lost revenue when there is a shortfall of inventory may result in scaling problems. There is a similar problem if your supplier cannot manufacture enough hardware to meet your demands because another supplier in the food chain does not have enough parts. You should consider second-sourcing and check out the entire supply chain for bottlenecks and other limitations if your business depends on it for success. The main point is to think ahead about downstream problems that may occur due to scaling your business to ensure that there are no show stoppers just as the company is getting traction in the marketplace.

Over the past decade, the software business model has shifted from software-as-a-product to software-as-a-service (SaaS) due to the advent of cloud computing. (The term "cloud computing" was adopted since many diagrams in the past would show the computer hardware in a cloud-shaped bubble with users connected to it through terminals.) This is transforming the way companies do business and reshaping the client-server model of the past. The cloud platform involves a set of infrastructure and services that allow a large number of users to access the resources and capabilities through the Internet. It consists of arrays of compute servers, data storage and software programs. Software companies are now delivering SaaS over the Internet and building scalable businesses using a subscription-based revenue model. There is a shift from the traditional bag-carrying field sales force to an inside sales force that generates leads using the phone and Internet in the comfort of the office. This new inside sales approach is much cheaper and often generates more predictable revenue, but the field sales force is able to close larger deals with bigger customers.

The subscription-based revenue model for SaaS in its complete form is complicated. However, the main features are relatively easy to grasp. It begins with the notion that customers will sign up for the service (movies, music, dashboards, etc.) and pay a monthly (or perhaps annual) fee. The metrics to assess the viability of such a business are collectively called Unit Economics, where the unit is one user or customer. These metrics are used to make decisions on how to get the company to profitability. Initially, SaaS businesses tend to incur cash flow problems as they develop the product, compete for customers and then try to retain them by offering a compelling value proposition and attractive upgrade options. All of this costs money. But in the long run, the goal is to acquire and retain enough customers to keep a steady flow of cash coming into the company to make it viable, scalable and profitable.

First-order metrics are best illustrated using an example. Assume that the subscription fee for a service is $50/month. This is referred to as the monthly recurring revenue (MRR). Customers can either subscribe (acquisition), continue with the service and perhaps upgrade (retention), or drop the service altogether (churn). The length of time they stay with the service is the customer lifetime in months (LTM). Let us assume this value is found to be 20 months.

The lifetime value (LTV) of the customer is simply:

LTV = MRR x LTM = $50/month x 20 months = $1000

The LTM is usually represented in terms of a churn rate:

LTM = 1/(churn rate)

Therefore,

LTV = MRR/(churn rate)

If 5% of the customers leave the subscription program each month, the churn rate is 0.05. A typical customer would participate as a subscriber for a length of time in months given by:

LTM = 1/0.05 = 20 months

That's the income side. There are also expenses to deal with. They are associated with the cost of sales and marketing to acquire customers, called the customer acquisition cost (CAC). The unit cost per new customer acquired is simply the total sales and marketing costs divided by the number of customers acquired in a given period of time:

CAC = (sales and marketing costs)/(# of new customers)

Assume that CAC=$200 in this case. The time to recover the customer acquisition cost (CACR) is:

CACR = CAC/MRR = $200/$50 = 4 months

The main issue of concern using these metrics is whether a subscription-based business is viable. The scalability and profitability depends on the unit cost of acquiring a customer (CAC) relative to the lifetime value of the customer (LTV). Consider the following table of values for five hypothetical startups delivering SaaS. Each one has a different business decision to make based on the listed customer traction metrics.

Start With a Minimum Viable Product 133

The KPI's (key performance indicators) are the LTV/CAC ratio and the CACR. Based on these examples, LTV/CAC should be greater than 3 for a scalable business and the CACR should be less than 12 months. These are rules of thumb that may vary depending on the type of business. If the values are not in the prescribed range, corrective action should be taken to improve the situation, as suggested in the table. Of course, these first-order metrics do not account for sales margins, varying MRR per account and all other important details, but they do convey the use of such metrics in decision making.

	Startup A	Startup B	Startup C	Startup D	Startup E
CAC	$200	$400	$600	$800	$1,400
Churn	5%	5%	8%	2%	1%
LTM	20	20	12.5	50	10
MRR	$50	$80	$100	$50	$100
CACR	4	5	6	16	14
LTV	$1,000	$1,600	$1,250	$2,500	$1,000
LTV/CAC	5	4	2.1	3.1	0.7
LTV/CAC > 3	Yes	Yes	No	Yes	No
CACR < 12	Yes	Yes	Yes	No	No
Possible Action	Scalable business: need to invest in the sales channel	Scalable business: reduce CAC, then invest in sales channel	Viable business: reduce churn by improving customer experience	Viable business: reduce CAC, increase MRR until CACR < 12	Risky business: Reduce CAC & churn, increase MRR, new markets

Advanced notes:
1. The CAC is a "killer metric" that the CEO and the sales and marketing team must monitor constantly. Typically, a number of different acquisition methods are attempted for single customers, small businesses, large enterprises, partners and international distributers. Each one may produce different LTV's and associated CAC's. It may be very expensive to experiment with all of them at once so the sequencing and selection to produce the highest LTV/CAC ratio is critical to success. The ratio of field sales people to inside sales people also impacts CAC and LTV.
2. The P&L costs of SaaS businesses are much lower than in traditional software since you do not have to support multiple versions as new versions are updated online rather than on-premise. The downside is data security. That is why some industries (like banks) will not buy SaaS, and some companies use hybrid clouds (online & on-premise). There are many big issues here so entrepreneurs interested in SaaS are well advised to dig deeper into these issues.
3. To beat the competition, SaaS companies must invest heavily in sales and marketing when they observe traction improving rapidly. This tends to reduce profits for the short term but payback is expected in the long term. They go from making some money to losing money to making more money to losing more money until they become profitable.
4. Detailed models for CAC and LTV are needed in the business plan to demonstrate potential customer traction. More accurate calculations of user metrics requires the inclusion of gross margins, average MRR's across many customers, variable MRR's over the lifetime of the customer, etc. Online resources should be consulted for further details.

CHAPTER 5
Get Properly Funded

5.1. **You Need Angels or VCs to Scale Your Business**

5.2. **Make Valuation a Win-Win Negotiation**

5.3. **Know What You're Getting for What You're Giving Up**

5.4. **Do Your Due Diligence on Angels and VCs**

5.5. **Understand the VC Landscape and Timing**

5.6. **VCs Expect a 20X ROI**

5.7. **Revenue Projections Determine Your Valuation**

5.8. **Liquidation Preference is about Who Gets Paid First**

5.9. **Convertible Notes Must be Handled with Extra Care**

Tip 5.1

You Need Angels or VCs to Scale Your Business

Summary: While building a business, there may come a time when bootstrapping the company is insufficient. Although you should bootstrap as long as possible, you may reach a point where sales are on the verge of growing faster than your infrastructure and processes can support. In that case, you have a scalable business that may quickly capture a large market share, but only if there is sufficient investment of capital. A fast-growing company needs a large infusion of cash to build the sales channel, fill the pipeline with products, hire people, support customers and implement scalable business processes. The primary sources of this working capital are angels and VCs. They provide "smart" money by offering a range of services and business connections, along with the investment, to help you grow faster. However, to secure their funds, you must achieve certain well-known milestones before approaching them. So while you are bootstrapping, you need to get all your ducks in a row so it is easier to obtain your first round of financing by the time you need it.

Key point: It is a highly-competitive process to secure funding from angels or VCs, and you will only be eligible if you fit their desired profiles. Angel investors are looking for potentially scalable companies with a working product, reference customers and initial revenue. VCs are interested in rapidly-growing companies that are ready to scale. A startup targeting a large market with a scalable product, a strong management team and several customers fits the criteria and has a high probability of securing funds from angels or VCs. In addition, VCs evaluate the future capital requirements (and hence potential dilution) of the business. In fact, most VCs consider the number of rounds needed to get to profitability as a very important factor in their final decision to fund a startup.

Tutorial: Investors are all looking for the same thing and only a few companies fit the profile out of every 1,000 business plans they receive. The most important factor is that the business has the characteristics of scalability: a potentially fast-growing company within 5-8 years of operation. If not, they will not be interested in funding the company. Angels fund early stage companies while VCs tend to favor later stage companies with a provable growth potential. If they are convinced there is a high-growth opportunity, they begin a due diligence process to decide whether to invest. It is important to know how you will be evaluated if you seek this type of funding.

First, they assess the quality of the team. The investors want to invest in a collaborative team that has the experience to execute on the strategy but is also adept at figuring out how to change direction and solve problems as they arise. Investors look for certain traits that define real entrepreneurs. For example, one desired trait is the ability to accomplish many goals before investor funding is pursued. The team must demonstrate the ability to motivate people to perform work for the company with little or no pay during the bootstrapping phase. They need to know that you can be frugal with cash. They will study the team dynamic and interactions during the pitch. They evaluate whether or not the team has shared values and a shared vision for the company. If the team is solid, they pass the first criterion for success.

The second requirement is a "must-have" product for a large market, with a tangible product/market fit. If there are sufficient barriers to entry built into the product and it does not have much competition, it passes another criterion. Third, if the product has high margins or high volume, it passes a first-order test of being scalable. This is the major hurdle that your startup must overcome to be on the short list of companies that move to the next stage of evaluation. They will also need to understand your "exit strategy". That is, they need to know how you plan to deliver their return-on-investment. You must specify whether you plan to stay private, have an IPO, or get acquired by a bigger company. They will require a list of companies that are potential acquirers if the startup does not get to an IPO within 5-8 years. If you satisfy all these requirements, you will likely be funded.

When you are bootstrapping with the intention of pursuing angel or VC financing, you should make sure you have all of these factors in place, not just one or two. In other words, you need a strong team AND a killer product with high margins AND a large market. This is not only to impress the VCs but because there is no other way to build a fast-growing company. Furthermore, the expected return-on-investment by angels and VCs cannot be delivered if you do not have a scalable business.

Securing these funds will not be easy. The bar has been set very high and the environment is very competitive with many startups vying for the same funds. Study a number of investment firms to find a match between your company and the investors. You will need investors that fully understand what you are doing. **The investment community is built on relationships, so you must have an advisor make introductions to suitable VCs or angels.** This is the only way to get your signal heard above all the noise since investors see a large number of potential deals every year. If you have any interested investors, prepare a presentation and pitch deck for the first meeting. The best approach is to be very well prepared before you go to the top VCs or angels. You have only one shot at getting a follow up meeting so your pitch must be carefully crafted.

Another way to prepare is to make sure you are working on a killer product. This will allow you to differentiate yourself from others who seek the same funding sources. It will enable you to attract top management and acquire beta customers. Work with beta customers to steer you towards a must-have product and have those customers act as references. Demonstrate there is a growth path for the company with this product. Show the company can be scaled to achieve high revenues in 5 years. Set realistic expectations about the potential of the company and identify the inherent risks. If you do not have all these pieces in place, they may still fund you if you can convince them that the company has potential and can be scaled with this product. If no firm is willing to fund you, then you should continue to bootstrap until you reach more milestones and have a higher confidence of success. The goal of getting funded is to grow the company rapidly, not to keep a sinking ship afloat. If you do not think that the company will make it, it is wise to shut down operations and start over on a new venture.

The day you obtain funding, life changes completely from your pre-funding days. You lose primary control of the company and the clock starts ticking for a liquidation event sometime in the future. In exchange for funding, you have committed to making the company successful. Now you will have to deal with impatient investors, along with a newly constituted Board of Directors. You have to hit milestones in an environment of "no excuses". People will be fired if they fail to execute. You are in the big leagues of business, not the bush leagues. If you do not like the environment associated with angel or VC financing, it is best to turn it down, or not pursue it altogether. But if you agree, you must make every attempt to get the company to a high-value exit in partnership with the investors. In other words, your pitch to the investors should not be a series of promises that you cannot keep. It should be a serious discussion of the strategy, plans and risks of the venture.

Advanced notes:
1. Angels and VCs receive up to a hundred business plans a month, and only a few will garner serious attention. An investor not engaging with you does not necessarily mean you do not have a fundable company. It may mean you did not make the short list of startups they have chosen to engage deeper with at that time. Most investors have passed on companies that have gone on to become very successful. Remain persistent if you believe that you have a potential home run.
2. Many founders fail to understand the real goal in their first investor pitch. The goal is to get to a second meeting with the other partners in the firm. Your pitch needs to be strong enough that they want to dig deeper and bring in more people to review your company. Do not expect to go deep into all the fine details of your company; they are screening

the high-level issues. The investor's decision at the first meeting is to either meet again to probe further or disengage.
3. Always create your pitch from the investor's point of view. Stay away from long technical details, of which they have no interest. They have their own questions they need you to answer to reach a funding decision, so answer those questions as clearly and concisely as possible. Imagine yourself in their place. Successful entrepreneurs who become investors often experience an epiphany the first time they sit on the other side of the table and receive a pitch from a founder asking them to part with their hard-earned money.
4. Be prepared for two key questions in your investor meeting: what is your unfair advantage and what big bet are you asking the investor to make. Your unfair advantage addresses why you will succeed while the other deals they have seen with the same plan will not. The big bet is what change in the technology, industry or market conditions you expect will lead to your company's success over the other deals in this space.
5. Exaggerations reduce your credibility and suggest a lack of expertise in your space and of your team. For example, if you are developing accounting software for small businesses, do not claim the market size for your product is multiple billions – the size of all accounting software for all size companies. And avoid guessing. If you do not know the answer definitively, put forward a reasonable estimate and an overview of the process used to make the estimate. They may be able to provide you with more data to make a better estimate.
6. The best way to get on the short list with any investment group is to already have one of their group members as an investor in or advisor for your company. Many angel groups allow companies to bypass initial screening criteria if a member has already agreed to invest. The investor can also help you fine-tune your presentation to have a better appeal

to the specific investment group and point out specific group members that might also like your company.

Take Away: After securing funding, you will be off trying to meet the next set of milestones for the company. In the back of your mind, you must remind yourself that someone has bet their money on you and your team, and you will pay them back at some point in the future by building a great company with their help. That is the contract you signed. Even though there is a tremendous amount of work to reach the point where you are funded, it will seem like the easy part later on. The road ahead is even more difficult, but you will have help through the investors, the Board and the new hires in the company. Regardless of the difficulty, you must be willing to put all of your energy into this newly-funded venture. If you do not feel you can make this level of commitment, it is best not to take the money and keep bootstrapping until profitability.

Tip 5.2

Make Valuation a Win-Win Negotiation

Summary: If you decide to raise funds from angel investors or venture capitalists, you are implicitly building a high-growth company. While pursuing these funds, there is a prevailing belief that obtaining a high valuation is the most important aspect of the deal but, in reality, getting enough cash should be a higher priority. The valuation is the total assessed dollar value of a startup that is used as a basis for funding and ownership. There are many methods to determine the valuation. Your approach and the investor's approach are likely to produce two different results. Typically, entrepreneurs do not know how to determine their own valuation but will attempt to negotiate a high value to retain more ownership. The assigned valuation by the investors may be lower but they use standard methods based on many years of experience. Battling investors over valuation is usually a losing proposition. In practice, the valuation does not change significantly during the negotiation. Both sides need to weigh many other factors to find a workable deal. The best way to obtain a high valuation is to build up value between rounds of financing and have several VCs competing for your deal.

Key point: The valuation of a startup is based on the milestones achieved, projected revenues and due diligence. Many investors are willing to share their evaluation process with you to help build up value prior to funding. It is important to know the major criteria for establishing a valuation soon after you start a company. However, the most important goal during the negotiation is to find a deal that provides enough funding to extend past the next set of achievable milestones without running out of cash. Do not let greed get in the way of good judgment. In fact, if the initial valuation is too high, you will likely face the scourge of a "down round" if you are unable to hit milestones. **Keep the negotiations on valuation as simple as possible and strive for a win-win outcome in the overall deal.**

Tutorial: Valuation is the term used by investors when assigning a dollar value to your startup in order to determine how much to invest and what percentage ownership to receive in exchange. It is difficult for founders to assign a value to a company that does not have revenue, or a completed product, or any customers for that matter. But sophisticated investors, such as angels and VCs, use their own methods to establish a fair valuation and those seeking financing should understand these methods. There are general guidelines and evaluation sheets that are used to quantify what is ostensibly a qualitative process.

The relationship between the pre-money valuation, investment requested and post-money valuation is as follows:

Post-Money Valuation = Pre-Money Valuation + Investment

In general, angel investors work with pre-money valuations, and venture capitalists work with post-money valuations. Angel investors typically invest in seed and first rounds to get a startup off the ground so their valuations are usually lower. They evaluate the company, assess its pre-money valuation, add the investment and derive the post-money valuation. VCs fund companies in the first round and subsequent rounds. They try to establish a post-money valuation based on revenue projections. Their valuations are necessarily higher since they are financing later stage companies. They are often involved in later rounds to help grow the company. They may also participate in a round to avoid dilution.

Once a valuation is established, the price per share for the preferred stock and common stock can be determined. For example, if the post-money valuation of a startup is $10M and the company has 20M shares fully-diluted, the strike price is set to $0.50/share for investors. They must pay this price for every preferred share purchased. If $4M is invested, the VCs will buy a total of 8M preferred shares and own 40% of the company in doing so. The common stock share price is typically set to one-tenth of the preferred stock price. In this case, it would be $0.05/share for the remaining 12M shares, which is intentionally kept low to attract employees. At a liquidation exit, the preferred shareholders are paid first, and then the common stock holders. This is why they are priced differently.

It is possible to extensively study the valuation calculations of investors and get lost in the details with little change in the outcome of a negotiation. Instead, it is better to recognize one simple fact: **the further along the path to success that you are, the higher the valuation**. You should carry out a self-assessment at each achieved milestone. Furthermore, you should attempt to put yourself in a position where multiple investors are competing for your deal. This is the most reliable way to drive up the valuation. So work hard to build up value in the company before you seek funding.

Angel investors are groups of wealthy individual investors that often pool their resources and fund startups in a seed or early round. They are risking their own money but fully understand the risk as sophisticated investors. If you are trying to raise $500K, then angel funding is a good option. Angel investors may give you a pre-money valuation of around $1.5M. Combined with the $500K that you are trying to raise, you have a post-money valuation of $2M. These are typical numbers for angels. They expect to make in the range of 3-5X return in 3-5 years. Generally speaking, the higher the total investment made by an angel group, the higher the expectations on the return.

Angel investors consider deals with pre-money valuations in a fairly tight range of $1-3M, although the full range may be larger depending on your geographical location and the specific angel group. The figure below illustrates their subjective perceptions of the investment opportunity relative to pre-money valuation levels. Note that the further along you are the higher the valuation, and the lower the investor ownership. In this example, they start with a target pre-money valuation of $2M and then evaluate the potential investment by examining the strengths and weaknesses of the team and the market opportunity.

```
$3M  ──product, CEO hired, revenue──  very low risk
$2.5M ──────product, CEO hired──────  low risk
$2M  ---------------------------  medium risk
       ────prototype, founding team───
$1.5M ──────────────────────────   high risk
       ──────idea , founding team─────
$1M  ──────────────────────────   very high risk
Pre-money
valuation
```

If the team is very strong and possesses both technical and management experience, the valuation increases. If not, it decreases. If the TAM (total available market), and SAM (serviceable market) are large enough, the valuation goes up. Otherwise it goes down. If the product is likely to do well in that market, the valuation goes up even further. If not, the valuation decreases. Other factors are also included to determine if the pre-money valuation is closer to $1M or $3M including a lengthy due diligence process. Then the amount requested is added to the pre-money valuation to produce the post-money valuation. It does not move around much once it is determined. Even though it is supposed to be a negotiation, the movement is relatively small in the end.

Venture capitalists, on the other hand, manage very large funds from which they finance startups. Their valuations are subject to larger variations because their numbers are simply larger and they consider a wide range of businesses at different stages of development. But their first round valuations do not move much after they present their term sheet. These investments may start at $1M but a typical value is closer to $2M-$4M. The post-money valuation depends on the revenue growth model and the projected exit value of the company, which are both speculative measures.

Venture capital valuations have well-established formulas based on the projected exit value (total value of company at IPO or acquisition). They may use two or three methods to establish bounds on the post-money valuation to get a reasonable handle on what their ownership should be for the requested amount. Usually, the funding level requested is kept constant while the post-money valuation is subject to negotiation, especially if you have multiple VC firms competing for your deal.

One approach to determining the valuation uses the following equation:

$$\text{Exit Value} = \text{Post-Money Valuation} \times \text{ROI}$$

where the ROI is the expected return on investment. For example, if you are trying to raise $2M and your business plan projects a revenue of $50M in the IPO year, the exit value can be taken as two times this value, or $100M. The desired ROI is 20X. Therefore,

$$\text{Post-Money Valuation} = \$100M/20X = \$5M$$

and

$$\text{Pre-Money Valuation} = \$5M - \$2M = \$3M$$

The ownership by the VCs in this case is 40% in Series A preferred shares. Of course, these simple calculations do not include effects of dilution in later rounds.

The major aspects of a term sheet are investment level, valuation, ownership percentage, liquidation preference, milestones and vesting schedules for founders. While you can try to negotiate a higher valuation, there must be specific reasons for the investors to raise the valuation. If you already meet their funding criteria, then you should be receiving a fair valuation. If not, you have to accept the proposed valuation or improve it's basis before going back to negotiate. If a high-quality CEO joins the team, you can request a higher valuation. The same is true if a high-profile customer is obtained. If the prototype product exceeds the expectations set in the business plan, the valuation may also increase. The amount of increase depends on the type of change from the last meeting with investors. Talking them up does not work. Getting two term sheets from other VC firms with higher valuations will work.

Shown below are two hypothetical VC cases to illustrate the deal selection process. Assume that you receive 4 term sheets from 4 different VC firms. Selecting the proper one for your company involves some careful thought.

Consider case (a): All have the same VC percentage ownership.

	VC1	VC2	VC3	VC4
Post-Money Valuation	$5M	$10M	$12.5M	$25M
Investment	$2M	$4M	$5M	$10M

The best deal is the $5M investment with a $12.5M valuation. Take the largest amount of cash possible up to a point. The $25M valuation is out of line relative to the other VCs. If you are unable to sustain the $25M valuation, you are staring in the face of a down round, which would be disastrous. The expectations for growth and performance will be well beyond reason. Investors at this level will not be patient when $10M has been invested. And when you burn through the cash and miss all the milestones, you will be unable to attract additional funding. As a result, you should not go for valuations that are not sustainable from a business perspective, as tempting as they may be.

Consider case (b): All have different VC percentage ownership.

	VC1	VC2	VC3	VC4
Post-Money Valuation	$5M	$8M	$9M	$15M
Investment	$2M	$4M	$5M	$10M

At first, the best deal appears to be the funding level of $2M with a $5M valuation. It is not wise to give up 50% of the company or more at Round 1. It may grow to 50% over the next few rounds (at a cheaper price) but **retaining control of the company in the early** stages is very important. That said, the case with a $4M investment with an $8M valuation may actually be a better option depending on the quality of the investors and climate that exists for raising funds. You can operate for an extra year with $4M in the bank before you have to go out and raise another round. It is better to have more money in the bank and use it to stay focused on building a company than to run out of money in a year and have to chase another round after perhaps missing many milestones.

There are negotiable terms other than valuation. Reduce the requested amount, change the milestones, modify vesting schedule, or adjust the liquidation preference. The investors may also pivot to these other items if they want to close the deal. Perhaps a workable solution can be reached if some middle ground can be found. Consider all other options in your back pocket before you walk away from a deal. If you really like the angel or VC team and they can add value, you are better off taking the deal than wondering how you are going to make payroll in 10 weeks. **Big picture: take all factors into account, not just valuation.** After all, you are trying to build a high-growth company and, for that, you are going to need plenty of funding and some solid partners.

Advanced notes:
1. When VCs begin negotiations, they will likely ask for a "no shop" agreement, meaning you will not negotiate with any other VC once discussion of terms begins. If, however, you already have discussions with multiple VCs, let them know you cannot sign, so they know they may be in a bidding war for your opportunity.
2. When raising funds from a VC, it is important to have experienced advisors familiar with the process. A part-time CFO can assist in scrubbing the details of your financials and make them match an investor's expectations. The VC may also interview the temporary CFO to validate the numbers in your plan. Advisors at this stage of the company are more likely to accept stock in return for services if they believe the company will be venture backed. They realize and accept that you are trying to conserve cash whenever you can.

3. Each round of financing dilutes previous shareholders by a percentage that depends on the valuation of the round. If the capital requirements to get to profitability are enormous and require multiple rounds, VCs may not be willing to accept the level of dilution and may pass on the deal. It is important to limit the number of rounds anticipated to get to positive cash flow in order to make the deal more attractive to investors.
4. Some angel groups are open to partnering with other angel groups. If you pursue this, make sure there is only one person you work with on the deal terms. The lead investor generally negotiates the terms for the group.
5. One factor some VCs may use when predicting an exit value for a startup is the ease of obtaining a sign-off in an acquisition by a large company in the industry. If a business group manager can sign off $25M deals, the VCs may use this information to project an exit value at about $25M for a small startup. If the Board of a large corporation must approve a higher value potential acquisition, its chances of being approved are lower.
6. Potential exit value is also predicted by the history in your industry. So be familiar with the acquisition values of prior startups in your industry, especially those in the past 3-5 years.

Take Away: The focus on valuation is often misplaced because successful negotiations are often gauged by others using this one metric. But in this context, money is a just commodity, and taking a higher valuation just because it is a higher number can be suboptimal if you can derive more value from the right connections/network/advice of a better VC with a lower valuation. Consider all factors including control, cash and the quality of assistance when evaluating a VC or angel deal.

Tip 5.3

Know What You're Getting for What You're Giving Up

Tutorial: When you incorporate a startup, you and your co-founders own 100% of the company. While this may be exciting and satisfying, the value of the company is typically $1,000 at that point depending on what each founder contributed to the company to start it. However, if you seek investor funding, you must sell equity in the company in exchange for cash to fuel your company's growth. When the first round of financing is closed, your percentage will drop dramatically. Therefore, you must carefully consider your decision to pursue this type of funding by knowing what you are getting in return for what you are giving up.

Consider the example of an IPO bound company in the bar chart below showing percentage ownership as a function of certain financing events.

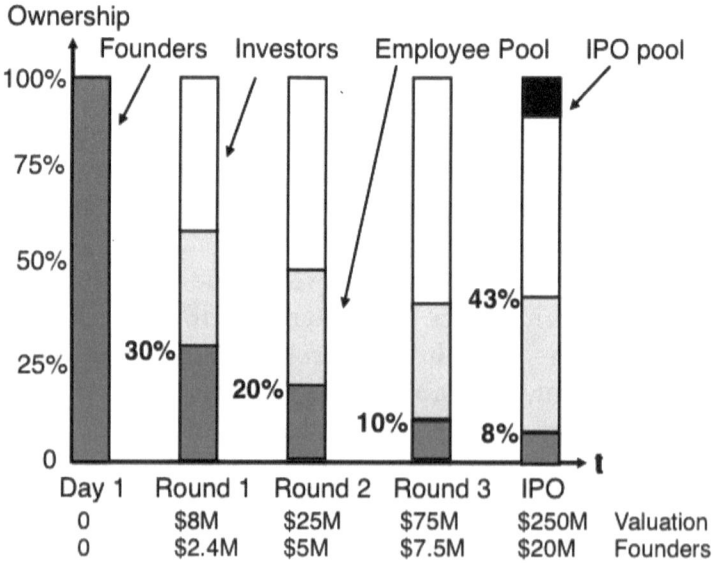

Get Properly Funded 151

These values are based on a successful company with a $250M valuation at the IPO in a 5-8 year period. The numbers for other companies will vary depending on the size of the market, the types of products, and perceived future value by the underwriters and the stock market. Such an IPO is considered a home run by VCs.

The first bar indicates founder ownership of 100% at incorporation. However, the second bar indicates this value reduces significantly due to two factors. First, the VCs own 40% of the company after investing $3.2M on a post-money valuation of $8M. In that case, the founders own the remaining 60%. Second, the ownership is further divided in half to create an employee stock option pool. An employee pool is set aside up front as way of avoiding dilution every time someone is hired. Therefore, the founder ownership effectively drops to 30% at the Round 1 (or Series A financing) as shown in the second bar of the chart. In essence, founders have given up 70% of the company at Round 1 in exchange for funding. The question is: what do you actually get for giving up 70% of the company?

The first piece of good news is that the founder ownership of 30% is valued at $2.4M on paper as opposed to $1,000 at incorporation. The bad news is you have to earn your percentage ownership by staying with the company for a number of years. This process of earning your shares back is called vesting. The standard vesting period is 4 years in most financing deals. It is possible to negotiate a deal where you get 1/5 fully vested if you have spent 1 year trying to get the company off the ground. However, the remaining 4/5 is still subject to vesting over the next four years. Usually, 1/48th of your shares will be earned every month for 48 months. **This vesting schedule is absolutely necessary to keep founders committed to the company.** This also clarifies how much stock is forfeited if a founder leaves the company early. Therefore, each founder has a strong incentive to stay with the company for many years and drive up the stock price by achieving milestones through hard work. It is very important to understand issues surrounding stock options, stock pricing, vesting schedules and tax consequences as part of raising funds for a startup.

In general, founders receive their equity ownership in the form of common stock over four years whereas investors receive preferred shares immediately for their investment. This means, if there is a liquidation event, the investors are paid first in accordance with the financing agreement and common-share holders are paid after that. However, the price of the common shares may be set to one-tenth of the price of the preferred shares. They are cheaper to buy and provide a mechanism for employees to have an ownership stake in the company. For example, preferred shares may cost $0.25/share for investors, called the strike price, whereas common stock may be priced at $0.03/share for employees. Since the price per share usually increases at every round of financing, and perhaps between rounds if the Board dictates, employees are given a strong incentive to join the company at a very early stage because the stock is cheaper. They are usually given stock options, that is, the option to buy stock at the price set when they join the company as part of the compensation package. The 4-year vesting schedule on stock options applies to all employees, including the CEO and management.

Given this arrangement, it is important to set aside a suitable percentage, in this case 30%, as an employee stock pool. This gives you the ability to hire the very best people using stock options without further dilution. The reason for the high percentage allocated to the pool is because you will need a large number of people to build a great company, and that is not going to come cheaply. In fact, greed has no place in the context of wealth creation. Each person will need to have a piece of the action as part of the compensation package to feel that they are working for themselves and the company at all times. This is the best way to engender a sense of teamwork and common purpose - through the issuance of common stock to all employees. As such, the value of the 30% stock pool is enormous.

For the remaining 40% equity given to investors, you are obviously receiving cash. Perhaps more importantly, you get a significant partner to help you build the company. Investors provide assistance for free from the time they fund you until there is an acquisition or

IPO. VCs, angels and other investors all vary in terms of how much they can help you and the type of help they offer. They may provide access to networks of people, customers, potential acquirers, Board members and consultants. They also may be able to provide insights on marketing and sales, and provide consulting visits from time to time to resolve immediate issues that occur outside of Board meetings. It is important to find a good match between your needs and the type of help the investors can offer.

The general rule is to understand what help an investor can provide before you take their money. If you select the right VC firm that understands your market and is able to connect you to the right business partners, you have a much better chance to succeed. Unfortunately, entrepreneurs often forget or forgo the use of this important resource. Building and maintaining strong relationships with the VCs and other investors is essential. Meet separately with investors to educate them on the product and customers. Meetings of this nature often elicit suggestions and alternatives that lead to better outcomes. Including investors in lunches, mixers and parties will also go a long way to building trust. It will get you through some tough times if you get to know your investors and they get to know you.

The value of a strong partnership with VCs should not be underestimated. If they truly understand your business, market, products and opportunity, they will likely continue to fund you. Depending on the VC firm, they will give you instant credibility with others and allow you to hire employees with a guarantee that they will be paid (until the company is no longer viable). But you also have a longer runway to succeed with deep-pocket VCs funding the company and that is extremely important when it comes to sales. Potential customers consider the purchase of products from a startup to be a risky proposition. Startups usually go out of business within 2 years so any manager who decides to buy a product from one wants to know the company will be around for many years. Their job may be on the line if they buy a product and the company disappears due to a bankruptcy or liquidation. There will be no further support, maintenance or upgrades of the product if that happens. The backing of a VC firm signals to the customer that your startup will likely be around for a while. They are more inclined to buy if they know that VCs have already checked you out and have given you sufficient funds to build and support the product, and will continue to fund you to grow the company.

As you take on future rounds of financing, you may experience more dilution. This is often viewed as an undesirable consequence of more funding. At Round 2, founder ownership may drop to 20%, and by Round 3, the founders may be down to a total of 10%, but the value of those shares on paper may be $7-8M. At the IPO, additional dilution will be experienced because new shares are floated to sell to various institutions. Typically, the total value of the founder's shares may be worth $20M. Dilution is only a negative event when the share price goes down. If it always goes up, it is in fact an accretive event with a net positive outcome.

It is useful to know the circumstances under which the price of the stock can go down in the second, third and later rounds. Often, the company does not meet some major milestones for a variety of reasons and begins to run out of money. When the CEO goes to raise the next round, investor interest begins to dwindle if the milestones seem unachievable even with more investment. No one wants to throw good money after bad. To continue, the company must accept a "flat round", where the valuation is the same as the previous round, or a "down round", where the valuation is lower than the previous round. The price of the stock will go down in this case, as indicated by its name. This is the cost of an over-valued previous round, or a set of overly-aggressive milestones that could not be met before running out of money.

If disaster has struck and new investors are invited to keep the company afloat (in a last-ditch effort to turn the company around), a down round is likely to occur and things can get quite nasty. The new investors will require previous investors to either participate on a pro-rata basis or be demoted to common shareholders. This is the so-called "pay-for-play" scenario. Lost in the shuffle of a down round is the significant dilution to all common stock holders, including any preferred stock holders who are demoted to common stock for failure to participate. Again, this is the price of the company not meeting expectations.

These situations are more common than an IPO or a high-value acquisition. It is prudent to understand the mechanics of the later down rounds and flat rounds. The best way to avoid the chaos of these later rounds is to ensure the company is not over-valued in early rounds, milestones are achievable between rounds, and the burn rate is kept as low as possible at all times. Of course, a working product with a large market potential is the best weapon to have when you walk into a financing negotiation in any round.

Clearly, the type of funding associated with VCs and angels is not for everyone. In fact, most startups may be better off growing organically to build a profitable business. The truth is not every entrepreneur or business is a fit for VC funding. But this does not mean that the business or idea is a bad one. It just means that it is not a business suited to venture backing. The objective must always be to build value for customers. However, the funding mechanism to meet this objective is not necessarily through sophisticated investors. The cost in equity may be too significant depending on the type of company being built. If your exit strategy is an acquisition at a modest but acceptable valuation, it may not require this type of funding at all. This can be a lucrative path if you have a key technology that is in demand by a few big companies. If you are developing such a technology and planning to sell it to a larger company, you may not need to build the infrastructure such as a sales channel, HR systems, financial systems, etc. It would be more efficient for the larger company to convert it to a product because they already have the needed infrastructure. However, if you are planning to become a high-growth company, there may be no option but to pursue VCs and angels.

Advanced notes:
1. Identify a good match before you contact a VC or angel group. Know which ones invest in your market to ensure that there is likely to be a match. Figure out which partner in the firm knows your market and ask to work with them in the initial phases of the evaluation. Decide if that person is the right fit for your team. Check out their other portfolio companies in your market to find out what kind of help they provide and their candid opinion of the firm.
2. Just as you need to understand what you are giving up when you accept financing, the VCs also weigh all the options on their side. They deal with such terms routinely as part of their business and know what interests they need to protect in their deals. The amount you can push on terms is a function of how many VCs are negotiating to fund you. Be sure to remain reasonable in your proposals and negotiations by keeping in mind the advantages of being funded by sophisticated investors.
3. A typical requirement in a financing agreement is that founders stay with the company for a minimum of one year to obtain any stock. This is the so-called one-year cliff-vesting schedule. At the one-year anniversary, each founder receives 25% of their shares fully vested, while the remaining 75% vests monthly for the next 3 years. If they leave the company for any reason before one year has elapsed, they will not receive any shares. This cliff-vesting requirement may be captured as a Repurchase Option in the financing agreement.
4. It is important to create and maintain a stock capitalization table, sometime referred to as a cap table for each round of financing. This table contains the number of shares and percentage ownership of founders, investors and employees. Often, the employee option pool will be broken out into used and unused portions. It also includes equity dilution and company valuation (pre-money, post-money and investment level) at each round. This table will be reviewed at Board meetings and managed by the CEO and CFO as the company grows.

Tip 5.4

Do Your Due Diligence on Angels and VCs

Tutorial: Due diligence is the process of checking the background and characteristics of businesses and persons before entering into a contracts with them. It is carried out with an extra level of care due to the importance of the contract. Usually VCs and angels carry out an extensive due diligence process on a startup, but it is equally important for the entrepreneur to carry out a similar due diligence on investors. The reason is most first-time entrepreneurs do not fully understand the financing process and may have many preconceived notions of investors that may not be correct. The investors will likely be involved with your company for many years so it is worth learning about them.

Not all angel groups and VC firms are created equal. There are many to choose from and you must check them out to separate the good ones from the rest. They are all made up of a group of individuals, so you must also identify the one person in each firm that you can work with. It is also important to understand the funding model and where the money comes from, as well as the steps in the process of getting funded. It is instructive to know what situations lead to conflicts between investors and entrepreneurs. Therefore, some investigation into professional and sophisticated investors is warranted prior to striking any deal. This investigation should be carried out initially to decide whether you are interested in this type of funding, and whether you should work with a specific firm if they express interest in funding your startup.

The first thing to recognize is where the money for the investment comes from. Angels are private investors using their own money, and venture capitalists are professional investors using somebody else's money. In both cases, it is real money. It does not fall from the sky or come up from some subterranean vault. It comes out of someone's pocket and they will do what is necessary to protect their investments. Therefore, you need to think differently about the process of securing funds from sophisticated or professional investors. There has been much written and much said about the nature of these investors in terms of their character, motives and behavior. In your mind, it should boil down to this: if you are funded, it is commitment to investors to build a great company and provide a return on investment.

Many founders view financing as a way of getting free money to chase their dreams. They want to take the money and run the company their own way. This is where they get it wrong. It is a partnership, not a dictatorship. When investors fund a company, they intend to provide as much help as possible to make it successful and do not intend, at the outset, to interfere with the strategy or plans of the entrepreneur but rather accelerate them. If you receive funding, the investors are making a bet on you and your team based on the business plan, presentation and due diligence. You pitch ideas and make a commitment to build a big company based on those ideas and they provide the funds to do it. That's the deal.

Unfortunately, one party usually breaks the deal. Think of it in this way: their part of the bargain is to provide you with funding and they deliver on their part of the deal; your part is to deliver on what you promised in the pitch; this is where the problem occurs. Usually, the company is unable to meet major milestones and eventually ends up on the verge of failure. The investors assert their control only when the company is in trouble because they have skin in the game and they want to preserve value for their investors or themselves. If it does fail, it is actually your responsibility, not the investor's responsibility.

To avoid failure in these types of cases, investors and the Board may step in and institute major changes. They may go as far as to remove the CEO or a founder in order to change the direction of the company and salvage their investment. But the entrepreneurs usually resist any such attempts by investors because they still want to run the business their way. They believe the interference of the investors is the norm rather than the exception because it happens frequently with other companies. Most startups make lots of mistakes that lead to failure and they want to pin the blame on the VCs or angels. This is why the reputation of the investors tends to be mostly negative. Many startups in this situation have ongoing conflicts with the investors and the Board. Conflicts should be avoided at all cost because the investors are the main reason you have a company. The best way to avoid the conflict is to keep the business running well, keep the promises and grow the company. Or choose not to take the funds in the first place if you have difficulty accepting the circumstances associated with funding.

Everyone must go into the investment negotiations with their eyes wide open and be operating from the same playbook. The investors are savvy business people who have seen a wide range of startups and are sometimes ruthless or heavy handed when they sense trouble. It is a matter of what expectations have been set in the business plan. Any attempt by the founders or management to exaggerate the possible outcomes, or stretch the truth or purposefully fool the investors into parting with their money, will only lead to conflict and failure down the road. Do not be a politician and make promises that you cannot keep. Set realistic expectations. The closer you come to telling investors the reality of the prospects of the company, the better off you are in the long run.

It is important to understand the details of VC and angel funding models to appreciate who will be paying your bills. Venture capitalists build their funds from university retirement systems, endowments, private investors and other financial institutions. They are expected to provide a healthy return to their investors by picking startups with a high probability of success. Their funding levels are in the range of $1M-$10M. They typically pursue companies involved in markets well beyond the range of $100M. However, only 1 in 10 funded startups actually succeed and the rate is even worse for startups without investor funding. Startups fail in many ways so they expect only one to hit a home run to make up for the nine that do not. A home run is either an IPO or a high-value acquisition. When a company is failing, VCs look for the closest exit ramp to at least recoup some of their investment, or deliver a modest return to their investors. In the process, they may end up in a fierce conflict with the management team or founders if the liquidation path is at odds with the company strategy.

Angels and angel groups are private investors who invest their own money. There is no middleman. Therefore, they tend to be more "hands on" and assist the entrepreneurs in many facets of building a company. The levels of investment are in the range of $150K-$500K per angel group. When angels pool their assets, funding levels can be as high as $2M. Market sizes greater than $50M are suitable for angel investments. They invest their own money and time, and they expect a healthy return by picking startups that have a high probability of success. Again, only 1 in 10 succeeds. This time, the investors have a personal interest in the exit because it is their own money. They will definitely want to preserve their investment and be paid back first. This is also a source of conflict because angels expect liquidity at some point along the way, usually in 3-5 years.

Given these statistics, it is surprising they continue to invest. But one home run is all that is needed out of 10 companies to get an acceptable return. The hard part is picking the right startups to fund, given that they all make claims of huge successes in a short time frame. Their selection process is relatively straight-forward. They start with the business plan and identify those that appear to be promising. This process requires 1 to 2 months. Next, they carry out their own "due diligence" to find out if the company seeking funds is viable. Actually, they are trying to validate all the various claims of the founders or management team. There are many exaggerations, tall tales and visions of grandeur that must be checked out. This requires 1 to 3 months. Many of the claims turn out to be false and the company is not funded. Exaggerations do not increase valuation or the likelihood of being funded; they just shorten the time to rejection.

Get Properly Funded 161

If they cannot find any red flags, they begin negotiations to determine if they can come to some agreement about valuation, ownership and funding level. A term sheet is a non-binding offer of interest that starts the negotiation process, which takes approximately a month. The total time can run anywhere from 3 to 6 months. Many VC deals have been known to occur in a much shorter time frame but it is better to allocate more time to the process. In fact, if you are going to run out of money, you should start several months ahead of that time. Otherwise, you will not be able to make your payroll. An example of a 6-month timeline and set of milestones is shown below.

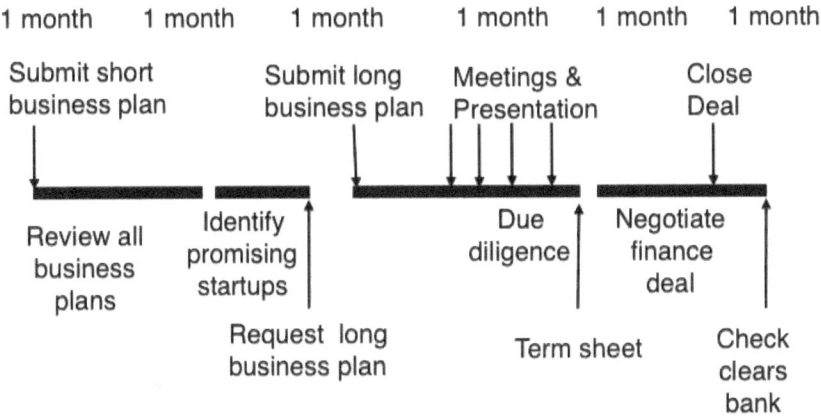

The top half of the schedule shows the founder milestones and the rest of the diagram shows the investor milestones. The tasks carried out by the investors are shown along the timeline. As mentioned before, each VC and angel investor group may vary both in timeline and milestones. It is best to check with the investors and work out the schedule accordingly.

Picking the right angel group or VC is very important and should be done through contacts. This is the only way to get in the back door or side door of an investment firm. You need to have these contacts as part of your network. Fundamentally, the relationship with the investment group matters. If you have connections that can make introductions for you, this already establishes a positive relationship. However, if you must go through the front door, you need to make a list of angel groups and VC firms in order of their prominence in the industry. Send your business plans to all the firms on the list. If you receive many responses, start pitching to smaller firms first and work up to the large firms. You need to play in Peoria before you go to Broadway.

Pitch your ideas and get feedback several times until your pitch and ability to handle Q&A has reached a professional level. **Ask them for feedback on what is missing and how to improve your plans at every meeting.** Then, pursue the high-end firms. At the end of the process, decide which of the firms, small or large, is the best match for your company. If you have only one option, then you will have to decide if it makes sense to work with them or pursue other options.

If you have more than one option, there are ways to find a good match. This is where some serious due diligence comes into play. It is important to get references, talk to portfolio companies of the firm "off the record" and find out how they are viewed by others. You should investigate their track record. Once you identify a short list, you need to pick the best match for your startup. Work with firms that know your industry, have access to large networks of people and understand the sales and marketing process. Within each firm, identify people who are compatible with your team. You must find someone you can work with for 5 years or more. They must be interested in helping your team to build a company. They must be easy to work with and accessible. You should try to develop a relationship with them outside of Board meetings. Building a strong relationship with the investors is one of the key foundations of building a great company.

Advanced notes:
1. The investor community is almost exclusively driven by relationships to reduce risk. One of the best ways to get a meeting with investors is to get an introduction from someone they already know well and trust.
2. Become familiar with the common terms used in a term sheet before you begin discussions with an investor. If you are well informed as to why the terms exist and can speak to what is appropriate to your situation, you have a better chance to receive more favorable terms.
3. Be sure there are no conflicts of interest. Do not approach an investor having investments in your competitor. Investors do not sign NDAs. Be sure your lawyer has no conflict with the investor. Your lawyer can become conflicted if you let them invest in the round.
4. VCs have deeper pockets than angels. So if you will need more funds, they will be more readily available from a VC. The amount of extra funds available will depend on the firm but, in general, VC firms are able to fund multiple rounds.
5. Many investors are either team-centric or market-centric. Team-centric investors believe that a strong team will be able to solve problems and pivot as necessary due to shifting market conditions. A market-centric investor believes that if the market opportunity shifts from good to poor, the needed ROI cannot be delivered regardless of the team. Therefore, a large market opportunity must exist to make the investment. It is important to understand what type of investors you are dealing with when preparing your pitch.
6. There are many "pitch deck" templates available on the Internet. They should be consulted when putting together your pitch. The number of slides and the ordering should be based on the priorities of the investor. The market (TAM/SAM/SOM), team, ROI and exit strategy are always important first slides. Unit economics and scalability proven with traction metrics are critical in making the SOM/ROI case believable. It is best to have an advisor review the slides prior to each presentation.

7. Customer traction metrics depend on the type of company being built. Typically, information is gathered regarding the number of users or customers, traffic to the website, units sold, sales margins, revenue, profits, etc. Growth in these numbers over several quarters is an indication that the product is "gaining traction". It is important to identify the proper metrics for your product to demonstrate customer adoption and momentum in the marketplace.

Tip 5.5

Understand the VC Landscape and Timing

Tutorial: Venture capital is the classic model for funding a startup. For more than half a century, startups have been launched using venture-backed financing. However, the landscape of venture financing has changed considerably over the past 20 years. This impacts the timing of when funds are available for startups so it is important to follow the trends in the VC world. In the mid-90's, money was free-flowing and you could still get funded with a business plan and a good pitch. There were approximately 5000 venture capitalists in 400 VC firms at the time. The Internet was in its infancy and VC funds were loaded up with cash so companies like Netscape, Amazon, Yahoo and many others were funded, alongside those who wanted to sell lipstick over the Internet. Good money quickly found bad companies in a landscape that resembled the Wild West.

Unfortunately, the hey-day of funding everything in sight, and money chasing anything that moved without proper due diligence, came to a crashing end when the Internet bubble burst in 2000. It was only a matter of time before everyone realized that having "dot com" in your name with 200 people hacking code in a building produced mostly vaporware and broken promises. Of course, the names that we recognize today survived that period and have become giants of the industry.

The VCs were not badly burned at first since many of their portfolio companies went public with over-inflated valuations prior to the crash even though they had no product, no sales and no future plans. The liquidity of the initial IPOs allowed them to sidestep the consequences of these questionable investments. The number of VC firms grew to about 1,000 in this period, with approximately 15,000 venture capitalists. However, the VCs did take on significant losses with their remaining portfolio companies that had no path to liquidity. A hard lesson learned! By 2001 the market for IPOs completely dried up. Their portfolio startups became shutdowns and, as they were moved out of the system, the VCs began to take a long hard look at the criteria used in all future investments. The ROI's had dwindled to single digits and in some cases to negative values. This was a very bad time to start a company in high-tech.

After the tech bubble burst, a higher bar was set for funding new startups. The startup required a product, revenue and a business plan to get to the next level. A thorough due diligence process (which resembles an annual physical examination, including a colonoscopy) was necessary before any funding could be finalized. The funding levels for startups also increased significantly as the VC funds themselves were larger and the investments were being made at a later stage of the company. Slowly but surely over time, the solid returns on investment were restored.

Then the housing bubble burst unexpectedly in 2008 and that would shake things up again in the venture capital world. This was another bad time to start a company. Funds were closed to new startups in order to continue to support additional rounds of funding for existing startups in their portfolio. Some startups encountering problems were liquidated through acquisition and some were wound down, depending on the return stated in the liquidation preference clause of the financing agreement. New funds were not initiated until the market began to recover, and some VC firms contemplated closing down business or at least scaling back. While the number of VC firms remained about the same, at around 900, the number of venture capitalists reduced to 6000 by 2014.

Another boom cycle began in 2014 with investment levels that have never been seen in the past. Hundreds of millions of dollars have been poured into a handful of companies by pooling the funds of multiple VC firms. These VC deals are extremely high risk with equally high rewards, and there will likely be big winners and big losers in 5-8 years. These over-hyped investments tend to skew the data greatly and imply the VCs are only interested in companies ready to go public. In fact, the enormous sizes of the VC funds have shifted the focus of some VC firms to expansion-stage companies with working business models. Angel groups have backfilled to fund early stage companies, and other options such as "crowd sourcing" sites are increasingly used. However, most VC firms will continue to fund promising startups of any size with products, customers and a path to profitability, as they have always done.

Another more subtle timing issue exists within a VC firm depending on when they are raising their own funds. Basically, the general partners (GPs) of the firm build a VC fund from a set of investors, collectively called limited partners (LPs), who manage endowments, retirement systems, trust funds and large financial funds and includes some individuals with high net worth. Typical VC funds are in the range of $100M-$400M, with an average capital under management at one time of about $200M.

The target level of a large VC fund today may be as high as $1B and it may last for up to 10 years before the funds are exhausted. When a target level is reached, it simply means that the LPs have committed to delivering the funds at a later date. The actual funds are drawn down over time upon request of the VCs and are used for startup seed rounds, first rounds and other subsequent rounds of financing. In parallel, the VCs close down a previous fund, while chasing the dollars for their next fund. As a result, it is useful to know which fund you may be drawing from and how many rounds can be sustained for your startup.

Three concurrent VC funds are shown below. The goal should be to get into the New Fund as early as possible so there is enough time in a 5-8 year window to raise a number of rounds of financing with the same VC.

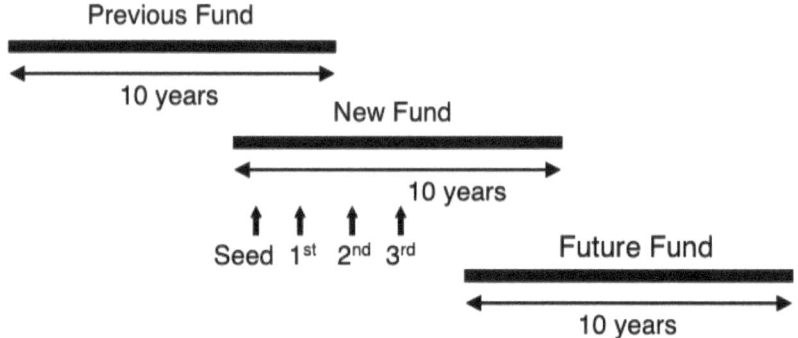

If you end up drawing funds from the Previous Fund, you would likely not have a 2ⁿᵈ or 3ʳᵈ round out of that same fund, and the VC may push to get the cash out at the end of the fund for their LPs - potentially before your company has reached its maximum exit value. However, the New Fund accommodates all the subsequent rounds and therefore provides a longer runway. Meanwhile, a Future Fund is still being constructed and is likely unavailable.

Clearly, it is important to understand the landscape of VC financing and the timing of the internal VC funds themselves. You need to know what part of the boom-and-bust cycle they happen to be in. To pursue funding, you must be a high-growth company ready to scale to the next level. **The key point is to try to seek funding in boom times from a VC firm that understands your industry.** Find out how many rounds they can support in the future. This will inform you that they do indeed have deep pockets and can participate in multiple subsequent rounds.

Advanced notes:
1. VCs have good reason to be selective on the size of deals they fund. They have limited bandwidth to help companies and expect large returns for their funds. If you need only a small amount of funding, your company is not worth their bandwidth as the final payout will be too small to be interesting, even if you succeed.
2. VCs do not like to lead subsequent rounds. They prefer a new VC to enter and negotiate terms of the new round. This acts as confirmation of their bet as well as distancing themselves from the negotiation of new terms. If they have to lead the round, it will likely be a flat or down round.
3. Beware of taking funds near the end of a fund. When the fund ends, the VCs like to close it out by delivering cash and shares to the LPs. You do not want to get caught by a VC needing to cash out your company in order to close their fund. This is another reason why it is important to know exactly which fund is being used to fund your startup.
4. As VCs need to deliver returns to investors, they do not like to spend time on companies that are not growing fast enough once they are funded. If your company is profitable, but not growing fast, they may push for an additional round of funding to resolve the company in one direction or the other: either shoot for the moon or crash to the ground. Either way the company will get off their books. These types of actions lead to the negative reputation that many VCs have gained over the years.
5. The CEO's job always includes fundraising, even if there is no current need for cash. The milestones and schedule for the next round must always be kept in mind. Given it may take up to 6 months to close a round, cash must last at least 6 months beyond the completion of the next round's milestones.

Tip 5.6

VCs Expect a 20X ROI

Tutorial: VC funding is not suitable for all startups and more difficult to obtain today. They expect a 10-30X return on investment (ROI) in 5-8 years. This is based on the typical proceeds of an IPO or an acquisition, where the valuation of the company is $100M or higher at the point of liquidity. Otherwise, it is not a viable enterprise for VC funding and you should pursue other sources of funds.

Some have found this level of expected return quite objectionable and the whole VC financing process unreasonable. The reason for these high multiples is that venture capitalists are expected to provide a healthy return to their investors by picking startups that have a high probability of success. Since only 1 in 10 funded startups actually succeeds, the one winner must return 10X just to break even across 10 companies. With a 20X return from the winner, the initial investment in 10 companies is doubled over 5-8 years, which is about 10% per year. But not all the other companies fail completely. Some are liquidated and part or all of the initial investment is returned. Others are acquired by larger companies and produce positive returns on the initial investment. The expected internal rate of return (IIR) is closer to 25% per year. This is why they target a high return rate in Series A financing when investing in a startup – most of them fail.

Venture capital firms raise funds from a variety of sources such as university retirement funds, endowments, private investors and other financial institutions. These entities expect very high returns that exceed stock market performance on these very risky investments. So the VCs must be able to select and fund startups that are likely to succeed, or their returns will be unacceptable to the investors. This will, in turn, jeopardize their ability to secure capital for their next fund.

Unfortunately, something inevitably goes wrong for most startups. No matter how much due diligence is carried out, an unexpected show-stopper manifests itself and forces an untimely end to the startup. Either the product has no market, or the product does not work, or the management team does not execute the strategy or pivot in time in the face of competition. A host of other reasons may cause failure. To mitigate risk, they require a business plan that offers a 10-30X return from each company. Essentially they are pooling the risk of all the startups. The one or two that succeed, in effect, pay for the other failures, but the resulting ROI is still acceptable, especially if the one winner is a "grand-slam", and another one is a "home run", to use baseball jargon that is commonly used in this field. Clearly, if more companies assembled strong teams and then built "must-have" products for large markets, the success rate would increase. However, since many first-time entrepreneurs do not figure this out until it is too late, the low success rate has remained the same for decades.

Angel investors are private investors or collections of private investors who put their own money into startups. Angel investors require anywhere from 3-5X to 10-20X ROI, depending on funding levels and their own internal statistics on funding successful startups. Their funding levels are lower but they are willing to provide seed funding if the startup is considered to be viable after due diligence. They can also provide more attractive terms, or invest in deals that VCs have declined for various reasons that may not have to do with the viability of the business. This is still a reasonable alternative for many startups, but does not always come with the credibility or the deep pockets of VC firms. However, angels may also be open to alternate return mechanisms, such as annual dividends. If you create a unique business and return model that makes sense, you may be able to structure an unconventional financing for your company.

To pursue VC funding, your business plan should reflect the fact that you can build a company that will deliver a 10-30X return within 5-8 years based on the revenue projections for the product being developed. Your business model drives the revenue projections, so that must be carefully thought out. In the 5th year of the sales projections, your revenue must be around 20X the initial investment that you are seeking in Series A financing. Let us assume you are able to raise $2M for a 40% stake in your company from a VC firm. This means your post-money valuation is $5M. Your business plan must show revenue in the range of $20M-$50M in Year 5. Using this information, the VCs will project your company to be valued at $100M. Their stake will be worth $40M at that point and they will have the 20X return on investment they seek. Note that these calculations will have to incorporate the dilutive effects of later rounds in order to realize the full 20X ROI.

It is the first VC round is where the 20X return is expected. In later rounds, Series B or C, the ROI expectations are lower so the returns can be in the range of 3-5X, especially if the company is selling product, building out a sales channel and planning a follow-on product. The risks have been greatly reduced by this time so the returns are necessarily lower. On the other hand, if the company is struggling and running out of money, you may end up with a down round, and be forced to give away more of the company at a lower price than in the previous round due to the inherent risks in the new investment. For this reason, it is important not to be too aggressive on the valuation of the company in each round because you may face the scourge of a down round at a later date.

Tip 5.7

Revenue Projections Determine Your Valuation

Summary: From a business perspective, revenue and a clear path to profitability are perhaps the two most important criteria to evaluate a company. However, when you start a company and begin to develop a product, there is no revenue to speak of. Therefore, the company is valued primarily on its revenue projections rather than actual revenue. These projections must be calculated using detailed top-down and bottom-up analyses. The results of such projections are used by investors to determine the valuation of the startup.

The top-down analysis should take into account the market size, share of the market expected and year-by-year growth. The bottom-up approach must consider the status of the product, length of the sales cycle, the number of customers that can be obtained in each year, price of the product, cost of goods sold and the bandwidth of the sales force. First-order bottom-up and top-down analyses in combination will give you a bound on the potential sales. Then you should use feedback from advisors to build a more credible revenue model. Ultimately, this tells you what type of company you can build and its projected valuation.

Key point: Companies with projected revenues of $20M-$100M in 5-8 years of operation are suitable for angel and VC financing. Revenues far less than $20M are not expected to deliver enough of a return for sophisticated investors, so they are more suited to friends and family (F&F) investments, government funding if available, or other instruments to bootstrap the company. Companies with projected revenues above $100M in 5-8 years are too big for angel groups because the investment level required is far above what they would typically be willing to risk. Such deals would likely require the involvement of multiple VC firms, both for funding and due diligence.

Tutorial: Even in the early stages of discussing your plans to start a company, it is important to think about revenue. This is the eventual funding source for the company. You sell product, you get revenue, you subtract off expenses and you have your profit before taxes (PBT). Initially you may have no idea of how much product you will sell, but you should still sit down at several different times and try to figure it out with a spreadsheet over a 5-year period. It may be especially difficult for startups in the B2C space that require customer traction metrics to project potential revenue, but many startups in the B2B space are more able to carry out such an analysis. Included in the analysis should be the point where the company becomes profitable, and there must be year-over-year growth in profits. In fact, the amount and type of funding will be largely determined by what comes out of the spreadsheet.

The revenue prediction model used by first-time founders is the classic "hockey stick" curve. This plot starts with no revenue in the first couple of years and then quickly rises to $20M or more in the next 3 years. It is fun to dream about this type of outcome but it will not impress the VCs. They receive over 1000 business plans each year, most of which feature the hockey stick curve. Unless there is an underlying credible basis for the projections, it presents an easy way to separate business plans that are real from ones that appear to be no more than pipe dreams. Avoid this spreadsheet game with fictitious revenues and ridiculous valuations. This is the serious part of building a startup, so get serious.

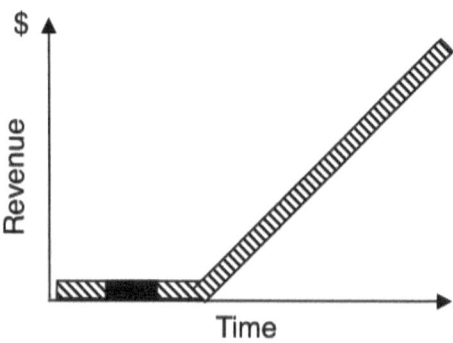

A better first-order revenue model can be devised by carrying out a top-down analysis. The top-down approach involves studying the market you are targeting for your product. You determine the total available market (TAM) and the portion of that market that you can realistically cover within 5 years, called the serviceable available market (SAM). Finally, the serviceable obtainable market (SOM) is the portion of the SAM that you can capture.

At first, the revenue projection is performed assuming no competition and no limitation on the bandwidth of the sales force. Consider a simple example of such a projection for a traditional software startup using a cost-based revenue model. If the TAM is $300M and your product has a SAM of $120M, then it would be reasonable to expect that you could gain 30% market share, or SOM, by Year 5 ($36M), 20% in Year 4 ($24M), 10% in Year 3 ($12M), 2% in Year 2 ($2.4M) and finally no revenue in Year 1 ($0M). This implies that you will need angel or VC financing to ramp up the company very quickly to take advantage of the market opportunity before other companies get the same idea. The VCs are interested in this type of high-growth opportunity. However, this top-down analysis is too simple minded to attract the VCs.

The purpose of the first-order approach is to get a feel for what type of company you are trying to build. If you fit the VC profile, a more detailed revenue projection must be carried out using a bottom-up analysis. To begin the analysis, you start with the price of the product, which could be based on other products in the same space, or the overall value provided by the product, or perhaps an amount based on the cost of production. Typically, the average selling price (ASP) is used in the bottom-up calculations. The ASP takes into account that the unit price of the product may vary due to volume discounts, product specification differences on orders, regional differences or other contributing factors. Since it is too early to determine revenue based on actual customer data, a suitable ASP is used in the analysis.

Assume you start a software company where the ASP is $300K per software license sold. Next, the schedule of product development is considered. The first year would essentially be used to develop the alpha product to begin in-house testing. Assuming the beta version of the product is available in the middle of the second year, it implies that there will be no revenue in the first year. In the second year, you plan to hire 2 sales people who will each close 4 accounts. The sales cycle in that second year would require 6 months: 1 month of pre-sales effort to contact many potential customers, 4 months for product evaluations, and 1 month to close 4 accounts each with completed purchase orders. The 8 accounts would produce revenues of $2.4M in the second year. This is shown in the chart below. Each fiscal year (FY) is labeled from FY1 to FY5. The initial revenue of $2.4M is obtained in FY2 from a target market segment called 'segment 1' in the chart.

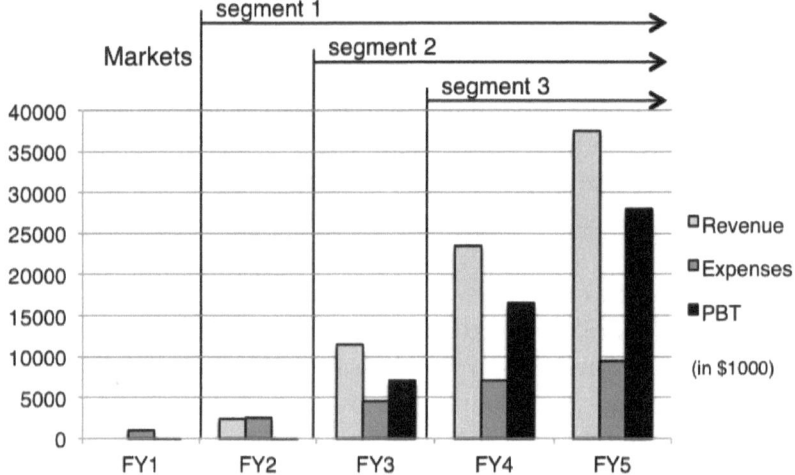

In FY3, the sales cycle is shorter since production software is released. With the addition of 2 sales people to obtain new customers from markets 'segment 1' and 'segment 2', a total of 30 new accounts can be closed, while post-sales support and maintenance charges are obtained from prior accounts. The revenue projected in FY3 is $11.5M. In FY4, $23.5M is projected due to the penetration into a very large market 'segment 3', which represents the mass market. Finally, revenues of $37.5M are projected in FY5.

Next, a first-order expense and profit calculation is carried out. Most of the annual expense of a startup is driven by headcount, especially in a software startup. The chart above assumes a fully loaded cost of $150K/year for each person hired and yields a first year expense of $1M (6-7 people) and a second year expense of $2.5M (15-16 people). Therefore, the funding level sought from VCs would be $3M-$4M to get through the first 2 years. The analysis would continue for FY3, FY4 and FY5 based on the headcount targets for each year. Using these numbers, the profit before tax (PBT) is computed. These values are also provided in the chart. Note that the company becomes profitable in FY3, but probably requires another round of funding to complete the management team, grow the sales channel, support customers and increase marketing.

These numbers are not final. They are merely a starting point for the next pass of analysis and iterative refinement. This first pass of number crunching is not sufficient to convince any knowledgeable investor you have a business because the results are too optimistic and somewhat unrealistic, especially on the expense side. At this stage, you are confirming for yourself whether you potentially have a business. The first-order analysis indicates that you do. But a very detailed bottom-up approach including the sales cycle, product cycle, headcount, customer list, etc., is needed to yield more accurate information. This is where a consultant CFO or CEO would be extremely useful to validate the numbers and add credibility when meeting with investors. In fact, you should meet with the advisors after every major revision of the financial plan as you drill deeper into the analysis.

One factor that most founders overlook is time and additional expense it takes to get the team in place and productive. It could be 3-6 months for R&D add-ons or 6-9 months for sales teams before they are up and running. If the number of customers increases, as implied by the increasing revenue, then the accounting and administration teams need to expand accordingly. Additional headcount in other parts of the company will add to the overall expenses. In effect, there would be little if any profit in FY3, and may actually occur in FY4 or FY5. The expenses are likely to double or triple compared to the initial estimates as more detail is added.

This is reflected in the more realistic projections below. After several discussions with a CFO consultant, the numbers will eventually converge to a credible plan that investors will accept as feasible.

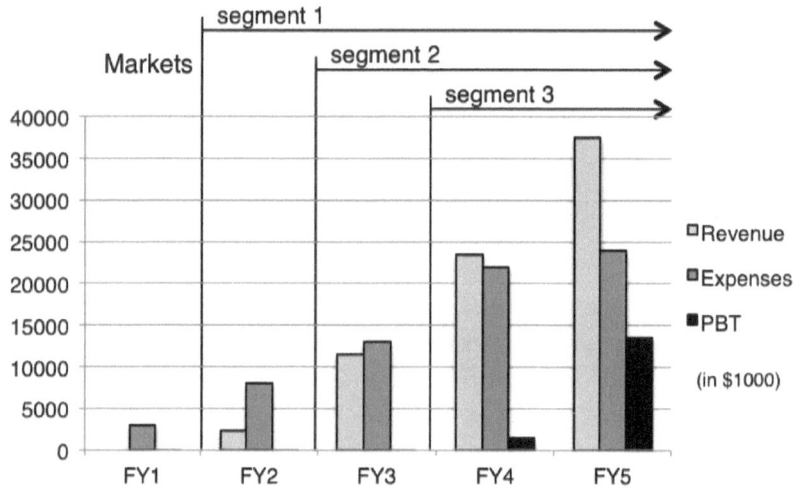

A key aspect to note in the chart is the timing of sales channel expansion to grow revenue. A sales channel is a combination of processes and people that allows the company to capture its target revenue. It involves direct methods to engage the customer using local sales people and international distributers, and indirect methods for lead generation. Sales force bandwidth is defined as the maximum rate at which customers can be acquired using the sales channel. The sales force must have the bandwidth and channels to access customers and obtain purchase orders within a time frame called the sales cycle. Increasing the channel bandwidth is expensive so the timing of the expansion must coincide with the timing of the expected rapid growth in revenue.

The tipping point for exponential revenue growth occurs somewhere in FY3 according to the chart. Clearly the FY4 and FY5 revenue numbers cannot be obtained unless the bandwidth of the sales channel is greatly increased. FY2 is the year that a CEO would make the decision to secure another round of financing to grow capacity in the sales channel. This is one of the critical timing decisions for the company. If the sales channel is increased too early, before the product is ready to go, the burn rate will be too high to be sustained and sales people will be laid off. If it is built too late, you will not be able to hit the target revenue numbers.

Advanced notes:
1. The financials will be heavily scrutinized. The investors want to know your expected "use of proceeds" of the funding and how you are going to make money. Their experience shows that most founders regularly underestimate the time and cost for product development. Founders also generally overestimate sales (both amount extracted from each account and speed to close deals). So do not be surprised if an investor derives a slower financial plan than your analysis would project on sales.
2. If customers prepay for a product or service, be sure to track the bookings, revenue and cash. You may be able to establish valuation based on bookings rather than revenue. Be sure to educate yourself on the basics of revenue recognition before you meet with an investor.
3. While detailed revenue projections are difficult to carry out at an early stage of a startup, the revenue model should be based on the type of business being built. Many options exist such as cost-based, value-based, subscription-based, advertising-based, etc. The selection of the proper revenue model is important for the viability of the company and capital requirements from investors.

Take Away: **VCs and angels establish a company valuation and their expected ROI on credible 5-year revenue projections.** They use a multiple of the revenue to determine funding levels and ownership requirements. This is where some level of rigor is expected. That is why it is important to spend enough time on the financials. Today, VCs and angels expect actual revenues or at least beta testing with actual customers and a high-growth path going forward. **Actual revenue is your biggest shield against having to raise another round of financing and your biggest weapon when you do go to raise the next round.**

Tip 5.8

Liquidation Preference is about Who Gets Paid First

Summary: One of the more important but subtle terms in a VC agreement is referred to as the liquidation preference. Here, liquidation refers to an event whereby the company is sold through acquisition (in the best case) or declares bankruptcy (in the worst case). Liquidation preference is a way to give downside protection to investors in case the company is sold before an IPO. It guarantees that any investors with preferred stock will be paid back first, often with a multiple on their investment. The founders and other common stock holders receive payment based on their pro rata common stock portions with what is left of the proceeds of the sale after investors are paid off. The liquidation preference clause does not apply if the company goes public - only if it is sold. But most companies are acquired which makes liquidation preference a very important clause in the agreement.

Key point: In the VC negotiations, the goal of the founders is to push the multiplier on liquidation preference as close to 1X as possible. A more typical value is 2X or 3X. A 3X multiple means that investors receive three times their investment if there is a liquidation event. If there are many VCs chasing your deal, it is possible to push the multiplier close to 1X because you have leverage. Otherwise, you will have to accept the standard terms as part of the price of doing business.

Tutorial: Imagine for a moment you are an investor in a startup. You use your own money to provide a seed or first round. Later on, if the company makes money and goes public, you expect a handsome return on the investment. But what happens if the company fails completely? Then, you lose your money. If it is acquired by another company or otherwise liquidated in some form, there will be proceeds of the liquidation. As an investor, you expect to at least get your money back, which is a 1X return. If the selling price is high enough, you expect to get a higher return before any non-investors get their portion of the proceeds because startups are very high-risk investments. These expectations are the basis for preferred shares and multiple liquidation preferences.

The same is true for VCs. But they do not invest their own money. They invest other people's money. So they require downside protection on the return in the form of a liquidation preference in case things go south. Otherwise, their investors are not going to like the returns and will be reluctant to participate in the next fund. The liquidation preference specifies the minimum return for investors upon any liquidation event. Typically, the multiple on the initial investment is 1X, 2X or 3X, depending on circumstances.

There are two forms of a 1X liquidation preference: non-participating and participating. In the non-participating 1X case, the investors are paid back with interest or can choose to be paid on a pro rata basis. In the participating 1X case, the investors can double dip by being paid back and then participate on a pro-rata basis on the rest of the proceeds with common shareholders. A cap is usually imposed on the maximum return on investment in this case. Of course, none of this applies if there is a very high value exit.

It is important to construct a graph of the liquidation preference payouts vs. liquidation amount to fully understand what the critical values are, and when common stock holders get some value above $0. This tells you the minimum selling price that would be acceptable to the VCs and the minimum that would be acceptable to the founders and management. The two will not be aligned, as the graph will tell you in no uncertain terms. However, you may be pressured into selling the company if you miss major milestones, or the market is weak, or the competition is winning in the marketplace. Investors may also lose patience or seize any opportunity to quickly obtain a return on their investment by finding a willing buyer. Whatever be the reason, if things are not going well, the investors may want out with whatever they can claw back of their investment - including the multiple that you agreed to give them.

Consider the following example for illustrative purposes. Let us assume that a 2X multiple is part of the liquidation preference clause in the financing contract. If you raise $2M with a $6M post-money valuation, then the VCs own 33% of the company. The 2X multiple means that the investors will receive a minimum of $4M upon liquidation. As a founder or CEO, you have to ensure the company sells for more than $4M or you will not see one penny. The VCs will take the first $4M of the sale price so they will be quite happy with the outcome, but founders and employees will be left with nothing. This is shown in the figure below:

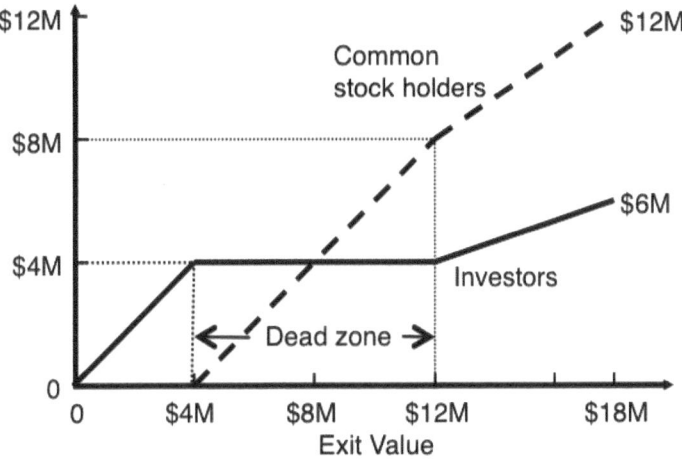

On the other hand, if the company sells for $12M, then the VCs still get paid $4M since they own 33% of the company. Anything above $12M and the VCs will not exercise their liquidation preference clause as they stand to make more by converting to common stock and taking 33% of the proceeds. At $18M, the investors are paid $6M, and the rest goes to common shareholders. Between $4M and $12M is a dead zone where the VCs are guaranteed $4M so they are somewhat indifferent to the value at liquidation. It is considered a danger zone for the founders and CEO if the VCs get impatient with the progress being made by the company and are able to find a willing buyer for an acquisition at any price above $4M.

When there are multiple rounds with different investors, the implications of a liquidation preference can be worked out but it will have many breakpoints and the minimum value for an employee-friendly sale price may go up significantly. The obvious implication is that no one holding common stock gets paid until all the investors holding preferred shares are paid their multiple in priority order. Once they are fully paid, the remainder is divided among common stock holders based on their pro rata share. If the sale price is low, some of the investors may not be paid back in full, but the common stock holders will not be paid at all.

Advanced note:
1. In unfortunate situations where liquidation preference applies, seniority becomes a critical issue. Seniority refers to who gets paid first. Later rounds of financing tend to be senior to earlier rounds. Bank loans are generally senior to preferred stock. Employee back wages are generally senior to loans, but this could vary from state to state.

Take Away: Liquidation preferences with differing priorities, convertible notes and multiple rounds should be carefully considered before closing each financing round. There may be too many hogs at the trough before you get to it if the total amount set by the liquidation preferences is at or near the sale price. Make sure you draw the graph and work out the minimum acceptable sale price and negotiate the multiplier to be an acceptable value to the founding team. Know this in advance of signing any agreements.

Tip 5.9

Convertible Notes Must Be Handled with Extra Care

Summary: Recently, there has been a trend of entrepreneurs entering into early financing deals using convertible notes because of their seemingly attractive terms. These are essentially pre-seed or bridge funds in the form of debt that can be converted into preferred shares at the next round of VC or angel financing. Convertible notes have a few advantages. The funds are often made available with no lead investor and the share price is set at the next round of financing so it avoids the issues of valuation, ownership and price per share. But there are inherent risks in these funding instruments because it complicates the negotiations with the VCs and may lead to unsatisfactory results for founders, note holders and VCs. Min/Max pricing, percentage discounts, multiple liquidation preferences and other terms may create downstream problems for a VC deal. Therefore, the actual terms of a convertible note should be considered carefully before entering into such agreements.

Key point: Do your homework on convertible notes before jumping at the chance to sign a term sheet. They are useful as pre-seed funds, a short-term bridge to the next round of financing, or leverage with the VCs. But they can also create downstream problems when negotiating with VCs and satisfying note holders, and may end in no deal. Typically uncapped notes (i.e., no max on valuation) and no accrued interest are good options to pursue for the company and VCs, but potentially bad options for note holders. Find out more about these instruments from your business advisors. You will be doing yourself a big favor later on when you sit down with the VCs.

Tutorial: When you start a company, you will need to get some short-term funding to get you to the point when you can go after VC funding. This is essentially pre-seed funding beyond bootstrapping. You may need substantial funding to reach a point where you are of interest to the VCs, such as having a more complete product and a few customers who would serve as references. However it is difficult, if not impossible, to put a proper valuation on a company prior to reaching this point. But cash is needed to get there so it becomes a chicken-and-egg problem.

Convertible notes, a funding vehicle in the form of debt from very early sophisticated or unsophisticated investors, have been used to resolve this problem. These instruments seem attractive because a valuation is not set until angels or VCs get together and decide what makes sense. Even in that case, valuation is subjective but can be based on various methods, metrics, rules-of-thumb and experience according to the contents of the business plan and extensive due diligence. Once the negotiations are completed, the valuation sets the preferred share price for the round, at which time all the outstanding convertible notes are folded in as preferred shares.

Another situation where a convertible note proves useful is when you are close to a set of milestones that, if achieved, will trigger another round of financing. Instead of running out of cash, a convertible note can be used to bridge the gap. This is perhaps the most common scenario for the convertible note, which is referred to as a bridge note if used in this context. If private investors, who believe in the company, can raise the needed funds, they can be part of the next round of financing. In addition, the funds associated with the note can be used as leverage to obtain a higher valuation at the next round. Keep in mind that this may be at odds with the note holders because a lower valuation produces a higher percentage ownership for them. Often, min/max valuations, called caps, are specified in the note to accommodate these conflicting interests.

When the note is converted to preferred shares, there may be a discount applied to the preferred share price depending on the terms of the convertible note agreement. A discount is used to recognize that the investment was made earlier at a higher risk. For example, if the price is set to $0.50/share at the next round and a 10% discount is part of the note agreement, the note holder would pay $0.45/share. Discounts can be offered on an elapsed time basis. For example, if the note is converted after 4 months, the discount may be in the range of 10-20%. Common share warrants (without liquidation preference) have been used in some cases to implement the discount portion of the transaction and to resolve conflicts, but this must be negotiated with the note holder.

The discounts, caps and elapsed time to the next round have all led to conflicts that could be difficult to resolve at the closing of the VC round. Consider an example where you are between two rounds of financing and need to raise a bridge amount of $150K to reach a set of milestones for an upcoming VC round. You approach a knowledgeable investor about a bridge note for that amount. You explain that your previous valuation was $3M and you are hoping to have a valuation of $6M at the next round in 4 months. The investor agrees to sign the note if there is a 20% discount and a $6M cap on valuation. If you take the deal, then you have unknowingly placed yourself into a rather difficult situation. If the VCs offer a $12M valuation, then the note holder will get a 50% discount due to the $6M cap. However, only 4 months have elapsed so the VCs will not accept this level of discount, although 20% may be more acceptable to them. But the note holder demands that the terms of the contract be honored since their $150K enabled the company reach to the $12M valuation. The VCs do not move from their position and the note holder digs in. Lowering the valuation to satisfy the investors will result in a significant loss in equity. Now you are trapped in a situation with no way to resolve the problem except to find new VCs who will accept the terms of the bridge note, which is not likely.

When setting up a convertible note, you have to make sure the terms are negotiated with the intent of simplifying future negotiations. VC do not like high discounts which often arise when the note has a cap on valuation or there is a short elapsed time from the signing of the note to the next VC round. However, knowledgeable investors will not agree to small discounts if their investment is the main reason for a large increase in valuation for the startup. They want a discount that reflects the impact of their investment. You will have to learn how to negotiate terms that are favorable to future rounds and set the proper expectations with any investor who agrees to sign a convertible note. You should seek investors who are flexible and have the big picture in mind. Otherwise, you will find yourself in a situation where funds are available but not accessible due to the convertible note terms.

If there are multiple convertible note holders who fund the company at different times, you could end up with several multiple liquidation preferences. This may mean that the company must sell at a very high exit value before you see any payoff for your efforts. If there is a variable discount based on the VC valuation at the next round, it complicates the negotiations since everyone wants the highest possible discount. Be aware that these are all realistic scenarios played out regularly between startups and investors. **VCs negotiate in their own best interest. They have no obligation to be kind to prior investors**. If you are desperate for money, they may ask you to agree to terms that are unfavorable to existing investors. Angels may also request specific terms to protect their investment from future VC terms. The best way to keep all investors happy is to meet milestones and create multiple funding options for your company.

Take Away: Clearly, the best advice is to avoid convertible notes if at all possible. But it is not always possible. It may be your only option for funding. In that case, the best approach is to have convertible notes with specific time frames for the conversion, specific discount rates at different time points prior to the next round, and specific mechanisms to implement the conversion and discount. Perhaps discussing these issues with your advisors, VCs and other investors in advance would be prudent. This avoids the prospects of a long, protracted, complex, multi-way negotiation at a future date that may be the proximate cause of the failure of the company or a significant loss of equity.

CHAPTER 6
Operate a Successful Startup

6.1. Start with a Solid Board of Directors

6.2. Startups Be Nimble, Startups Be Quick

6.3. Bad Hires Cost Time and Money

6.4. Get the Right CEO

6.5. Cooperate Internally, Compete Externally

6.6. Systems and Processes Save Time and Money

6.7. Always Negotiate Win-Win Outcomes

6.8. Exude Confidence, Not Arrogance

6.9. Leave Marketing Strategy to the CEO

Tip 6.1

Start with a Solid Board of Directors

Tutorial: When professional investors fund your startup, a formal Board of Directors is required. At incorporation, usually the founders are the Board members, but now the Board is reconstituted. Typically one of the founders will remain on the Board to represent the founding team. And while all founders may believe they have a right to remain on the Board, they should rethink their proper roles and responsibilities in terms of making the company successful in ways that do not include serving on the Board. Even the goal of learning how a Board works and the curiosity factor of what happens in Board meetings do not justify being a Board member or observer. It is a very important responsibility that should be given to outside members who add tangible value to the company by bringing business experience and good judgment in difficult situations the company will likely face.

The Board of Directors is a group of company advisors having a fiduciary responsibility to deliver value to shareholders. Their main power is to hire and fire the CEO. As such, they must ensure the CEO is working diligently to make the company successful. They also approve major events of the company such as the IPO, M&A, pursuing financing and adding or removing Board members.

Their main value is their experience, the network of people they access, and their ability to give guidance on business issues as they arise. At all times, they are assessing the progress of the company against stated goals, and the abilities of the CEO and management team to execute the strategy. If they observe the company beginning to falter, or they lose confidence in the CEO or strategy, they will step in and try to make changes in order to set the company on a better path. That is their primary responsibility, and they take that role seriously.

Operate a Successful Startup 191

When negotiating your first financing agreement, it is prudent to consider issues related to ownership percentages, board seats and voting classes. They all impact who gets the final say on any decisions for the company. Founders should not get caught up on valuation but instead should shift their attention to control of the enterprise, especially in the early stages. Being master of your own destiny may not be all that important when everything is going well, but can be very important if you want to lead your company all the way to an exit. There will be many rough patches along the way so giving up control at Series A to the Board and the investors is not wise. Over time, this will change as more investment is made and more equity is distributed out. But at the outset, you should ensure that control is maintained in terms of ownership, voting classes and the Board level.

With this backdrop in mind, it is very important that a high-quality Board be constructed at the outset. One Board member will be a founder. Another Board member (or two) will represent the investors. At this point, discussions begin with the investors regarding other potential candidates for a Board seat. For example, an additional outside member should be a CEO-level person who understands the industry and business models. Another outside member could be a technical person with a strong background in startups. Once suitable members are identified, they are contacted regarding their level of interest and recruited to join the Board as soon as possible. One thing to keep in mind is to ensure they intend to have an active role on the Board and can be present at meetings.

When constructing the Board, investors want to ensure it is comprised of members who can make difficult decisions such as firing the CEO. Therefore, they will not accept a Board dominated by founders and their friends. On the contrary, investors will insist on a Board dominated by outside members. To show willingness to work with the founders, a typical proposal may be to have a balance of founders/management and VCs and a tie breaking member that will be jointly selected by both – a mutually acceptable outside member.

A group of three or five Board members is ideal to start. Each brings a different value to the table. They should be well known in industry or academia. Try to recruit the cream of the crop. They should all be the best people you can find. Ideally, you should select people who are 1 or 2 degrees of separation from you. Otherwise, you are working with strangers. In that case, get to know them very well. Remember that you will be living with them for five years or longer. **Select people you can work with who will provide high-quality feedback in all phases of a startup. This is a very important overall success factor.**

Next, a Chairman is selected. In the early days, it is usually one of the founders. Later on, it is likely to be the CEO. This role is filled based on agreement at the initial Board meeting. One role of the Chairman is to call a regular Board meeting to monitor the progress of the startup. **It is important to be well-prepared for such meetings.** They can be very intense at times because there are so many moving parts and things do not usually go according to plan.

Since you may be meeting monthly for 3-4 hours (often longer if discussions begin to unravel), it is important to be organized and have a strategy for Board meetings. Identify key issues of the company relative to the milestones that have been set. Provide information about the current situation, and discuss the decisions that your team has made to resolve the problems. Issues of importance in the early days will center on hiring/headcount, burn rate, product status, customer status, space requirements, stock grants and personnel issues.

As time evolves, discussions begin to shift to the business strategy, sales channel capacity, product issues in the marketplace, revenues, expenses, hiring management and plans to grow the business. It is important to be decisive on most matters. The Board is examining the leadership and management skills of the team. It is under constant scrutiny. The more decisions you make on your own, and the more progress you make, the less involved the Board will be on day-to-day operations. The Board will mainly assert its control when you seem uncertain in decision-making, or the company is beginning to flounder, or a series of bad decisions are made.

It is important for the CEO to meet with Board members separately and beforehand on issues that may be controversial or create major debates and conflict at an upcoming Board meeting. By gauging the members individually and getting their unfiltered opinions, it is possible to develop solutions that can be communicated back to the members in advance and then discussed further at the Board meeting itself. This avoids unnecessary Board conflicts or CEO decisions that are shot down in a manner akin to a firing squad. It is also useful to keep Board members updated in between meetings on any important developments. The key message is to manage the Board and have a rule of "No surprises at the Board meeting." Not even good news.

The face time with the Board at meetings is a valuable asset and not to be wasted, so the meetings should be organized in advance. Send out material before the meeting itself. In the early days of a startup, the Board packet is relatively small and can be sent 1-2 days in advance and serves as a reminder to very busy Board members. It should include an agenda, date/time, a list of participants, minutes of the previous meeting and information that needs to be read before the actual meeting. After a few years, there will be more material to send, so it may need to go out as much as a week in advance.

The Board meeting should not be used as a "kitchen-sink" discussion forum. It should be used to convey the current status of the company, the open issues, the decisions to address the issues, and some mention of what should happen by the next Board meeting. Team members can be asked to present as needed. Everyone should rehearse their short talk in advance. If you are running the company, make sure you have an answer to every possible question you can think of. Never walk in cold. You must be on your game at every Board meeting. That simply means that you have to prepare well in advance and put in long hours the day before to be on top of everything that is going on. It's a tall order, but that's why you get the big bucks. It will never be perfect, but it will never be a disaster either. Make notes afterwards about how to improve for the next time and take care of any action items that result from Board meetings.

There should be one or two agenda items each quarter to discuss either long-term strategic issues or short-term pressing tactical issues. But is it important to keep the meeting on point at all times. Avoid endless discussions that do not solve a real problem. As a general rule, anything you present to the Board may be questioned and may open up a can of worms. So use the Board's time wisely when you need feedback on decisions you and your team are making. They will likely grill the CEO in private sessions if the company is off course. And don't worry - they will let you know when you are off course. They are not usually shrinking violets when it comes to the business of the company. The Board meetings are often referred to as the monthly beatings but it does not have to be that way if you set expectations, control the agenda, anticipate likely questions and maximize the value of Board members at each meeting.

Tip 6.2

Startups Be Nimble, Startups Be Quick

Tutorial: Startups have one characteristic that makes them more creative and more productive than large companies - the ability to respond rapidly to external events. They are agile entities because the hierarchy is relatively flat. Decisions happen quickly and actions follow immediately. The characteristics of being nimble and quick depend solely on the nature of the people, both individually as employees and collectively as a team in the startup. This is one aspect of a startup environment that must be embraced by everyone because its survival depends on it.

The first step in building an environment promoting agility is to hire people in management who are team players. They must be very experienced and highly qualified, but they must also believe the strength of the startup is in the agility of the team. A bunch of outstanding individuals in the same room who are Prima Donnas will produce mostly arguments, not results. **In a startup, team chemistry is extremely important.** If the team works well together, they will be able to quickly figure out how to solve problems and there will be no challenge that is too great. If they are constantly at odds with each other, it erodes the ability to solve problems and take action. Every wasted minute is a delay element on the critical path to success.

Agility in a startup is about a team-oriented mindset. Team players are solution-centric, not problem-centric. They want to point the way forward, not engage in finger pointing. They prefer to solve a problem, not dwell on how they got into it. They trust each other to get the job done. They respect each other's talents. They love challenges. So when a market changes, or a business model does not work, or there is a problem with the product at a customer site, they are ready to meet and figure out a way to solve the problem. A cohesive team that truly believes in the mission of the company is critical to success because this is the only path to fast decision-making and quick actions. In addition to working with the team in the office, consider ways to socialize with the team outside the office to build stronger bridges between team members.

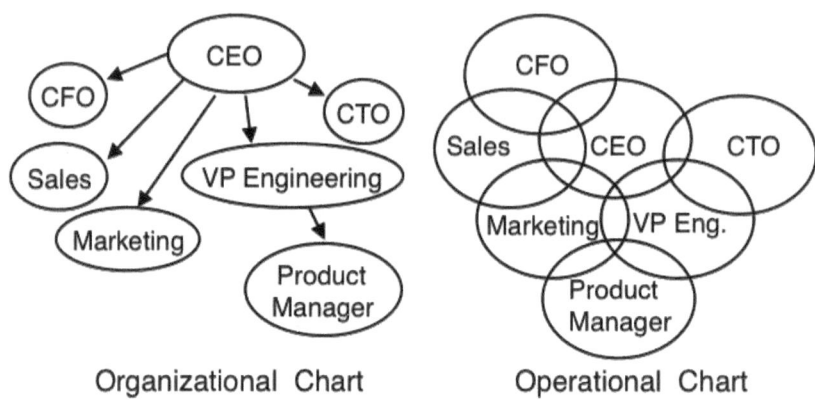

Organizational Chart   Operational Chart

One way to view the process of building team strength is to examine the organizational chart versus the operational chart. The classic organizational chart is a hierarchical reporting structure. It indicates who owns the decisions for each department and who can override those decisions. Those who own the decisions are called decision makers. Those who report to the decision makers are called decision influencers.

In a startup, the operational chart is more important. It illustrates the overlap in skill sets and decision-making between team members. It indicates how problems are solved. It emphasizes the fact that there is strength in numbers as compared to the isolated individuals in the organizational chart. The ultimate decision maker is the same but decisions are made through collaboration rather than by edict. This is the power of the startup and must be exploited to beat the slower processes within larger competitors that are often bureaucratic and political. Of course, the operational chart eventually settles into the organizational chart as the company grows. So take advantage of it while you can.

When hiring people in upper management, ensure they are team players with overlapping skill-sets. The CEO must be technically inclined so the details of the product can be understood. The VP of Engineering must understand business issues. The marketing person must understand business and technical issues. Everyone collectively must understand the customer and the competition. In management, team-oriented people with overlapping skills are two of the most important requirements.

The agile startup can rapidly respond to external and internal events. It begins with a strategy followed by a plan and then the execution of the plan. But as the plan is being executed, the team members must be ever vigilant about what the competition is doing, how the customers are responding to the product, what market forces are at play and how well the business model is working. Even though each of these tasks may belong to one particular person, it is the team responsibility to identify any problems on the horizon or any problems needing immediate attention. Anyone on the team must be able to recognize the problem and then everyone on the team must be responsible to solve the problem. The response may require a change in the plan or strategy or execution. There may also be internal events requiring team to act quickly.

The nature of an agile startup is captured in the figure below. The normal flow is to strategize, plan and then execute. The conceptual diagram is intended to reflect the fact that external and internal events tend to change the best-laid plans. Making the right adjustments at the right time in the presence of these events can be the difference between success and failure.

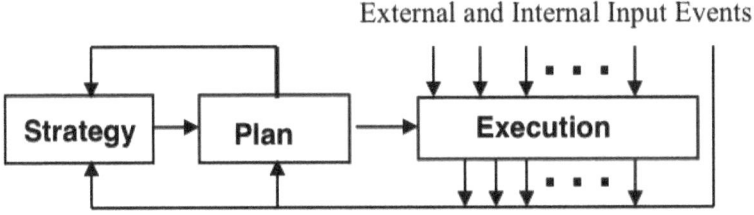

There are numerous situations when the strategy or plan must be modified. When the business model is not working, that may force a change in strategy, plan and execution. When the competition produces a new feature, it may force changes to the plan and execution. If a customer finds a problem in the product, it must be fixed immediately and then the plan updated to reflect a change in the schedule. If someone resigns, this internal event sets hiring plans into motion and current resources are reassigned to stay on schedule. These are all examples of where a rapid-response team is important for success.

In reality, many startups have a collection of individuals who think they know it all. They are too busy trying to be right instead of thinking about what issues may lie ahead. They think about how to get the upper hand on someone in the company or how to get their way. Political alliances form in order to marshal resources in a different direction from the stated goals. The conflicts, arguments and endless discussions sap the energy of the company and eventually it ends when someone has had enough and quits. Many companies have failed due to such conflicts because management did not take advantage of the main strength of a startup. For this reason, investors evaluate startups primarily on the quality of the team to try to avoid this type of outcome.

Tip 6.3

Bad Hires Cost Time and Money

Tutorial: Two company resources that cannot be wasted are time and money. Hiring the wrong person wastes both. That is why it is important to hire the best people into the key positions of the company. The business plan contains the target headcount for each year or by quarter to grow the company. You will not only have to find people to interview who fit the job description, you will also have to identify the best fit for the positions available. If you miss the targets, you risk falling behind schedule and that could also be very costly. It is a time-consuming activity but will pay off it if done properly.

Everyone tells you to hire the best people. But exactly what does that mean and how do you know they are the best? The statement is really a warning of the cost of hiring the wrong person, especially in those positions critical to the company's success. The hiring process costs the company time and money. And if the wrong person is hired, it will cost the company even more time and more money. In some cases, it has led to failure because expenses are largely driven by headcount, and every bad hire shortens the runway and delays the product.

Use these rules for employees, consultants and part-timers:

Rule 1 - Hire the best people.
Rule 2 - Correct a hiring mistake as soon as possible.
Rule 3 - Never fill a key position with a second-rate hire.
Rule 4 - Reward excellence to retain the best employees.

There are a number of efficient and effective methods used to achieve the goal of hiring the best people. The first thing to recognize is that your effort level in hiring should be commensurate with the expected impact of the position being filled. Three categories of hiring can be defined as follows:

1. High Impact players   (critical to company's success)
2. Medium Impact players   (important to company's success)
3. Low Impact players   (important to functions in the company)

You should optimize your time and effort primarily on the first two categories. That does not imply you accept sub-par employees in any category. All positions must be filled with the best talent available. It simply means the number of candidates interviewed and the number of interviewers can be reduced as you move from category 1 to category 3.

For example, you may need an executive recruiter in the first category. Make sure you have a long list of resumes to select potential candidates. Ensure the interview process involves many people and select the best candidate from the short-listed individuals. In the second category, you may use a regular recruiter to screen candidates to develop a short list. In the third category, you may reduce the number of candidates and the number of interviewers to save time without sacrificing quality.

Of course, it would be great to hire the perfect person in all positions, but that is not realistic. Mistakes will be made. People can be unpredictable and their life circumstances may change. As a result, 10% of the hires turn out to be the wrong decision, and 10% turn out to be a lot better than you expected. But this assumes you have a hiring process in place to ensure very high hit rates.

If you put the effort into positions critical or important and make only a few mistakes on these hires, you have increased your probability of success. The smart hires in those positions will figure out how to solve the problems they encounter, and that is the key requirement. A young startup has multiple fire drills every day and those who are "quick on the uptake" and respond rapidly are the type of people you seek. You need to find them, keep them, and reward them as the company grows.

A second effective method is to hire people in your own network. In the very early stages of the company, the first set of hires should be people who you already know to be outstanding. Not just good, but outstanding. The reason why previous acquaintances are important at this stage is that you already know what you are getting. There is no guesswork. Trust is built-in for these hires. But you will have to sell them on your small company and provide enough salary and stock incentives for them to leave their current employment. Even in these cases, you should follow a hiring process. They may need to be pulled away from their current employer and need to know more about your startup. Since you may have to disclose sensitive information to them, such as your "unfair" advantages, make sure they all sign non-disclosure agreements (NDAs) even prior to being interviewed. If you can hire some very good people you already know at the start, you will be faster out of the gate.

Another source of early hires is friends and family who are trustworthy and reliable. Office work and miscellaneous activity can be done by those in your inner circle. Expectations should be set that it is temporary until there is funding to hire full-time people. A maximum time limit of one year should be placed on these hires. Others may also be hired as consultants so work can be done before full-time employees are brought in for positions in marketing, sales or operations.

Once you have exhausted the short list of colleagues, friends and family, you will need a professional recruiter or use the employment websites available. This is where the trouble begins. It is difficult to hire that next great employee. Most people don't want to take a risk on your new startup. But you shouldn't hire those people anyway. Some people may want to work for you because they cannot find any other employment. If you hire them, you will find out why they are not already employed. In desperation, you will probably hire one or two anyway. Big mistake. Instead, ask your current employees, contacts, advisors and recent hires to identify potential new hires for a bonus, and go after them hard. Be persistent. It will pay off better than taking the easy way out with a bad hire.

Another effective way to hire great people is to find a great CEO or other executives for the company. Hire the best people at the top of the company and they will steer top talent to the company. They will hire a great VP of Sales, VP of Marketing, CFO, and so on. The best and brightest usually hire the best and brightest people to report to them and provide leads to other potential hires in a domino-like effect. The floodgates open and high-quality people start joining in large numbers. This is how you build up a high-performance team in the company.

As a general rule, try to hire someone who is as good as you, or better. In effect, this will bring up the average. This will increase your own confidence in the success of the company. When you see employees who are better at their jobs than you would be, it raises your confidence. Of course, you need to ensure their lifestyle allows for the long and unending hours of work required in a startup before they are hired.

If you cannot find the right person for a key position, there is always the option to restart the search. Never hire in desperation because you need a "warm body". You will pay later in time and money. However, if it is a critical position that must be filled in a short time frame, there are some alternatives to consider. The first one is to fill the position with an existing qualified employee and then back fill the open position just vacated. A second option is to hire a temporary consultant to perform the tasks while the search continues. A third option is to hire two people who together would cover the position but are also able to perform other tasks as part of their job description. Each of these solutions, and other creative options, has some inherent limitation and may not be suitable except in the case of an urgent need that must be filled.

In certain situations, a new hire may not be a good fit but it becomes clear only after they have been hired. If you realize a mistake was made, let the employee know it is not working out here. Set timelines for such a decision such as 3 months from the date of hire. Follow business protocols and guidelines about letting an employee go to ensure it is done legally and in a short time frame. And if an employee quits, it presents an opportunity to try to upgrade that position. The revolving door of employees going in and out of the company is normal operating procedure.

A final effective method to ensure most of the hires are of high quality is to use a hiring process. While you will occasionally make hiring mistakes, you can reduce the likelihood by involving more people. A simple process starts with a detailed job description followed by a job posting after approval by the hiring manager. If possible, develop a set of evaluation criteria that would produce the ideal candidate. A list of potential hires should be compiled, followed by interview dates and a list of interviewers. Finally, a group meeting of all the interviewers is held to provide input after which a decision is made, and an offer is extended or a letter indicating there is not a fit at the company. The details of such a process can be found from many sources. The main point is to have a hiring process in place.

Tip 6.4

Get the Right CEO

Summary: The lead founder often wants to keep running the company as CEO after being in the driver's seat for a year. This is usually the wrong decision - perhaps not for everyone, but for inexperienced first-time founders. The primary reason for starting the company is to change the world by building great products. It relies on the unique expertise of the founders. But somewhere along the way the goal changes to running a business with very little experience. This is a high-risk move. It is better to have a CEO with business experience. If you have lots of experience, you and the Board will be in agreement about who should run the company. One alternative to take to the Board is to hire a second person with business experience to help you run the company. But be prepared to have that option turned down. In fact, the Board hires and fires the CEO. This is the one point of control the Board holds.

Key point: If you decide to hire a CEO, it is wise to do it around the time you secure a seed or first round of financing and you have developed a working prototype. This situation will attract the best CEO candidates and give them a long runway to bring in revenue or the next round of financing or both. You are also effectively hiring the acting CFO, VP of Sales and VP of Marketing all-in-one, so keep that in mind. Their job will be to hire others to fill these positions and build a strong management team.

Tutorial: When you start a company as leader of the team, you are actually CEO, President, CFO, COO, VP of Marketing, VP of Sales, VP of Engineering, VP of R&D, Head of HR, CTO and CHC (Chief Hacker of Code). You will have to let most of these titles go over time and focus on the position that provides the greatest value to the company. In fact, all the founders usually experience the

Operate a Successful Startup   205

"Reverse Peter Principle" in that they descend to their highest level of competence. This implies that no one is fully qualified to be CEO. There are two possible solutions to this problem.

One solution is to the hire a CEO. But if the interim CEO/founder does not agree with this decision, there will be great difficulty ahead. Usually, the interim CEO tries to convince the Board they should continue. The Board disagrees and eventually, after a heated Boardroom battle, a CEO is hired. Conflicts between the new CEO and the former CEO occur on many issues. Everyone is painfully aware of what is going on and it starts to tear the company apart. This type of situation has resulted in the failure of an uncountable number of companies. Make sure you are not one of them.

With a CEO in place, you have to decide which role you are best suited for within the company. If you want to battle for supremacy for a few years, then you are no longer interested in the success of the company, but instead fulfilling personal ambitions. Your lack of experience as CEO will be costly every time you make a mistake. And your desire for power and control will seal the fate of the company.

There is a second option for a founder who wants to remain as CEO. In some cases, the Board may decide to let the founder continue as CEO as long as a second person with significant business experience is hired. This arrangement can be made to work if the two people can work cooperatively, and the roles and responsibilities are clearly delineated. There are also cases where two founders have decided run the company together as co-CEOs. While these alternatives also lead to successful companies, they are somewhat more complicated. In the end, the Board will make the final decision on the CEO.

The initial goals of the CEO are to reduce the time-to-revenue, raise the next round of financing to keep the company rolling, and to hire people to fill out the team, as needed. **It is better to hire the CEO before a VP of Marketing or a VP of Sales** since the CEO will hire their own people after sizing up the situation in the startup. So be aware of the ordering problem - CEO first, and then let them build up the management team. There are exceptions to this rule and the Board can advise you on the proper decision. Of course, when they are all hired, life in the startup will change dramatically. With a new management team in place, the simple days of a small startup are over. There are many more people hired very quickly and a new organizational chart is published soon after. But that is exactly what is needed to grow the company.

The tasks of a CEO change every year in a fast-growing startup. **First and foremost, the CEO must manage the burn rate in between rounds of financing and keep it low enough to get to profitability or the next round, whichever comes first.** This is the highest priority task in the pre-revenue and pre-profit phase of the company. Since initially you will be in a negative cash flow situation, it is important that the CEO watch and micro-manage the spending habits with a Director of Finance, and later a CFO. Managing the growth of a young company through careful and judicious use of cash is as much an art as it is a science. You do not want to be doing this. After all, you started the company to change the world. A company doesn't change the world – the products change the world. So you should stay focused on the products and customers.

The CEO must define the business model for the company. This involves issues of market segmentation, customer acquisition and retention, sales, expenses, product pricing and revenue recognition. It includes accounting issues related to bookings (customer commitment but no payment as yet), billing (request for payment), backlog (orders not filled), churn (lost customers in a subscription-based model), revenue (payment received for work completed or product delivered) and payments (when to pay which bills). The CEO must manage these issues in accordance with industry standards and federal laws. They must also anticipate potential problems to determine if a business model pivot is necessary to optimize revenue. Likewise, the CEO may consider market pivoting if the product is not gaining traction in the target market segment.

Later in the development of the startup, it is common for the CEO of a company to maintain a dashboard that is used to quickly monitor the status of key indicators of the company. The dashboard contains brief data that is generally reviewed in detail by the Board at Board meetings. The dashboard content depends on the specific nature of the business, but may include:

- Monthly, quarterly and annual sales and revenue plan and actuals.
- Monthly, quarterly and annual expense plan and actuals.
- Monthly and quarterly cash flow forecast and actuals.
- Monthly and quarterly margins and income plan and actuals.
- Status of fundraising activities.
- Sales pipeline waterfall chart by month or quarter.
- Status of top 10 key pipeline engagements.
- Status of top 10 existing customer relationships.
- Internal and field sales cycle length.
- Top reasons for failing to close business deals.
- Days Sales Outstanding (DSO) and list of significant late accounts.
- Days Payable Outstanding (DPO) and top upcoming payments.
- Days Inventory Outstanding (DIO).
- Headcount plan and actuals.
- Web site metrics (visitors, conversion rate, bounce rate, top referrals, top pages).
- SaaS metrics (CAC, LTV, churn, LTM, MRR, LTV/CAC)

The CEO must decide exactly when to build the sales channel. The timing of this decision is critical – done too early and the burn rate sky-rockets, done too late and revenue is left on the table. The tipping point for exponential revenue growth involves many factors that must be fully understood, so there is no place for amateurs here. The CEO must be able to forecast sales by gauging the product demand in the marketplace, the customers in the pipeline and the length of the sales cycle. It is the job of the CEO to get this right. The CEO is also responsible for developing the compensation package for sales team, which involves a base salary and commission based on sales with the appropriate incentives to deliver required revenue levels. All these issues are interrelated and therefore must be addressed in a coherent manner.

Selecting the CEO is one of the top five critical decisions for the company so it must be done with careful thought and discussion with the Board. An executive recruiter will be necessary to identify the short list of candidates. Often, the right CEO is only 1 or 2 degrees of separation from you. This means that you, or someone on the Board, or one of your technical advisors, or one of your business friends, know someone who would be ideal for the job. It could be a recommendation of a Board member who is also a major player in your industry and knows all the *Who's Who* in your industry. They can make recommendations based on their experience and the needs of the company.

It is important that the CEO be from your industry. Otherwise they have to come up to speed on the challenges of your industry and pretend to know what's going on – that's too high a risk to take on. You are not selling Coca-Cola or Pepsi. If it is a business-to-business (B2B) company, they need to also know the customers and have established relationships with them. In fact, the CEO will give the startup instant credibility with customers in the marketplace, something that should not be underestimated. They bring their virtual rolodex (a list of all their contacts in industry and academia) with them. You are actually bringing their knowledge and their network into the company.

The CEO must have hands-on experience with technology at some point in their career. They cannot be learning on the job, except for the specific technology and products you are bringing to the market. They must have a detailed understanding of the market, business models, sales cycle and revenue recognition models in the industry. As such, they must be in upper management at their current employment and looking to move up. A highly-ambitious individual who has not yet reached their peak in their career is an ideal candidate. The person should be located in the region (or expected to move there) and be well known to many others.

The exit strategy should be discussed with the prospective CEO to ensure alignment with the company goals. If the goal is to build value and sell the company, you should set expectations appropriately. They should also expect to put in long hours at the office for many years. A first-time CEO is potentially a good candidate because they will put every ounce of energy into the company. Of course, a very experienced CEO with a proven track record should never be turned down if you can convince them to join. Either way, there should be a 3-month transition period when they take over operations as you refocus your energy on the product.

A final characteristic to look for in a prospective CEO is an X-factor. It is hard to describe exactly what an X-factor is but you will know it when you see it. It is an intangible "extra" the person brings to the table and makes them stand out from the crowd. It is not essential but important to consider in the final decision. What is essential is that you make the decision yourself, in consultation with your team, and then get your decision approved by the Board. You will be the best judge of the right person for the job, and then you can explain your decision to the Board. Ultimately, it is the Board that hires and fires the CEO. The compensation package for the CEO is also developed in consultation with the Board and will depend on many factors. There is no general guidance to be offered here on compensation except that advisors should be consulted and that the stock position is often in the range of the founders.

If the goal is to build a fast-growing company, the first significant milestone by which to judge the CEO is the next round of funding. If the CEO can secure the funding, then it becomes a matter of growing the company commensurate with the business plan and revenue. Subsequent rounds of financing and taking the company to an M&A or IPO are the ultimate goals. As lead founder and the decision maker on hiring the CEO, your job is to make sure that the CEO is successful in meeting whatever objectives you have set.

Advanced notes:
1. One reason the employee stock option pool needs to be large is that the right CEO will take a significant portion of it. A CEO could require up to 10% of the company. Other executives require an order of magnitude less.
2. CEO integrity is critical. Many startups have been effectively killed by opportunistic greedy CEOs. They can steal the company from naive founders or spend the company cash on themselves. A quality experienced Board is able to easily spot and eliminate these candidates.
3. Experience managing sales compensation plans is important for a CEO. These plans must be structured carefully. Be careful what you ask sales for, because you might get it. Sales people are great at meeting the letter of the compensation plan as opposed to the intent. For example, a sales booking goal can be met by a multi-year contract in which actual revenue cannot be recognized until the end of the contract. An experienced CEO knows when commissions should be paid on revenue rather than bookings.

Take Away: If you are hiring a CEO, ask them interview questions in the areas of funding, hiring, marketing and sales. Have they raised a round before? What customers can they get you in to see? What are the marketing and sales plans for the product? Are there good people they can recruit to the company? In reality, you are interviewing to find someone who brings significant and complementary value to the company – especially given the stock position they will hold when they join the company.

Tip 6.5

Cooperate Internally, Compete Externally

Tutorial: Even small companies have people issues. In fact, there are as many people issues as there are people. These issues often overtake business issues on a day-to-day basis. Every person has a unique style and different motivation. Some are driven by titles, others by recognition of their work and still others by stock and salary levels. Some are highly ambitious and looking for shortcuts to rise up the ladder. Others are hard working and want to produce something that has a "Wow-factor." Some are attracted to a small company because there are many opportunities to seize control and power. There are introverts, extroverts and everything in between as well as other personality traits that result in varying wants, needs, expectations and energy levels. For better or for worse, these are the people you will be counting on to build a successful company.

It is important to realize that proper management of people is a key success factor for startups. This is often overlooked because startups begin with a handful of people and no hierarchy. But as the company grows, management skills become very important because you are dealing with people, tasks and deadlines. Without oversight and management, things can quickly go off the rails because of a lack of focus of the employees. Keeping people highly motivated and productive are perhaps the two most important aspects of managing people in a small startup. But there is no one-size-fits-all management approach to achieve this. In fact, management is more about realizing everyone is unique and different. This means that you will have to understand each person and develop the so-called "soft" skills to maximize their contribution to the company.

There are a few simple management techniques that have been found to be very effective as listed below.

1. **Assign the right people to the right jobs** – match people to the job they are best equipped to handle and are passionate about to produce the optimal results for the company.
2. **Reward people based on what motivates them** and what they value the most, and they will give the most back to the company.
3. **Keep people growing and learning** in their position by continuing to provide challenging work and delegating more responsibility to them. This is how you increase the talent of the company.
4. **Mentor, coach and teach people, especially junior employees. Provide feedback on things they do well and areas of improvement on a regular basis, not just once a year.** It is very important to take a strong interest in their work and contribution. This is how you increase their contribution to the company.

In addition, if someone is upset, you need to work with that person to find out if their concerns can be resolved. When it is clear that it cannot be resolved, it is best to let them go. Their negativity may affect the morale of others in the company.

To succeed as a company, you must reinforce a company culture of everyone pulling in the same direction. Company culture is a combination of the work environment and company values of the startup. The leadership group must establish the vision, the mission and a set of values for the company very early on. Many companies, including startups, are dysfunctional and chaotic environments. If you make your company a synergistic, "team-first" environment, you will have a huge advantage over other companies. It will not be easy to do this because people may say they have heard it all before. So teamwork must be articulated as often as possible, encouraged by the company leaders through their own actions and rewarded through employee compensation.

Unfortunately, politics creeps into the company as more and more people are hired. This is the norm in so many businesses that people are conditioned to behave in their own self-interest. But if you can convince people that the company's survival depends on the whole team working together, then you have an advantage over other companies and even other startups. This survival mentality and the mindset of continuously striving to make progress are ingredients for successful enterprises, and it can only be done as a team. It has been shown that if an employee does something that helps themselves AND the company, this will optimize the overall result.

The leadership must make it clear internal politics hurts the company. Create an open environment that encourages people to voice their concerns and identify potential problems that may affect the company or the working environment. Have communication meetings frequently to answer questions and keep people informed. Encourage team building and reward those who excel at delivering results as part of a team.

Personal conflicts will erupt from time to time in the pressure-packed environment of a startup. The appropriate managers must act to de-escalate and diffuse such situations. They should attempt to resolve problems through mediation. If the problem cannot be resolved, the CEO should become involved, but only if it impacts the company in a negative way. There will be other situations that can be resolved by the employees themselves and they should be trained to do so. At the same time, the rules on the use of email and company email etiquette should also be discussed in a training session. Email has been the source of many misunderstandings and confusion. Its primary use is for the distribution of company related information. Email for coordination, communication and clarification is legitimate. However, venting, flame-throwing, bullying and inappropriate jokes are off limits. Face-to-face discussions are much more productive than running dialogues on email. Require email be used in a professional context only.

To keep people focused on the real adversary, hold company meetings to talk about the competition as a threat to your startup.

Identify all the competition by name. People rally around a common purpose if there is a serious existential threat to survival. Make sure they know who is trying to beat you in the marketplace. Ensure the most competitive people are put into positions where they can be used against the outside forces and their products. For the rest, their competitive spirit should be channeled towards building something better than the competition. Everyone needs to be reminded that the survival of the company depends on their ingenuity.

In the end, it's all about internal alignment. Think of each person as an arrow that can be pointed in any direction. Initially, they assume a random position based on their own interests. Your goal as a leader is to harness all the energies of a diverse set of people and get all the arrows pointing in the same direction over time, with the head of the arrows collectively pointing directly at the competition. Although this takes time to accomplish and it is not possible to get all the arrows pointing the same way, the idea is to convince most people to focus their competitive nature on the competition and not on those within the four walls of the company. There must be a constant reminder to "cooperate internally with team members and compete externally against the enemy (i.e. the competition)."

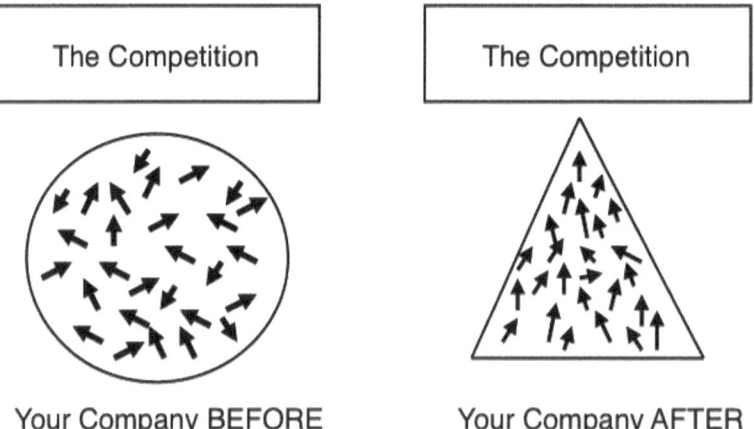

Another way to build a sense of common purpose is to celebrate all the milestones. You want to create an atmosphere of excitement and optimism. Pessimism in the company can spread faster than optimism. It has often been said that, while the pessimist and the optimist may eventually end up in the same place, the optimist has more fun along the way. In reality, the optimist usually ends up in a better place.

There are plenty of milestones to celebrate: the day of incorporation, the first time you move into a new space, the first round of financing, when the prototype product solves a customer problem, when the product is ready to be shipped and so on. It is an effective way to acknowledge the progress of the company and the accomplishments of the team while getting to know each other outside the office setting. It signals that you have a company culture of getting things done and then celebrating when it gets done. Work hard and play hard. It is just part of being in a startup.

Tip 6.6

Systems and Processes Save Time and Money

Tutorial: When you get your first office space for the company, it will likely be relatively small. This office should be big enough to get you through a year or so. Although small, this first office needs to be organized. It sets the tone for the future of the company. You need to create an environment that enables people to be successful, and you want to instill in everyone that things are going to operate in an organized and efficient manner, not in a chaotic and free-wheeling approach. Those days ended when you left someone's house that served as the temporary address for your fledgling startup. The benefit of operating in an organized manner is improved productivity and enhanced agility, the hallmarks of a successful startup.

It is always a good idea to introduce a process or a system to a startup, but it should be timed based on when it makes the biggest impact on productivity. In the early stages, organization of the office space is most important. As the company grows, processes must be introduced to increase efficiency. Then, when the company is large enough, a combination of office organization, processes and systems must be introduced to make the entire company efficient and productive.

A process is a repeatable, step-by-step procedure to complete a task. It has the details of who is responsible for each step, actions to be taken, timelines and outcomes. It must be written down and stored on the company's internal website. It reduces the training period of new employees, reduces confusion and increases the efficiency of current employees. The rule is that if something can be converted to a process, it should. If this sounds boring or tedious, you are missing one of the key ingredients of a successful company.

The same applies for systems. These are software programs that help businesses manage information in the company. An accounting system to track revenue, expenses, payroll and stock grants is essential as the company grows. A spreadsheet may work for a while but eventually you will have to switch over. Initially you will have to hire a consultant CFO to help you with a review of the business plan numbers, and then later to manage expenses when the company is started. Eventually, the CEO will hire a Director of Finance or CFO to take care of these responsibilities.

Computer systems to handle internal networks, firewalls, security, email, etc., need to be installed. An IT person may be needed in the early stages. Usually, the founders build their own computer environment but it can get out of hand if the company is growing quickly. Offload tasks to a new hire brought in specifically to handle IT issues. Otherwise, the founders and engineers will spend valuable time building infrastructure rather than building product. Many other systems should be installed over time as needs arise.

Here are a set of policies, processes and systems to consider:

HR	Hiring process, Performance Reviews, Termination or Layoff Process
G&A	Procurement/Expenses Process
G&A	Internal Organizational Chart
G&A	Financial Accounting and Stock Management
G&A	Email/Social Media Rules and Policies
G&A	General Company Policies including Benefits
G&A	Supplies, Equipment, Organization of Office Space
G&A	Process for Board Meetings, Executive Meeting, Staff Meetings
IT	Computer Installation, Software, Networking, Phones
Eng	Product Release Processes and Protocols
Eng	Software Development Process, Coding Standard
Eng	Hardware Development Process
Sales	Customer Engagements, Evaluation & Sales, Support

Tip 6.7

Always Negotiate Win-Win Outcomes

Tutorial: First-time entrepreneurs are always surprised about the amount of negotiation one must engage in when starting a company. They are used to writing code or building hardware by themselves in a garage, dorm room or perhaps a lab. But what they find when they start a company is that everything is a negotiation. For example, deciding on founder ownership levels and titles will be one of the first of many negotiations. The compensation packages of employees will be negotiated when you start hiring people. Office space and subleases can be negotiated under certain circumstances. Seed and first round valuations, along with many other terms in the financing agreement, are part of long and potentially stressful negotiations. Project schedules are usually negotiated. Product roadmaps are heatedly debated and finally negotiated. After a while, you begin to realize that everything in business is a negotiation.

You need to develop and sharpen your abilities to negotiate in the business world. There are a number of good books available and insightful commentary provided online that you should seek out and read thoroughly if you have not done a lot of negotiating in your past. If one of the founders is particularly well suited to this activity, they should be assigned the role of chief negotiator. However, all founders should continue to improve their negotiating skills over time.

You may find yourself negotiating many times per week for a significant period of time. Sometimes these negotiations will have a formal setting where it is obvious what is going on. For these situations, you must prepare beforehand to figure out what alternative outcomes are possible and then carefully think through the negotiating process. Other times it may be a conversation in the hallway where you may agree to squeeze the schedule for product delivery without realizing the consequences. That is a decision that should have been treated as a negotiation.

There are four possible outcomes of a negotiation: win-win, win-lose, lose-win, lose-lose. We can dispense with lose-lose for obvious reasons. However, the other three cases are typical outcomes of most negotiations. **The one that you should strive for is win-win.** If you shoot for win-lose, eventually the other party will realize that they have been short-changed. They may come back to re-negotiate, try to sue you, or refuse to do business with you again. If you end up accepting a lose-win outcome, you may have created a future problem for yourself and the company if it is a key negotiation. The other party often attempts to produce a lose-win outcome against you if you are not experienced enough and they recognize it. That is why you must have the courage to walk away from potential lose-win negotiations, or pay for it later. Cleary lose-win and win-lose end up in a lose-lose proposition.

There are some important examples where win-win is critical. For example, if you are negotiating with investors, both parties need to realize they are working towards the common goal of building a successful enterprise. In fact, investors want the founding or management team to maintain enough ownership to keep them incentivized. If this were not the case, eventually the team members would leave the company because the payoff is not worth the effort. This is why angels and VCs try to strike a fair and balanced deal at all times, although you must still ensure the deal is in your company's best interest.

Another situation is when you hire a new employee. Imagine if you negotiated a win-lose outcome, how the employee would feel when they find out they have been undervalued and underpaid. You will have lit a fuse that will eventually blow up and affect the company. Ensure all employees, consultants and advisors have fair compensation packages. If you are underpaying employees, they will need to be offered more stock to compensate for a lower salary. If you are providing market rates for salary, then the stock position can be set based on the position being filled. The best approach is to consult with the Board and develop standard packages for each level in the company, and adjustments based on market conditions and the cash position of the startup.

Win-win is the only acceptable outcome for two negotiating parties. Sometimes a win-win outcome may later turn out to be win-lose or lose-win and, in those cases, you could contact the other party and develop a new agreement. The timing of a follow-up negotiation can be based on which side of the win-lose or lose-win outcome you are on. But the goal should always be a win-win outcome.

The way to engage the other party in a negotiation is to first try to understand the terms they seek and their constraints. Then let them know the terms you seek and your constraints. This should be followed by a discussion of how to find a middle ground that makes both parties satisfied with the outcome. By doing this, you have built a bridge between you and the other party and now you are sitting on the same side of the table. While it is difficult to get to this point, it is important to keep this metaphor in mind because the negotiations can get heated, stalled, delayed or even halted if you do not really understand each other's positions at the outset. If you cannot come to an agreement, you need to consider your best alternative to a negotiated settlement. In fact, you should enter into a negotiation with an alternative in your back pocket, which you may or may not share with your counterpart. If you have no alternative, you should adjust as many terms as possible to close the deal. In the end, you must produce a win-win deal or have the courage to walk away if the terms of the deal are not acceptable. Never accept a lose-win proposition.

The outcome of a business negotiation is a contract. This means that you also have to become an expert at reading contracts with complicated legal language. For the first few months, you need to read all these contracts, or have a team member adept at contracts read them. It is important to know how business contracts are developed and negotiated. In addition, seek the advice of a corporate lawyer during the negotiations and have them approve the final contract. In fact, you will need legal services for a variety of company issues and therefore it is best to retain a corporate lawyer. And when you hire the lawyer, make sure you negotiate a good deal for your cash strapped startup.

Tip 6.8

Exude Confidence, Not Arrogance

Tutorial: When you start a company, you must have a great deal of confidence in its success. Otherwise you would not have started it in the first place. You must exude that same level of confidence within the company when it is up and running and maintain it at all times. Confidence is conveyed by remaining calm in a crisis, working on fixing problems, understanding the technology and products, studying the marketplace and communicating that your product is a game changer for the customers. Confidence is not conveyed by shouting louder, hammering on the table, storming out of meetings, and making grand sweeping pronouncements with nothing to back them up. If you behave in this way, you are following the wrong role models.

Your confidence and credibility will be tested often so you must work in areas where you are an expert so you can speak authoritatively about a subject. Confidence is built by doing your homework, always being prepared and putting in the hard work. You need to study the market and know that it is large enough to build a successful company. Then you must work with the customers to find out what type of problems they have and the solutions they seek. Next, you need to identify a pain killer product for that market, and one or two follow-up products that would also serve the market. The products must have certain barriers to entry and an "unfair" advantage to fend off competitors. You need to write a business plan to understand timelines, revenue, expenses and profitability so you can determine if you have a scalable business. You need to hire the best people and pull a strong team together to execute the business plan. Having all of these in place will give you confidence in the success of the company and this confidence will be on display for others to see.

To build confidence in employees, the environment within the company must be one of excitement and optimism. Team confidence is built by frequently communicating the vision and goals of the company, and by celebrating the milestones as you achieve them. The way to increase confidence is to develop a working product that actually solves a customer problem. It must be demonstrated to the employees at your site and later to early customers at their sites. These events must be communicated to the whole company because they are the first major steps towards being a viable company.

Confidence of the employees grows when the next round of financing is brought in to keep the company going and to hire more people. It is even higher when revenue starts to come in and when the company becomes profitable. Confidence within the company is built by tangible events moving the company forward, not by saying "Don't worry. It will all work out in the end." Your own confidence can be enhanced by knowing you have an action plan, a backup plan and a contingency plan. It is reinforced by delivering high quality results on a consistent basis, by not over promising and under delivering. Wishful thinking does not solve problems. It is about setting the right expectations and then meeting them. It is simply hard work, a high level of execution, a belief there is no obstacle too big to overcome and no fear of failure.

Confidence is also infused throughout the company if the management team is outstanding and visibly operating as a team. People take their cues from a leadership team that can execute the plan and hit the milestones. There are very few secrets in a small company. Everyone knows who creates trouble and nothing goes unnoticed. There is very little room for emotional outbursts and personal conflicts within the company. It wastes a lot of time, demoralizes the team and erodes confidence. All of this wasted energy should be used instead to build up the company and stay ahead of the competition.

Tip 6.9

Leave Marketing Strategy to the CEO

Tutorial: Marketing is usually a relatively new area for first-time entrepreneurs. It is taken as some form of advertising or public relations (PR) activity. But marketing actually encompasses a variety of different activities within a company. It may require new and inexpensive techniques using social media, or the traditional but expensive techniques of the past. The most critical one for success is the marketing strategy. As such, the proper marketing strategy is the subject of many discussions. The reality is that marketing is very product dependent and industry dependent. It is difficult to develop generic marketing strategies. It requires some in-depth knowledge of the customer base, market characteristics, the industry supply chain, the competitors and the partners. Therefore, the CEO must have a strong marketing background as part of their experience. At the appropriate time, they must hire a new team member - a Director or VP of Marketing to head up the development and execution of the marketing strategy. The path to success may well be due to the marketing strategy defined by the CEO and the execution of that strategy by the marketing team.

Founders engage in many forms of marketing early on without knowing it. The market analysis to determine the market size and market share is part of marketing, as is the study of the competitive landscape. These two aspects are required in the business plan so the founders have their first experience with marketing in the process of writing it in the business plan. Understanding the needs of the customer is also done under the banner of marketing. These needs are converted into functional requirements for the product as it is being developed. If this aspect of marketing is not done right, it will lead to failure. The founders must determine if the product can win in the marketplace. This is the primary objective of the early marketing effort.

There is another aspect of marketing often overlooked by the founding team. It is the so-called go-to-market strategy. This is the process of converting the product into a revenue stream. While the CEO is largely responsible for the development and execution of the strategy, there may not be a CEO hired at the time the product is ready to be beta-site tested. Therefore, **it is important that the initial team consider issues of initial market segment, suitable business model, product pricing, customer lead generation, identification of the decision makers and the customer acquisition process.** This is the second important piece that must be done right. Without paying customers, it will be difficult to validate the product and attract investors or a CEO. Once the first few customers are obtained and a CEO is hired, the whole process will be handed off to the CEO. Therefore, this is one key qualification that the CEO must possess – the ability to define the marketing strategy.

A recent marketing technique for websites is to use A/B testing. This involves experimenting with two or more different website layouts and features to determine which is best. Typically, this is used by software-as-a-service (SaaS) businesses. The steps in A/B testing are: split up the web traffic so they have different landing pages; measure which pages produce the best results using web data analytics; use the better option to increase the conversion rate and reduce the overall cost of acquiring a customer (CAC).

Another category of marketing is associated with advertising and branding. This is especially important for the consumer market. If not done properly, a startup may fail because it was not able to get enough attention to create a demand for their B2C product. However, for enterprise B2B products, mainstream advertising is not typically used or needed. Instead, it is done in the trade journals via technical articles about launching the company and its products. Careful consideration is needed when letting everyone know you exist. Certainly it is important when building customer awareness to build a beta program or obtain new customers. However, the competition will also be alerted to your presence. Ensure the PR for the product launch is carried out only after the product is working in two beta sites. A PR firm is usually retained to connect you to editors to place articles before an upcoming trade show. The marketing department is responsible for creating a "buzz" before the trade show and then taking care of all logistics associated with the trade show. Usually, a number of customer leads are generated from the show and the sales force follows up on the leads as the first step in the sales process.

There is a tendency in some startups to overuse the PR machine to give visibility to the company. The allure of the cameras and your name in print is hard to resist, but it requires time away from the pressing issues of the company. What is more important is the company P&L not the company PR. Therefore, it is important to ask if the PR helps the P&L. If so, it is worth doing. If not, it is best to be avoided. Company launches, product launches and trade shows are the right place to use PR.

On the other hand, strategic marketing is always an important part of a successful company. Loosely defined, it is the strategy by which you will greatly increase the number of potential customers for your product. You may be able to sell your product to a few customers, but the goal is to expand the customer base to a large number that enables significant revenue growth. In many cases, it will increase the burn rate so it must be switched on at the right time in the company's evolution. It should only be employed if the product is actually working and the initial sales numbers look promising. One key aspect of strategic marketing is to determine how to move from the early adopters to the mass market. Early adopters are customers who are willing to try anything that may solve an immediate and critical problem. The mass market is looking for turn-key solutions. This must be well understood by founders and early management before developing the proper strategy.

Your early customers will likely be heavily involved in the specification of the essential features of the initial product. They will tolerate many problems in the product if it actually solves their problem. But this is not a characteristic of the mass-market customer. They may need a new product that is full-featured, easy to use, easy to install and runs without bugs or errors. You may have to re-work your old product for this market or provide education programs to "evangelize" its value to large groups of potential customers. The early adopters can be pointed to as reference customers who understand the need and value of the product when selling to the mass market. A detailed marketing plan must be developed to capture the mass market, which is the only path to high growth.

Another aspect of strategic marketing is to form a joint venture (JV) with various partners in the supply chain of the industry. It may be possible to develop relationships with vendors at different points in the supply chain and to identify areas of common interest that would enable revenue growth for both parties. One possibility is the use of a sales channel for joint selling of products. This is not usually to the advantage of the startup because it relies on the sales force of the partner and may be costly in royalties, but may be an alternative to building a sales channel too early. A second possibility is to position your product to play an important role in the supply chain in your industry through the creation of a de facto standard interface. This is more difficult because it requires the cooperation of certain key companies to adopt the standard and then promote it to their customers. A third possibility is to integrate your product into an industry standard through software APIs or hardware protocols established by large companies to make your product more accessible. This is the reverse of the previous approach and much easier to implement because the bigger companies would benefit when other companies use their interfaces and protocols.

Many other possibilities exist - so many that strategic marketing is best left to the CEO and the marketing team. The main goal is to increase the pool of potential customers in the presence of competitors through creative strategies that enable more companies to use your products. As a founder, your role is to contribute to the conversation rather than develop a strategy for the company. Note that any plan will require additional resources and increase the burn rate, so the timing of this plan is very important.

CHAPTER 7
Improve Your Success

7.1. Ten Decisions Determine Your Destiny

7.2. Keep Your Priorities Straight

7.3. Work on Things that are Important but not Urgent

7.4. Always have Action, Backup and Contingency Plans

7.5. It's a Marathon AND a Sprint so Stay Healthy

7.6. Avoid Legal Entanglements

7.7. Selling Your Company is a Business Decision

7.8. Make Your Own Luck

7.9. Embrace Change to Support Growth

Tip 7.1

Ten Decisions Determine Your Destiny

Tutorial: There are ten big decisions that ultimately control the fate of a startup. Five of them are usually made by the founders and the other five by the CEO. The first **five important decisions made by founders** are:

1. Selection of the Founding Team
2. Identification of Market Segment
3. Initial Product Selection
4. Choice of Bootstrap, Angel or VC Funding
5. Hiring a CEO

If you are able to make the right decision on all five of these issues, you have a very high probability of success. Get one wrong and it can sink the company. This is why you have to get every one of these decisions right. Of course, it is possible to correct mistakes on each of these areas, but that costs time and money. While a corrected situation still has a good chance of success, it is not as high as the right decision in each case.

There are **five important decisions typically made by the CEO** in consultation with founders and management that also have a significant impact:

6. Management Team
7. Business Model
8. Board of Directors
9. Timing of Building Sales Channel
10. Marketing Strategy

If you are able to make the right decisions on all 10 issues, you are likely to go public or have a high-valuation M&A exit. Therefore, it is very important to go deep in all areas and spend more time thinking about these issues on your active priority list. It will keep you focused only on what is important. Each of the 10 decisions is discussed in more detail below.

Selection of the Founding Team: The selection of the founding team is the first and perhaps most important decision in starting the company. The founding team must be technically competent, extremely passionate about starting a company, trustworthy, reliable and have a strong work ethic. You will be living with them for years so team chemistry is very important. The core competence of the company is based on the founding team. Business experience with strong technical skills is the best combination for a startup.

Identification of Market Segment: You must carefully choose a large market and ensure customers demand the product in that market. The product/market fit and the product timing for that market are critical to success. The market size must be greater than $100M to build a fast-growing company seeking angel or venture capital financing. Markets smaller than $50M are not likely to produce a fast-growing company but they may present opportunities for smaller, slow-growth companies. The biggest opportunities exist in large fragmented markets with many small players and weak products. If one or two large companies dominate a market, it will be difficult to unseat them in the customer base.

Initial Product Selection: Make sure your product is a pain killer and not a vitamin pill. The development of "must-have" products leads to a successful company. For "nice-to-have" products, it must help the customer to reduce their costs, reduce their time-to-market, or enhance their own product in some manner. Otherwise, it will not succeed. You must also define the minimum first product you can sell into the target market. Ensure you have an "unfair" advantage in the product in order to beat the competition. It must also have high margins or high volume sales to reach profitability.

Choice of Bootstrapping, Angel or VC Funding: Most startups begin by bootstrapping the company. Typically, the initial funds are contributed by the founders, and later by a small group of investors comprised of friends and family. The goal of bootstrapping a company is to build value and grow organically until you reach profitability. If you are building a fast-growing company, you will need to pursue knowledgeable investors with deep pockets at some point. You should identify angels or venture capitalists that have in depth knowledge of your industry and have the key expertise to help build your company. Angel funding levels are in the range of $150K-$500K per angel group, and total $200K-$1M when a number of angel groups pool their assets. Venture capital financing starts in the range of $1-10M with a very high bar to secure funding. Both expect equity in return. If revenues grow exponentially, you may need to pursue angels or VCs for funding to scale your business.

Hiring a CEO: It will be necessary for one of the founders to carry out the duties of a CEO until you decide to hire one. An inexperienced founder should not attempt to run the company for a lengthy period of time because it will decrease the probability of success. If you choose to take on this responsibility or work with another employee who can serve as President to assist you, keep the following in mind. The CEO must manage the burn rate between rounds of financing and keep it low enough to get to profitability or the next round, whichever comes first. The CEO is responsible for raising the next round of financing when necessary. The CEO must hire the management team and define the business model for the company. The CEO must also decide exactly when to build the sales channel. Managing the sales force and implementing revenue recognition policies are also part of the job description. The CEO and CFO must manage the Profit and Loss (P&L) of the company on a quarterly basis and present the company status to the Board of Directors on a monthly basis. As such, the complexity of the job requires a CEO to be hired, or a founder CEO with an experienced second person to assist them on all matters.

Management Team: Leadership is about knowing what to do. Management is about knowing how to do it. In a startup, the leadership and management must be agile and quickly respond to changing events. The key factor in building an environment that promotes agility is to hire people in management who are team players. The executive management team includes the CEO, CFO, VP of Engineering, VP of Sales, VP of Marketing and the CTO. Each of these hires must be among the best people available. They must be experienced and highly qualified, and must have access to a large network of people they can attract to the company. They must also believe the strength of the startup is in the team. In a startup, team chemistry is extremely important. When hiring people in upper management, ensure their skill sets overlap. Everyone collectively must understand the market, the product, the customer and the competition. Overlap and team-oriented people in management are two of the most important requirements for these positions.

Business Model: This is about how you are going to make money. The key to a proper business model is to ensure the business is scalable. This means that there exists a tipping point at which the revenue curve goes exponential and there is a direct path to profitability. A scalable business has lots of customers, high margins or high volume, where the margin is defined as the difference between the product price (revenue) and the cost of goods sold (expense). If the sales cycle is very long, the cost of goods sold is high or the margins are small, it will be difficult to reach profitability. Eventually the company will run out of money. However, if the sales cycle is reduced and the cost of acquiring a customer is small relative to the lifetime value of the customer, the business is scalable.

Board of Directors: The Board of Directors is a group of company advisors with a fiduciary responsibility to deliver value to the shareholders. Their main power is to hire and fire the CEO. They also approve major events of the company such as the IPO, M&A events, pursuing another round of financing and adding or removing Board members. It is very important that a high-quality Board be constructed at the outset. A group of three or five Board members is ideal to start off. Each one must bring value to the table. They should be experienced in business and well-known, from either industry or academia.

Timing of Building Sales Channel: A sales channel is defined as a combination of processes and people that enables the company to capture its target revenue. It is the mechanism by which you gain a market share. It involves direct methods to engage the customer using local sales people and international distributers, and indirect methods for lead generation. The sales force must have the channel bandwidth to access customers and obtain purchase orders within a given time frame. The sales bandwidth is defined as the maximum rate at which customers can be acquired using the sales channel. If the sales channel bandwidth is increased too early, before the product is ready to go, the burn rate will be too high to be sustained and sales people will be laid off. If it is built too late, you will not be able to hit the revenue numbers. This makes its timing one of the most important decisions during the growth period of the company. Additional considerations exist if a hardware company does not manage its inventory properly after the sales channel has been expanded. The cost of excessive warehousing of inventory or the lost revenue when there is a shortfall of inventory may result in scaling problems. There is a similar problem if any supplier cannot manufacture enough hardware to meet the channel demands.

Marketing Strategy: Strategic marketing is an important part of a successful company. One key aspect of strategic marketing in business is to determine how to move from the early adopters to the mass market. Early adopters are the first few customers willing to try anything that may solve an immediate and critical problem. On the other hand, the mass market is looking for turn-key solutions. This must be well understood before developing the proper strategy. This aspect of marketing will increase the burn rate so it must be switched on at the right time in the company's evolution. It should only be employed if the product is actually working and the initial sales numbers look promising.

Tip 7.2

Keep Your Priorities Straight

Tutorial: Time is a precious resource that cannot be wasted, and you only have a finite amount of energy each day to do tasks and make decisions. When the company is up and running, it is easy to lose track of your priorities with fire drills every day and at least one or two crises per week. Meetings, deadlines and new problems seem to occur at the same time. All the while, you are pulled in every direction for help.

There are two ways to stay focused. First, keep your highest priority in your head at all times. Remind yourself of what it is every morning. It should not be the priority of the day but rather a long-term priority. Work on that long-term priority at some point during the day to move the ball forward. Second, be aware of how every part of the company is doing and identify trouble spots. Then figure out how to fix the problems. Unfortunately, there are usually competing priorities to deal with and they are often interdependent. For example, assume your priority is to secure the next round of funding. In order to get funded, you need revenue, which means you need customers. In order to get customers, the product must be ready for beta-site testing. Therefore, you need to check on the status of the product, talk to customers and arrange for the beta-test evaluation criteria. In the meantime, you may need to hire a CEO to signal to potential investors you have a solid company with proper management. If you do these tasks out of order, or in random order, you will waste valuable time.

To be more efficient, you must **know the critical path, rate-limiting step and unexpected bottlenecks** in the company at all times. The critical path is the longest path through a series of interdependent tasks associated with a deadline or a set of milestones. It will determine the overall length of the schedule and must be monitored

Build Something Great!

at all times. The rate-limiting step is a task that has a fixed processing rate, or bandwidth, so nothing can be done faster than this rate unless more bandwidth is added. Finally, a bottleneck is a stall in a task that is delaying the schedule and needs immediate attention. While all these concepts are well known, it is important for entrepreneurs to be vigilant and apply these concepts on a continuous basis.

As an example, assume the next round of financing is contingent upon meeting the following milestones in the next four months:

- Hiring a CEO
- Completing the beta version of the product
- Obtaining two beta-site customers

A schedule of tasks can be built as shown below. A simple diagram of this sort should reside in your head at all times until the objectives are met. It is very important to think of key milestones in this way to ensure that you never fail to meet the deadline. It is an effective way to identify your critical path, bottleneck and rate-limiting step.

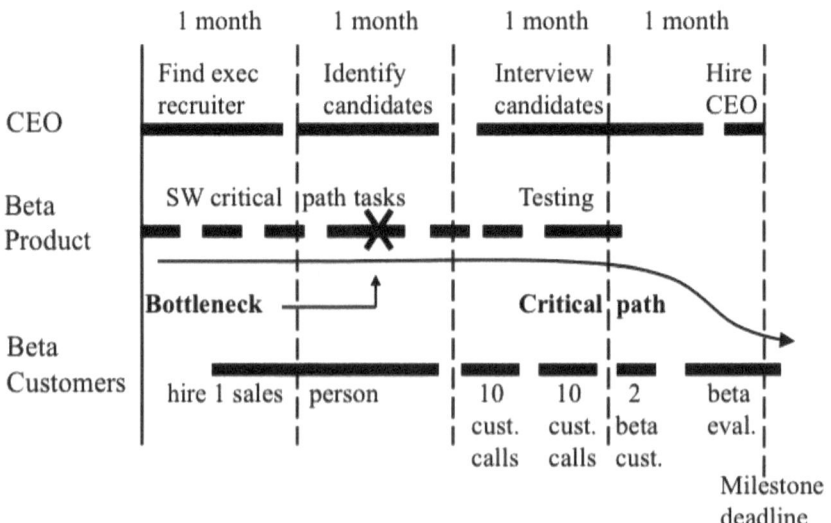

The critical path here is the completion of the beta product followed by beta-site testing with two customers. The process of hiring the CEO, as outlined in the figure, is not on the critical path but you must have the beta product ready to attract the right CEO. Therefore, it is scheduled concurrently with product development. The most important priority is to deliver the beta product on time. Otherwise, customers will be hard to obtain and a top CEO would be hard to attract.

Obtaining two beta customers requires some thought because the sales process entails significant effort. Among the potential customers are tire kickers, the curious and those who are just leading you on. If you do not have time to pursue a sufficient number of customers, this will become a rate-limiting step in the process of reaching the milestones. Therefore, you need to hire one sales person dedicated to delivering two beta customers during beta product development. A second sales person could be hired to increase the bandwidth, but that would increase the burn rate. This is not a good idea when you have no revenue or customers. Instead, it is better to start the process of contacting potential customers two months before the deadline, and identify the two beta customers just as the beta product is being completed. As a result, one sales person must be hired in the first 2 months of the schedule.

Most of the critical path goes through the software (SW) development schedule. Any tasks on the critical path must be monitored to ensure the overall schedule can be achieved. The bottleneck or stall in this critical path, illustrated with an "X" in the diagram, is a software issue in implementing a key feature that is not working. Here, another developer must be re-assigned to the task to help solve the problem. And you must stay on top of this issue until it is fully resolved.

Once the bottleneck is removed, you should continue to monitor the SW critical path while ensuring the selection of 2 beta customers is on track. The sales person should make 10 customers calls each month in order to identify 2 suitable beta sites for the product. In parallel, the CEO candidates should be short listed and interviewed.

When the right CEO is found and hired, they can further assist with the beta sites and close two accounts to meet the milestone objectives for the next round of financing.

Unless you keep track of your highest priority and are aware of your critical path, rate-limiting step, and bottlenecks, you will be under constant pressure to fix problems reactively. Often, it may be too late. These basic concepts should be applied by those in management. Keep track of the highest priority, build a schedule, find the critical path, identify the rate-limiting step and focus on removing unexpected bottlenecks. By doing this, everyone is on top of what is going on in their corner of the company and keeping all priorities straight.

More generally, you should view your time and energy as precious resources that cannot be wasted. It is important to be fully aware of how you use the limited amounts of time and energy that you have each day. Identify the highest impact activities to the company and work on them exclusively. If you have a choice of attending a meeting out of interest or ensuring that the product is on schedule by consulting with product managers, you have to decide which one is more valuable to the company's bottom line and long-term success. The meeting may be interesting in the short term but it will not likely uncover some major issues that would hold up a product release. Furthermore, you will be better informed about the product status by talking to the managers rather than sitting through a long presentation that does not help the company. Always look for the highest impact activity when you have multiple options as to how to spend your time and energy. Then, imagine the significant benefits to the company if everyone operated in the same manner.

Tip 7.3

Work on Things that are Important but not Urgent

Tutorial: Steven Covey's "7 Habits for Highly-Effective People" is a self-help book with concepts that also apply to startups. For example, "Begin with the end in mind" can be adjusted to "Determine your exit strategy." Each one of the 7 habits has a useful counterpart for startups. A useful exercise is to figure out how to convert each habit intended for a person into a habit to use in a startup.

Of particular interest is his four-quadrant system categorizing the importance and urgency of an activity. As shown below, each task of a startup can be placed in one of the four quadrants. Most tasks are usually placed in Quadrant 1, which is filled with Important and Urgent tasks. Everything seems like priority one, but this is not actually true. There are other priorities of the company that are important but not urgent. These are usually postponed or ignored because they can always be done next week or next month or at some point in the future.

	Urgent	Not Urgent
Important	Deadlines Customer problems Certain meetings Unexpected crises	Roadmap development Improve processes Team building Mentoring Improve communication
Not Important	Some meetings Some phone calls Meeting a conference paper deadline	Feature creep Analysis paralysis Side research projects "Skunk works" project Writing journal papers

But these tasks are important to the success of the company and must be placed in Covey's Quadrant 2. They deliver long-term benefits to the company if enough time is spent on them.

A number of sample items are shown in Quadrant 2. These items are to be allotted a certain amount of time each month. You must decide for yourself what to place in this quadrant and how much time to allocate, but some items must be listed there. For example, the company roadmap should be included because it contains pivoting strategies in case the product or business model is not working. The roadmap should also specify product and business responses to the competition. It is a defensive style of planning because something always goes wrong with the product or business model and you do not want to be in reactive mode when it does.

The processes in the company should undergo continuous improvement and therefore should be listed in Quadrant 2. Some processes can start small and then, as the company grows, new and improved versions can be introduced. Every year, the processes should be reviewed and improved. The payoff of improved productivity is immeasurable. Most startups do not have any processes in place so the atmosphere is one of constant fire-fighting, many misunderstandings and multiple do-overs. Continuous improvement for processes tailored to your environment is the best solution to avoid these problems while saving time and money.

Team building is another important activity that is important but never urgent. You must keep the morale of the company at a high level through tough times. When you sense the team is not functioning cohesively, get everyone together for a fun event, a group dinner, or have an open discussion of the issues. Off-site meetings, training programs and group think sessions are also effective. If the group is operating as a team, it may be time to recognize and reward the team. Also, ensure that mentoring is an ongoing process to grow the junior talent in the company. People want to feel they are progressing in the company, learning all the time and being supported by management. In addition, having open communication meetings frequently is important so that everyone feels they know what is going on. Create an environment where team members feel comfortable expressing their concerns. Each employee should be able to talk to their managers about any issues that may risk missing a company milestone or deadline. A pleasant and efficient workplace reduces misunderstandings and conflicts.

Quadrant 4 contains many activities occurring often in a startup, but should be discouraged. One example is when the product is packed with more features than needed to sell in the marketplace. This common occurrence is called "feature creep" and is usually wasted effort. Another time sink is when excessive analysis and effort is used to produce an optimal solution for some small portion of the product that does not increase sales. This form of "analysis paralysis" prevents rapid progress and should be avoided. There are also side research projects, "skunk works" and journal paper writing for those who are academically inclined. If they are not approved projects and do not contribute directly to the bottom line of the company, they should not be pursued on company time.

Quadrant 3 contains day-to-day activities that are urgent but not important to the success of the company. Examples include unnecessarily long phone calls or a meeting you don't need to attend. A quick favor that someone else asks of you or a side task that you decide to undertake may also be Quadrant 3 activities. Some academically-oriented employees may get the urge to meet a conference paper deadline to continue publishing. While all these tasks are harmless in nature, it is useful to monitor Quadrant 3 tasks and ensure they are limited in the first year or two.

The four-quadrant system of Covey is a powerful tool to manage your time and the company's time over the first two years. After this point, if you have hired enough people, developed a working product and obtained initial revenue, it is up to you whether you continue to use this valuable tool. By that time, it will be second nature, so you will likely use it without consciously knowing it.

Tip 7.4

Always have Action, Backup and Contingency Plans

Tutorial: There are a number of critical decisions for a startup where the wrong decision can lead to failure. For example, the selection of the first product to build and the timing of next round of financing are both critical decisions. If the product does not work or the company runs out of cash, the outcome is usually disastrous. To improve the likelihood of success even under these conditions, you need to think about what you will do if your initial plan is not successful. You need to have a backup plan and a contingency plan to mitigate your risk.

The primary plan is called the action plan. It is high risk but provides a high reward, if successful. A backup plan is enabled only if the action plan fails. The backup plan has medium risk and medium reward. But if this also fails, you need to consider a "red-zone" contingency plan. This is the lowest risk option, but the return is also low. However, it prevents the company from completely failing. You also need to consider the triggers that activate the backup and contingency plans.

This approach of having three plans is sometimes referred to as the ABC method of planning. In some cases, the backup and contingency plans are not as fully developed as the action plan but there is enough consideration to know what to do if they are triggered. This method is not needed for all plans – only the ones that are deemed important or critical to the success of the company.

To summarize, the three plans are as follows:

o Action Plan – what you are trying to do
 = **high-risk/high-reward**
o Backup Plan – if the Action Plan fails
 = **medium-risk/medium-reward**
o Contingency – if the Backup plan fails
 = **low-risk/low-reward**

A simple example of the ABC method is illustrated when hiring a CEO. The first step is to meet with the Board of Directors to discuss the time frame to hire the CEO. Once established, an executive recruiter must be retained, typically at the suggestion of a Board member or investor. The recruiter assembles a long list of candidates and you wean that to a short list of five candidates. If you interview all five candidates and find two suitable candidates, the next step is to hire one of them. You may prefer one over the other, but there is no guarantee your first choice will accept an offer until they examine it in detail and make personal decisions to leave their current position and join a fledgling startup. In fact, there are no guarantees they will join even after a verbal acceptance. Things may change between the time they accept the job and the time they are expected to join. The one rule to follow in a startup is that no one is actually hired until they are sitting in the chair and working. They must be contacted repeatedly between the verbal acceptance and their actual arrival. Because of this, you must have three plans, as follows:

o Action Plan – hire CEO candidate #1
o Backup Plan – hire CEO candidate #2
o Contingency – continue as interim CEO and restart the search

This is an obvious case where the ABC plan is implicit, but the advantage is that you have already worked out the three plans and can present them to the Board to receive the "go ahead." In fact, the Board expects three plans in many important cases, unless there are unusual circumstances. This is how you manage the risk of a critical decision. To complete the hiring process, the recruiter will inform those not suitable, and keep the other two candidates interested in the position to provide time to choose one of them. For each case, you need to work with the Board to determine the appropriate compensation package for the CEO.

Another situation suitable for the ABC method is the process of raising funds. The amount of funds needed for a given startup can vary from $100K to $10M or more, depending on the nature of the business. Assume that your startup is need of a mid-range figure of $4M within 6 months. If you pursue VC financing of $4M and are unable to complete the deal for any reason, you will run out of money and may have to close the doors of the company. Instead, you should pursue multiple VCs as the action plan. In parallel, you need to pursue angel financing or an investor willing to sign a convertible note of $150K to bridge you to a more significant milestone. If that falls through, you need to raise a small family and friends (F&F) round of $50K to give you more time to pursue angel funds and the convertible note. The F&F plan must be pursued first to ensure you have committed funds to act as a safety net. Then you should pursue VC and angel financing in parallel. If neither is possible, then funding using a convertible note should be pursued. A simplified version of the ABC method is as follows:

- Action Plan – Raise a VC round – $4M Series A round
- Backup Plan – Raise $150K convertible note or angel round
- Contingency – Reduce burn rate and pursue F&F funds - $50K

The advantage of having three plans in this case is it increases the likelihood of being funded in some manner because you can decide what needs to be done in parallel and what needs to be done serially. The timing of each is based on how quickly you can obtain a response. You are able to assess the probability of success of each plan as you gather more information. By using this approach, you know every effort is being made to keep the company funded rather than lamenting the fact that you should have tried other alternatives after it is too late.

If you use the discipline of having three plans, you avoid being in a reactive mode when an important plan does not go as expected. Knowing you have two other options worked out in advance mitigates risk and allows you to be more confident the company will succeed in some manner. Others in management and certain key employees should use the same method. Always ask your team what the backup and contingency plans are for any key deliverables on the critical path that have a significant impact on the success of the company.

Tip 7.5

It's a Marathon AND a Sprint so Stay Healthy

Tutorial: Starting a company is not easy. It is one of the most difficult things to do successfully. But once you get it up and running, things get a lot harder. It is a long and arduous 5-8 year endeavor, most of which requires your undivided attention 24/7/365. In the first two years especially, there will be more work to do than is humanly possible by the founders and the initial hires. It can be stressful and emotionally draining. You will be running hard to survive and running for a long time to meet a never-ending set of milestones on the road to success.

The one lesson to heed is to **take care of your own health**. This is the real secret to handling the endurance test of a startup that often goes unmentioned. This is how you can get through difficult times. It allows you to avoid burn out. You are able to make good decisions on a consistent basis. You enjoy the whole process of starting a company and watching it grow. You are an enthusiastic participant in a great adventure. It allows you to be confident and optimistic even in the toughest times. And you are more resilient after setbacks. The payoff is significant for taking care of your personal health and well-being. While it is difficult to have a balanced lifestyle, it is quite feasible to have a sustainable lifestyle, and that is what you should seek to attain. This can be done using 4 simple steps: get regular sleep, eat well, exercise frequently and relax.

First, get enough sleep. People need differing amounts of sleep. Figure out how much you need to function optimally and make sure you get enough. If you are tired all the time or seem to be having trouble solving difficult problems, you are probably not getting enough sleep. If you know you did not get enough sleep the night before, it may be a good idea to use the day for the less difficult tasks on your to-do list and put off any really difficult work or tough decisions until the next day when you're well rested. There may be many exceptions at the beginning when you start the company but you need 6-8 hours of sleep every night. This is when your body relaxes, heals and builds up energy for the next day. Lack of sleep is very costly and not sustainable. Bad decisions are made when you do not get enough sleep. You are more irritable and conflicts will be commonplace if you are tired all the time. You need to sleep at roughly the same time and wake up at roughly the same time every day. Be efficient during the day and get a good night's sleep.

Second, eat healthy and nutritious foods. You need a reliable source of energy to do your work. Each person is unique and will have to decide for themselves what to eat and when to eat it. However, the company should offer healthy alternatives wherever food is provided. There are many Internet sites with great tips on health and nutrition. Seek out these sites and follow their guidelines. Usually, the tips are simple and the advice is sound. Most people do not follow the advice but one thing is certain - you can last longer and avoid burn out if you eat right on a daily basis.

Third, exercise regularly. This is an important part of stress reduction. Walking away from your desk and going to the gym can be an excellent way to solve problems. Your brain will keep working on the problem you're trying to solve while you are working out. It is often suggested that 20 minutes a day of various types of exercise are enough to keep you going but each person must determine what activities are best-suited for them. Options include stretching, aerobics, resistance training, weights, dance, yoga, tai chi and other activities that are fun like ping-pong. Registration at a local fitness club may encourage you to exercise regularly. This can be done at home for most sessions, and perhaps a visit to a fitness club on the weekends. It is okay to skip a day or two, but it should otherwise be a regular part of your day.

And fourth, take time off to recharge the batteries at appropriate times. One of the other founders can cover for you during short breaks. This will allow you to be more effective while in the office, and have guilt-free breaks while out of the office. Without these breaks, you may burn out in the first three to four years.

Many founders regret the fact they did not take care of their own health. Lack of sleep and lack of rest are usually the two most often referenced factors in their inability to perform at a high level. However, all four aspects are important for general well-being. You have to figure out what works best for you and how to integrate these four steps into your schedule for yourself. There is plenty of information to help you in bookstores and on the Internet. You can either include it as part of your lifestyle, or be less effective over time and potentially burn out in a few years. If you are in it for the long haul, you might as well keep your mind and body in top condition. Also, encourage those around you to do the same. The health of the company depends on the health of all of the people working there.

Finally, it is worth mentioning that pressure and stress are part of life in a startup. But stress and emotional ups and downs are manifestations of how we perceive the events around us. You should not internalize setbacks because there will be many. Nor should you dwell on what you could have done differently. Instead, if you have a laser-like focus on how to solve the next problem, move the ball forward and hit the next set of milestones, you will cope with the daily pressure cooker that is a startup. Some have been able to cope by reminding themselves they are on a great adventure and the events, both good and bad, are just part of the journey. Keep the "big picture" in mind and consider the progress you have made rather than dwelling on the setbacks that have occurred in the short term.

Beyond this, there are no simple solutions except to say that emotional upheavals and worrying do not solve problems – thinking clearly and rationally does. If you experience every bump in the road, you wear out quickly. Your family relationships must also be kept intact during this process as they can often be a source of encouragement when things are going badly. If you do not get too high or too low, no matter what happens, you can last a very long time.

Tip 7.6

Avoid Legal Entanglements

Tutorial: One of the unexpected challenges of a startup is the highly-litigious environment of the business world. To protect the management team and Board of Directors from lawsuits, frivolous or otherwise, it is best to retain legal counsel early in the process of forming a company. You need lawyers for financing, contracts, leases, licensing and a host of other issues. There are also safeguards and prudent steps to avoid legal entanglements that can cause the company to fail.

First and foremost, leave your previous employer with "clean hands". Legally, no resources of your prior employer can be used to develop your ideas. Otherwise it belongs to them. Any proprietary material from the prior employer must stay with the prior employer. To be precise, any ideas in a company notebook or on a company computer belong to the previous employer. This intellectual property (IP) is theirs, not yours. Clearly, if your ideas are not related to the business of the employer, then it is more of a cut-and-dry situation. Your employment agreement should have the details of these issues and any other non-compete clauses. Read it before you leave to avoid a lawsuit.

Second, avoid infringing known patents and avoid the use of IP of other companies. When you have new ideas, try to file a patent. There is a sequence of steps involved in filing a provisional patent, continuations, and eventually being granted the patent. During that process, related patents may be encountered. You must not infringe any patents you find. In fact, it is better not to find them! If you knowingly infringe a patent in your product, you may be subject to a significant lawsuit. There may be pending patents granted just as you start to get traction in the marketplace. Countless companies have tried to put a startup out of business by filing patent-infringement lawsuits. One resolution of such a lawsuit is to cross-license patents from the other party rather than filing a countersuit. Consult your lawyer or advisors for guidance on patent-related issues. Usually a startup does not file lawsuits, as it is an expensive distraction to management.

Third, avoid reverse-engineering the competitor's product and replicating its look-and-feel. This raises a red flag in the competitor and their wheels start to turn towards a lawsuit. It will only be a matter of time. Even if they do not have a legal case, you will lose time and money. However, they will have a strong case against you if you use copyrighted music, videos, or TV programs as part of the digital streaming content of your products. Do not beg, borrow or steal content that does not belong to you. This will be the end of your company if there is any hint you are using illegal content. This advice also applies in cases where a founding team is dissolved and the rights to the IP are in dispute. Lawsuits have stopped startups in their tracks in these situations.

And fourth, when you hire employees from another company you must ensure they do not inadvertently supply you with any IP from that company. IP contamination is too common and has led to an abrupt end to startups, sometimes in the form of an acquisition at a low price. It is also important to ensure customer licenses have clauses that allow you to integrate any solutions developed in conjunction with the customer into your products, or there may be a lawsuit from the customer against your company for IP violations. Likewise, have your new employees sign non-disclosure agreements indicating they will not disclose your IP to the competitors or anyone else, and they will not quit and compete against you. This happens frequently in fast-growing industries with lots of new ideas floating around the high-tech hub. The best way to proceed is to ensure your IP and technology legally belong to you, avoid knowingly violating patents and avoid the use of copyrighted content not belonging to you.

Tip 7.7

Selling Your Company is a Business Decision

Tutorial: One of the first few considerations when starting a company is to determine your "exit strategy." This refers to the end goal of your business. Investors use this term often because they are usually the ones taking the exit ramp at a liquidity event. For the founders, it is not as much an exit strategy as it is a basis for the key initial decisions for the company. There are four possible outcomes of a successful startup:

- An initial public offering (IPO)
- A product company acquired by another company (M&A)
- A technology company acquired by another company (M&A)
- A stand-alone private business

Every big company decision should be made in the context of reaching one of these destinations. The reason to define your exit strategy up front is because each one is built in a different manner depending on the intended outcome. The common theme in all cases is to deliver value to the customer and continue to build up the value within the company. How you actually do that will depend on where you are headed.

The reality here is that although we call these goals "exits", your involvement with the company will likely continue and the pressure to continue delivering revenue and growth may increase. These exits are merely milestones in your involvement with the company. Fortunately, the milestone includes a significant reduction in financial risk. It may take an additional 6 months to several years to fully extract yourself from the company and reap the financial rewards you have earned. The true simple exit of cash or marketable securities with no ongoing duties or responsibilities is generally enjoyed only by your investors.

For an IPO bound company, there are usually multiple founders involved who make decisions intended to lead to a fast-growing company. It requires a large infusion of cash over many rounds of financing. Therefore, funding is pursued from high-end angel groups or top-flight VC firms. At every stage, it is operated with the express goal of going public. For the founders, this involves bringing in experienced management, relinquishing control to a seasoned Board, and taking on roles in the company that best suit their talents and the needs of the company. The business must be made scalable within 5-8 years. A large amount of infrastructure is built including financial systems, human resources systems, computer infrastructure and other systems at the appropriate time. A sales channel is built and a market strategy is defined to capture a large market share. A family of products is developed to drive revenue growth. And a large number of outstanding people are attracted to the company through stock incentives.

At the other end of the spectrum is a stand-alone private business. This is usually started by a lead founder who wants to retain control of the company and prefers to bootstrap the entire operation. The ownership is closely held by only one or two people, along with stock incentives for key employees. There is slow growth based on revenue and income until it reaches a steady-state operating condition. The outcome is a profitable business grown organically without the involvement of investors, or the concerns of hitting the quarterly revenue numbers to satisfy the Board of Directors or Wall Street. Liquidity is usually in the form of profit sharing for the ownership group on an annual basis. As such, there is no desire for the company to go public.

The most common outcome of an investor-funded startup, by far, is an acquisition. Anytime a company is sold, it is referred to as an M&A deal, where the acronym stands for mergers and acquisitions. Usually, a merger is associated with two companies that are roughly the same size, either in revenue or personnel, or both. An acquisition is more of a big fish swallowing a little fish. A startup is obviously the little fish. So, in this context, selling your company means being acquired by a bigger company – hopefully, a publicly-traded company or a company with a path to an IPO or high-value acquisition in the future. Potential acquirers include other vendors, partners, competitors and customers. It is important for the CEO to develop connections to friendly parties who may be interested in a future M&A deal and keep them updated on the progress of the company, especially after achieving key milestones.

In all M&A transactions, there is extensive due diligence performed by the acquirer to ensure that the startup meets all expectations in terms of products, P&L, personnel and legal issues. Any use of copyrighted software, or infringement on patent rights of a third party, or questionable bookkeeping may result in the termination of the intent to acquire. This is an important reason to ensure that your IP is clean and your books are all in order. Otherwise, an acquisition exit may not be possible and the company will likely run into funding problems at the next round, which will lead eventually to failure. The acquisition is finalized only when a lengthy, often intrusive, due diligence is completed and all the paperwork is signed off. Prior to that, the outcome of the negotiations is uncertain even if an agreement is reached in principle. The offer to acquire can be retracted for a variety of reasons at any time.

One typical M&A case is when a startup builds a technology that is in demand by an industry and then sells it to the highest bidder, or works with a specific company to create and transfer the technology at a negotiated price. These are usually low-value acquisitions but are quite lucrative for the founders and some employees because the sale occurs within the first 2-3 years of operation. The requirement to build infrastructure is minimal. It is possible to operate on a shoestring budget in many cases and work quickly using agile methods to develop working technology. A large market analysis or complete business plan is not necessary. However, some interaction with potential buyers is necessary to ensure that a suitable technology is being built.

Another M&A option is to build a product company with a stated goal of selling the business to a larger company. The larger company may be a competitor, a customer or a company that would like to remove that product from the market for its own internal use or to keep it away from their competitors. In this case, there is some requirement to build infrastructure and seek angel financing, or VC funding depending on the type of product. Each company in this category must decide how much effort should be spent building the infrastructure versus building the product. The focus is mainly on the product with minimal infrastructure to allow beta-site testing and initial sales. Usually, potential buyers are consulted to gauge and maintain their interest level at various points in time. The key reason that this model works is that startups tend to innovate quickly and large companies prefer to grow by acquiring startups when they have a product that has tangible value. Typically, large companies tend to stall because they do not usually have an environment that promotes continuous innovation. Some large startups also acquire smaller startups to build up their portfolio of products if they are on a path to an IPO. The smaller startups recognize there is a faster path to liquidity and decide to join forces with the larger startup to reach critical mass quickly without as much effort.

Because the acquisition route is the most common and most lucrative in many cases, it is worth considering this decision in more detail. When a founder or CEO of a startup comes face to face with the prospects of selling the company to a larger company, many reactions begin to influence the final decision. A typical one is to think of how it would feel to sell something that you have spent many years building up. It is your baby and you do not want to let it go. This emotional reaction is often related to maintaining power and control, which are being handed off to the acquiring company. This is at the heart of why some CEOs or founders refuse to let go. Second, the demotion and loss of control defeats the whole purpose of starting a company in the first place. And finally, there is the issue of greed, which is always lurking. No offer sounds right when you have a much higher number in mind. But make no mistake – this is a business decision, pure and simple. Viewed any other way will produce suboptimal results.

You have to think differently about the possibility of an acquisition. This is the most likely outcome of a successful startup. An IPO is a noble goal and a few companies may have the necessary ingredients to get there, but on the path to the IPO, there will likely be many offers to buy the company. Think carefully before turning any offer down. If greed is driving you, then you should think about the liquidity that it offers you and every employee in the company. If it is power and control you seek, start another company and run it. But the current company must be sold to do that. And if you are emotional, then remember your objective in starting the company was to build value for customers, employees, investors and other shareholders. An offer to buy is recognition of its value. If the offer is a fair market value, you should seriously consider it.

Life in the startup changes when you agree to sell. Everyone in the company will likely change their title, and some will be let go due to redundancy. Products will find new homes in the larger company, and lines of reporting will change as people are absorbed into the new environment. There will be difficult issues in the merger process for most people on both sides of the merger. But from a business perspective, it is often the right thing to do.

Of course, negotiating the right valuation is difficult but there are many ways to triangulate on the current and future value of the company. If you let greed get in the way, you may be setting yourself up for failure. Understand how energetic your team is at the time of the offer. They may be experiencing burn out at that point. Decide whether the business plan is working as expected. Consider whether or not the business is truly scalable by looking at the length of the sales cycle, cost of goods sold, customer support costs and the cost of growing the company itself. Examine whether you have saturated the market with your product and if the next product can rebuild the revenue stream. Investigate whether there is synergy between your strategy and the acquirer's strategy. These are the real questions to ask in making a decision. If the company is controlled chaos as opposed to a well-oiled machine running on automatic, you need to seriously consider selling, but only at the fair market valuation.

If the valuation of the company is below what you believe to be fair and reasonable, you can choose not to consider the offer any further. But if you are in conflict with your Board about selling, or the investors are not thrilled with another round of financing, you must read the tea leaves and make the right decision. Use your business sense and business savvy to consider all possible outcomes including unexpected world events that could upset all plans before the company realizes its full potential. If you are forced to shut the doors of the company due to unforeseen events, you may lament the day you did not take the offer. Many founders have misjudged the opportunity to sell the company because it is not an easy decision to make if the company is making slow but steady progress.

If the company is truly struggling and a low-ball offer arrives to sell the company, the investors may push for a sale due to multiple liquidation preference rights in the financing agreement. If the investors receive a multiple on their initial investment under the terms of the agreement, they may be able to convince other Board members to vote to sell the company. This is something to watch out for because investors are quick on the draw for liquidation if they can reduce the time to receive a return on a seemingly bad investment.

Consider the following example for illustrative purposes. You raise $2M from VCs in exchange for 33% of the company. Let us assume that a 2X multiple is part of the liquidation preference clause in the financing contract. The 2X multiple means the investors will receive a minimum payment of $4M upon liquidation. As a founder or CEO, you must ensure the company sells for more than $4M or you will not see one penny. The VCs take the first $4M of the sale price so they will be quite happy with the outcome of a sale as low as $4M, but the founders and employees will be left with nothing.

258   Build Something Great!

Consider the following figure:

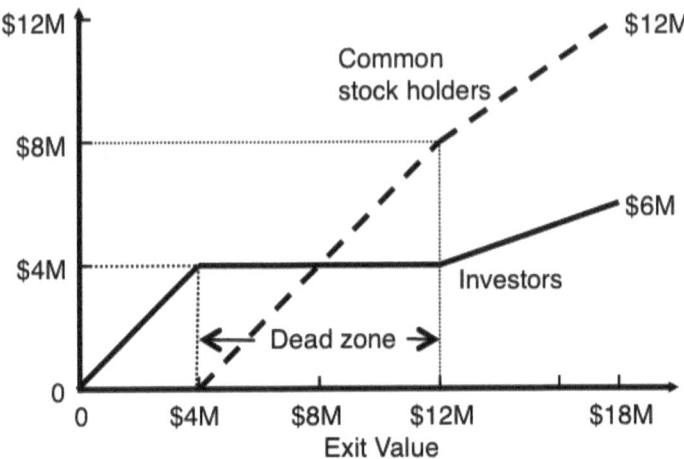

Between $4M and $12M is a dead zone where VCs are guaranteed $4M so they are somewhat indifferent to the valuation at liquidation. It may also be considered a danger zone for the founders and CEO. If the VCs get impatient with the progress being made by the company, they may try to find a willing suitor for an acquisition at any price above $4M. The backdrop to this situation is that the company has not met its milestones, either due to poor execution, no market, bad pivoting strategies and so on. This is the range where the management and Board have major differences of opinion on the next step and the Boardroom battle begins. Rather than battle the Board, it may be time to cut bait and move on to the next company. Unfortunately, the final decision is in the hands of the Board, not the management team.

On the other hand, if the company is making good progress, the Board will not consider selling the company because of the possibility of much higher returns. For any sale above $12M, the VCs will not exercise their liquidation preference clause as they stand to make more by converting to common stock and taking 33% of the proceeds. For example, at $18M the investors are paid $6M, and the rest goes to common shareholders. Therefore, the best way to avoid the dead zone is to keep the company on track until its valuation exceeds the final breakpoint in the liquidation preference graph. If a sale occurs beyond that point, everyone shares in the proceeds based on their stock ownership percentage.

In reality, any acquisition is recognition of value so consider the offer seriously if it meets all of the business requirements and is of fair market value. This is the most likely outcome of a successful startup. You have to know when an exit makes sense and when to enjoy the fruits of your labor. In the meantime, continue to build up the value of the company quarter by quarter until the next offer comes along. And even though an IPO may not be your exit strategy, it is important to be aware of the criteria for an IPO to improve your company.

Advanced notes:
1. Many startups are given milestones to meet even after they are acquired in order to receive their full payout. These are called earn-outs. It protects the buyer from potentially false claims by making sure the acquired team continues to deliver on the expected benefits of the deal beyond the acquisition date. They are an important aspect of the negotiations.
2. Sales and revenue earn-outs are important to frame properly in the deal. The contract structure of future product sales and associated revenue credit may impact the ability to achieve milestones. The acquirer's sales team may have little incentive to sell your product, which would limit your ability to hit any target revenues established in the contract. For you, the acquisition is not complete until you have met all milestones for your earn-outs.
3. Carefully structure the form of sales-based earn-outs. Your acquirer may have agreements with customers giving them a large discount off list price. You may find your revenue decreasing with larger volume because your Average Sales Price (ASP) declines in the acquirer's sales channel. Be sure earn-outs are structured to protect you from such situations.

4. Your ability to achieve earn-outs may depend on your existing resource plans, which you expect to continue after the acquisition. To ensure you will receive the expected resources, be sure to add a clause in the negotiation that if your resource plans are reduced after the acquisition, your earn-outs will automatically be satisfied as a consequence.
5. An acquisition is not done until it is done! Terms may require enough of your employees to sign new employment agreements. Don't take this for granted. Acquisitions have failed when employees did not sign new employment agreements on the deal-closing day.
6. Certain key employees could be designated as a critical part of the acquisition. They may be required to sign multi-year employment agreements including special non-compete clauses in exchange for additional compensation.

Tip 7.8

Make Your Own Luck

Tutorial: It is often stated that the success of a startup is mostly luck. But is that really true? Not quite. You do have a lot of control over the outcome. Consider the analogy of a spider trying to catch a fly. If the spider snatches a fly right out of the air, it is definitely luck. But if it builds a small web, it increases its chances of catching the fly and relies less on luck. A very large web, or multiple webs, would lead us to say that luck was only a small part of catching the fly.

Likewise, with a startup, you need to set up big "webs" to rely less on luck and more on execution. So how do you construct large webs to catch the proverbial fly? Here's how:

- Start the company with three founders to ensure coverage of most technical and business issues and to minimize gaps.
- Build up knowledge of industry trends and make sure your product is timed with an industry inflection point or a growing market need with a solid product/market fit.
- Identify any regulatory or supply chain barriers that would prevent your product from succeeding when deployed in the marketplace.
- Make sure you are working with customers early on to develop a "pain killer" product and have two backup plans in case you need to pivot to a related product or market.
- Build in "unfair" competitive advantages into your product that form high barriers to entry to block the competition and maintain a competitive edge at all times.
- Have technical and business advisors help you with tough decisions and use them as often as needed.

- Follow the VC and angel funding trends to see if the timing is right or even feasible to raise a seed or first round in your industry if you want to pursue professional investors.
- Build a large network of people who you can attract to the company and maintain strong business relationships with them.
- Attract and hire the best people in the industry to manage the company and have them hire the best people to work for the company.
- Think ahead about the business models in the company roadmap to maintain a competitive edge and develop pivoting strategies well before problems occur.
- Always have three plans: an action plan, a backup plan and a contingency plan.
- Figure out how to scale the company revenue based on the price point, shrinking the sales cycle, lowering the cost of goods sold, and reducing need for significant training and support of customers.
- Keep customers happy with enough support, training and maintenance so you will receive feedback on new products and potentially new orders.
- Think ahead to when you will have lots of customers or users to predict what kind of scaling problems you may experience in handling a large number of users in terms of hardware and/or software.

This is how you make your own luck. Each one of these factors reduces the dependence on luck. It is like building lots of large spider webs – after you build them, you expect to catch the fly. At that point, it boils down to the degree of execution rather than luck. Of course, things happen beyond the control of the company, and outside forces may conspire against you. But at least you can increase the probability of success by doing as many of these things as possible, and hope some luck comes in and takes you across the finish line.

Tip 7.9

Embrace Change as a Way of Life

Tutorial: In a fast-moving startup, things change almost every day, sometimes a couple of times a day. So you must embrace a life of constant change. There is always something exciting going on, or some new and unexpected problem to solve, especially in the early days. But there are distinct points in the evolution of a company when things change dramatically. It is a moment when there is a step-function change in the life of the company. The CEO and management team should examine the systems and processes in place after each of these events and upgrade them accordingly.

There are six notable rapid transition points as listed below along with some of the major characteristics of each phase that follows. Some of these transition points are more dramatic than others but they all signal a significant change ahead for the company and its employees. Each one has a different "feel" and you will never go back to the way it was before. Embrace the change of the next phase because it means that you are growing. And figure out when you want to take the exit ramp to start your next one!

When you incorporate:

- o You have given birth to an exciting new company.
- o You move into some real office space.
- o You have many 18 hours days ahead.
- o You have a fancy new title and you are an employee now.
- o You own a large chunk of the company but it's worth almost nothing.
- o You have lots of innovative ideas to implement.

When you take financing from angels or VCs:

- The IPO clock starts ticking.
- You own less of the company. Far less. But it's worth much more.
- You now answer to the Board of Directors.
- You have to hit milestones or else things may change again but in a bad way.
- Things get a lot more serious now. The fun and games are over.

When you bring in management:

- You have to deal with new people who have even larger egos.
- Processes get put into place and this improves productivity.
- You encounter a lot of politics unless you nip it in the bud.
- Team members must raise their level of execution or they will be fired.

When you release the first product and have customers:

- You have to answer to the customer demands now.
- The amount of work increases due to customer support and maintenance.
- Your product decisions are driven more by customers.
- You have to find many more customers to get more revenue.

When you acquire or get acquired:

- You have to integrate two company cultures.
- You have to integrate two or more product lines.
- You have to layoff people who are redundant.
- Many will change their business cards and titles.
- If a public company acquires you, everyone finally has liquidity.
- It is a successful exit if the valuation is high enough.

<u>When you go public:</u>

- There is a large infusion of cash from the initial public offering.
- You have the glare of Wall Street watching your every move.
- You have to hit your numbers every quarter or the stock drops.
- More time is spent on PR and with investment bankers than on the P&L.
- There is liquidity for investors and employees, but not upper management.

CHAPTER 8
Think Differently

This book presents the best tips for startups based on our many years of experience. We are confident these tips will set you in the right direction. Through these tips, we are providing you with a framework to succeed. Our recommendation is to focus on tips most valuable to your particular situation. It is up to you to identify the tips of greatest value that resonate with your instincts and have immediate use. You should use these tips as a foundation to pursue additional resources to help you dig deeper for information you need to make critical decisions. And every time you apply one of these tips, you are increasing your probability of success.

The tips are also intended to make you think about important success factors and failure mechanisms of startups. There are so many ways to fail and only a few paths to success. It is essential to know what they are. Even if one tip is something you did not know, or helps you move your startup forward, our basic objectives have been met. If this collection of tips helps you succeed, our vision has been realized.

The message is clear. Most startups do not succeed. The main reason is most first-time entrepreneurs think the same way. They think they have the inside track and strongly believe they know what they are doing while others do not. As a result they end up making the same series of mistakes that lead to failure. The first step towards being successful is to **change the way you think**. The tips in this book have been designed to help you do just that. If every startup worked, the book would be telling you to "think the same". Most fail. So if you want to succeed, you need to **rewire your brain** and start thinking differently.

Beyond thinking differently, you need to **transform yourself** in short order into a business person. You are moving from the technical world to the business world where things are highly competitive. If you have a favorite Olympic sport, imagine yourself trying to compete for gold in that sport without any practice, workouts or a trainer. Starting a business without any prior experience is similar. You will be trying to build up a company and competing for customers with little or no preparation. Change that quickly! You need to read a lot, talk to advisors, watch videos, attend courses and study material on best business practices. You must view every decision in a startup, including technical ones, from a business perspective. Once you have transformed yourself into a person making crisp business decisions, you have a chance to succeed.

When you decide to start a company to build a product, you need to flip another switch in your head and **become customer-driven**. However, your vision should not be controlled by the customer. It is the one thing you own as a founder and entrepreneur. On the other hand, the value proposition you offer is controlled by the customer. If they do not need the product, they will let you know. There is no amount of marketing that would convince them otherwise because they are constrained by budgets. Impulse buying is suitable for consumer products where marketing and branding are critical. However, for enterprise B2B products, no amount of coercion will work. What does work is to engage the customer early in the process, and loop back several times to ensure you are building a "must-have" product that meets their needs and they are satisfied with the value it delivers.

Ultimately, the success of a startup boils down to people, products and profits. You need to build teams of people committed to the same goal of winning in the marketplace by beating the competition. This involves hiring the best and brightest. They will in turn hire great people and create high-performance teams in the company. The product is the vehicle for taking market share away from the competition. It must be a killer product to do this. When it gets traction in the marketplace, you can get to profitability if you are able to manage expenses and keep the costs of goods sold well below revenue. And if the business model is scalable, you may need to seek venture financing to grow the business.

In the end, the success or failure of your startup is in your hands. The proper use of these tips will get you very far, but it depends on whether you start to think differently about your role in the venture, whether you transform yourself into a business person and whether you work actively with the customer. As a founder, you are actually the Chief Architect of the venture. If your expertise is technical, you have to start making business decisions. You must build a scalable product and business. You must build relationships with investors and Board members. You must build teams within the company and have everyone pulling in the same direction. You must engage customers early and often. And you must understand and respond quickly to market forces and the competitive landscape at play in your industry. With all of these changes in your self, your thinking and your approach, we believe you have a very good chance to succeed.

Good luck on your next venture! Hopefully, with this book at your side, you won't need to rely as much on luck.

David Overhauser
Resve Saleh

Visit our website: www.BuildSomethingGreat.biz

Authors' Biographies

David Overhauser, Ph.D. (University of Illinois, Urbana-Champaign), began working with startups in 1980. He has been involved in over 20 startups in a variety of roles over 35 years, including engineer, Vice President, Founder, Board member, investor, consultant and business advisor. He has also worked at IBM, AT&T, Texas Instruments and Cadence Design Systems. Dr. Overhauser was an Assistant Professor in Electrical Engineering at Duke University, where he founded the Design Automation Technology Center. During his professional career he published 3 books and over 40 technical papers, and has been granted 13 patents. His degrees are in Mathematics, Computer Science and Electrical Engineering. He is a member of IEEE and the Band of Angels, has held several leadership positions in Boy Scouts, and is an endowment trustee for Alpha Phi Omega, a national service fraternity.

Resve Saleh, Ph.D. (University of California, Berkeley), began his professional career working in a startup in 1979. He was Founder of 4 startups including Simplex Solutions where he served as CEO for one year, Vice President of Engineering for 3 years and Chairman of the Board of Directors for 5 years. Subsequently, he was involved in 6 startups as a consultant, advisor or investor. In his 10 years in industry, he worked at Mitel, Tektronix, Toshiba, Nortel, PMC-Sierra and Cadence Design Systems. He served in academia for 20 years in the Department of Electrical and Computer Engineering. Dr. Saleh was Assistant and Associate Professor at the University of Illinois, Visiting Professor at Stanford University and Full Professor at the University of British Columbia where he established the System-on-Chip Research Laboratory. He published 4 books and over 120 journal and conference papers, and was granted 1 patent. He received multiple awards and distinctions, including the prestigious Presidential Young Investigator Award (1989) and IEEE Fellow (2006).

www.ingramcontent.com/pod-product-compliance
Lightning Source LLC
Chambersburg PA
CBHW032019230426
43671CB00005B/139